Also by Rosamond Bernier

Matisse, Picasso, Miró—as I Knew Them

Some of My Lives

Some of My Lives

A Scrapbook Memoir

Rosamond Bernier

Farrar, Straus and Giroux   *New York*

Farrar, Straus and Giroux
18 West 18th Street, New York 10011

Copyright © 2011 by Rosamond Bernier
All rights reserved
Distributed in Canada by D&M Publishers, Inc.
Printed in the United States of America
First edition, 2011

Grateful acknowledgment is made for permission to reprint the following material: "Irving Penn" from *Irving Penn: A Career in Photography*, edited by Colin Westerbeck, copyright © 1997 by The Art Institute of Chicago. Reprinted by permission of the publisher. Transcript of Jerome Robbins interview from the public-television program "Choreography by Jerome Robbins with the NYC Ballet" (1986). Reprinted by permission of Thirteen.

Library of Congress Cataloging-in-Publication Data
Bernier, Rosamond.
     Some of my lives : a scrapbook memoir / Rosamond Bernier.— 1st ed.
         p.   cm.
     Includes bibliographical references.
     ISBN 978-0-374-26661-5 (cloth : alk. paper)
     1. Bernier, Rosamond.   2. Art critics—United States—Biography.   3. Arts, Modern—20th century.   I. Title.

NX640.5.B47 A3 2011
709.2—dc22
[B]
                                                                                    2011007503

Designed by Jonathan D. Lippincott

www.fsgbooks.com

5   7   9   10   8   6   4

Every word is for John

Contents

Some of My Lives

Disgrace

My English mother, Rosamond Rawlins, left her native shores to marry my father, Samuel R. Rosenbaum, the eldest son of Hungarian Jewish immigrants, at the beginning of World War I. He was brilliant, the president of his class at the University of Pennsylvania, president of his year at law school, editor of the law review, Phi Beta Kappa. And what did he do but marry my mother, an Episcopalian. His family said the Kaddish over him and never met my mother. I hardly ever saw them.

I was born in 1916, two years into World War I, in Philadelphia. My mother was quintessentially English and patriotic. Her brother Hugh had been killed fighting in the trenches. His photograph in uniform, a handsome sensitive face, hung over our staircase.

I was brought up like a little English girl: riding lessons began at age four. I went for my lessons to Foley's Riding Academy, where Miss Eleanor Foley in admirably fitted jodhpurs guided my efforts from a leading rein. I won my first medal at six. A photograph records me on my pony Teddy happily holding my silver cup. It was only second place—but there was a cup to go with it! Two years later there was a blue medal for jumping, first place!

Naturally, I had to have a governess; a French governess would be best. Both parents were excellent linguists. Because my mother missed her family and her country, we went to England several times a year, sailing on one of the ships of the Royal Mail Lines. We stayed at Aunt Queenie's in London. I was very impressed because the toilet in her flat was at the end of a corridor, not part of the bathroom. I had never seen this before. Her daughter was called Aunt Olive. She was always described as the picture of rectitude.

Many years later, in 1949, I opened a copy of *Time*, and there was an article about Aunt Olive: she had been murdered by someone who came to be called Haigh the Vampire—dissolved in a vat of acid. I gained considerable credit with my ten-year-old stepson when I took him to Madame Tussaud's wax museum in London and could point out my family connection to one of the exhibits.

On one of our visits to London, my mother was interviewing candidates for a French governess. I was six at the time and extremely shy. I was called in to meet the favored candidate, and, wordlessly, I stood on my head. This is a skill I had acquired on my own, and I thought it best to show myself to my advantage.

A disgraceful episode dates from two years earlier. At that time English children, boys and girls, were dressed in what were called sailor suits, navy blue of course, and part of the outfit was a metal whistle on a white cord. It was Empire Day, when there was a great procession of various elements of the British army and navy with their bands. I marched along with my mother, following the parade, carried away by the marching music and the sight of a drummer with a big tiger skin bravely making resounding whacks on a huge drum.

The parade ended in a church, where there was a Thanksgiving service for the troops. As I have said, I was a shy child, so it was completely out of character when, intoxicated by the music, I lifted my whistle to my lips and let out a shrill blast. I was hurried out of church in disgrace and never allowed to wear my whistle again.

A few years later, I am ten years old and enrolled, to my dismay, in an English boarding school, Sherborne School for Girls. My mother had died two years before, and this had been her wish. I would come back to Philadelphia for the Christmas and summer holidays. Before these departures, the entire school, at chapel, sang the encouraging words "Oh, hear us when we cry to Thee, for those in peril on the sea." I was the only transatlantic student; foreign students were still a great novelty.

It was time to return for the autumn term. I was booked with my governess, Mademoiselle, to sail on the family's favorite line, the Royal Mail, on the *Orduna*.

At the last moment Mademoiselle fell gravely ill, no question of traveling. But my father saw no reason to postpone my return to school. He took me to New York for a farewell dinner, at the old

Waldorf. I had black-currant ice and was totally miserable. I kept my misery to myself.

My father knew the purser of the *Orduna* because of my mother's frequent transatlantic trips. I was taken to the boat, introduced to him, and, I felt, abandoned.

I discovered that my cabin had three bunks, which encouraged me. I slept in a different bunk each night. I had my place in the dining room at the purser's table. Each night I would put on my one party dress (silk), my white silk socks, and my patent-leather slippers and go down to the dining room. The others at the table were quite jolly, and soon I was enjoying my favorite dish at the time: cold smoked tongue. Since there was no one to curb me, I had tongue at every meal and felt this indeed was high living. After dinner, I would go up to the smoking room and gamble. The gambling consisted of choosing a wooden horse; a throw of the dice would indicate whether the horse could advance along a stretch of canvas marked with divisions or stay in place. I had spectacular luck. People came to see which horse I had chosen. I won my term's pocket money many times over.

It was something of a letdown when my grandmother met me at Plymouth and hurried me away to Sherborne.

A welcome illness ended my English boarding school days and brought me back to Philadelphia and my bed.

This was before the days of streptomycin and antibiotics. For TB patients it was bed rest and practically force-feeding.

When finally I was fully vertical again, it was Sarah Lawrence for three happy years. I had the great good fortune of having Professor Jacques Barzun for my don. Many years later we were both speakers on a program for Glimmerglass Opera, in Cooperstown, New York. As I said to Jacques (by then, he was Jacques to me): I had never expected to share any platform with him, not even a subway platform.

Even later, I was lecturing at the McNay Art Museum in San Antonio, Texas, on Diaghilev. And who was sitting in the front row but Jacques Barzun? His first wife had died, he had remarried, and his second wife came from that part of the country.

After the lecture he and his wife took me out for some memorable margaritas.

Some Musicians I Have Known

I was brought up in a bath of music. My father was a lawyer by profession, but music was what counted for him. His enormous collection of records, lovingly cataloged and constantly expanded, filled my young ears with everything from late Beethoven quartets and German lieder to Stravinsky and de Falla. He used to play the themes from Wagner's operas on the piano before taking me to a performance.

As my father was head of the Board of Directors of the Philadelphia Orchestra, I got to go to concerts, even rehearsals, at an early age.

There were archaic blue laws in Philadelphia, which meant that on Sunday everything was closed tight, no cinemas, no restaurants, nothing to do. So, visiting conductors and soloists were delighted to be asked to our house for a Sunday lunch. We had a pretty eighteenth-century house just outside of Philadelphia, with fireplaces in almost every room and a big garden, so it was a welcome change from hotels.

Note: it may be just as well they only came for one meal. The English cook, impractically imported by my father, had shot her bolt with the Sunday roast and Yorkshire pudding. Weekdays, my father away at his office, we alternated for dessert between anemic stewed pears and discouraging stewed prunes.

There was no feminine hand at the helm, so I presided as hostess long before my teens, to a fascinating array of guests.

I was most impressed by Otto Klemperer, not only because he was enormously tall, way over six feet, but also because of the jocular way he threw butterballs at his wife at table.

It seems he became more and more eccentric. I learned from his biographer that while being honored in Australia at an endless dinner followed by dancing, he was excruciatingly bored. Dutifully, he danced with his hostess, but desperate, he suddenly grabbed her and gave her an enormous kiss. "Dr. Klemperer, you really cannot do that *here*," gasped his astonished partner. "Then VERE?" he bellowed.

But his *Fidelio*, his Mahler, were unforgettable.

As a young Debussy fan, I was thrilled to meet Walter Gieseking, the incomparable interpreter of that composer. I remember going with him into our rose garden and choosing a particularly pretty bud for his buttonhole.

Nathan Milstein made his American debut with the Philadelphia Orchestra playing an old favorite of his, the Glazunov Concerto. I went with my father wearing my best party dress. The seductive, full-blooded Russian tone really moved me. Milstein was one of the last pupils of the great Hungarian violin teacher Leopold Auer, I learned later.

Sergei Rachmaninoff was the soloist with the orchestra, playing his Fourth Piano Concerto. Not even rapturous applause melted his icy demeanor.

When he came to our house, he could not be persuaded to take off his fur-lined coat.

Another guest conductor was Issay Dobrowen. He was the regular conductor of the Oslo Philharmonic at the time.

The day he came to us, there had been a heavy snowfall, and we were able to hire a sled drawn by two horses, with tinkling bells, to drive us, cozy under fur rugs, through a car-less Fairmount Park. I remember the ecstatic look on his face.

During the ride Dobrowen revealed an unexpected fact: he had played Beethoven's *Appassionata* Sonata for Lenin, whose favorite piece of music it was.

The pianist José Iturbi, who always crossed himself backstage before going on, was another guest soloist. He was a handsome, stocky Spaniard with an eye for the ladies. He appeared in several pictures in Hollywood, playing himself.

After a Sunday lunch at our house in Philadelphia (I was a college student by then), he offered to drive me back to New York.

During the journey, it became clear that he counted on the drive being prolonged by dinner and something more.

I hopped out nimbly at my destination.

Eugene Ormandy was a Hungarian whose real name was Jenö Blau. He took his stage name from the ship on which he had traveled to America: the *Normandy.*

He was a violinist and first earned his keep playing in the orchestra of the Capitol Theatre in New York, which accompanied silent movies.

Ormandy followed Leopold Stokowski as conductor of the Philadelphia Orchestra and remained there for forty-two years.

Those were the days before air-conditioning, and we had a screened-in sleeping porch. One summer when we were away, my father lent it to Ormandy, who was conducting the summer season, to escape the stifling Philadelphia heat. But he soon gave it up and moved indoors. He had absolute pitch, and he complained that "those damn birds all sing out of tune."

He was not given to understatement. When he returned from conducting the orchestra on tour, my father would ask him, "How did it go, Gene?"

And Gene invariably answered, "I was a zenzation!"

The Philadelphia Orchestra was my extended family. Its members saw me grow up. Every Christmas, the old timpanist, Papa Schwar, as we called him, gave me liquor-filled chocolates from his native Germany.

The greatest oboe player of them all, still a legend, was Marcel Tabuteau. His phrasing was so perfect, so musical, that it influenced all the other chairs. He was a jolly French bon vivant and a superb cook. He asked us back to his apartment for supper after a concert one night and made us kidneys flambé in a chafing dish that have never been equaled, even in Paris. Every summer he would go to Monte Carlo and lose all his money, and my father would wire him the funds for his fare home.

He called his wife Chocolat, and she called him Penguin.

I had been studying the harp for several years and graduated to study with the number-one harp teacher in America, a Frenchman from the Basque Country, Carlos Salzedo—a compatriot of Ravel's.

He divided his time between the Curtis Institute in Philadelphia and Juilliard in New York, where he had a few private pupils. I used to come to New York from Sarah Lawrence once a week for my lesson and joined his summer colony at Camden, Maine. He was a short, Napoleonic figure—the old-fashioned music teacher who ruled over us tyrannically. We addressed him as "Maître" and stood up when he came into the room.

My theory was that he married the best pupil and the next best became his mistress. Every now and then there were improvements, so everyone moved up a notch. I was at the bottom rung of the ladder. Many of the other pupils already had jobs in symphony orchestras.

An exception to this pecking order was his most eminent pupil, Edna Phillips. When she was still in her twenties, Stokowski invited her to join the Philadelphia Orchestra as First Harpist. She was the first woman to join an American symphony orchestra. Later she became my stepmother.

We Salzedo pupils were mostly lodged in boardinghouses along Mountain Street, in Camden, and if you walked up Mountain Street, you would probably eventually hear a whole composition—Ravel's Introduction and Allegro, for instance, because Salzedo had us all practicing parts of the same piece.

Salzedo was fascinated by new technology. Radios in cars were the hot new thing. The best radio reception in Camden was at the cemetery, at night. Salzedo would drive up to our boardinghouse windows in his big old-fashioned car and honk to bring us down. We would scurry down, coats over our nightgowns, and pile in to be driven to the cemetery to listen to some uninspiring work he would not have dreamed of listening to under normal circumstances—the Grieg concerto, for instance.

He was a close friend of the composer Edgard Varèse and named his little rowboat *Arcane* after a Varèse composition. I got an allée in his garden named after me. Of more consequence, Salzedo was an early and very active member of the League of Composers, championing new music. In a recent concert of Elliott Carter's music, one composition, for harp and quartet, was dedicated to Salzedo, and there was a warm note about Salzedo in the program.

Salzedo, a quintessential European, did his best to fit in as a Maine summer householder. He joined the local organization of the Lions Club, which met weekly. Proceedings were started by all the members giving their best efforts at a roar, and Salzedo roared away with the best of them.

In my mind's eye, I can still see Salzedo on his hands and knees on his driveway, a woman's comb holding back a lock of very black (dyed?) hair, wielding a pair of manicure scissors as he minutely adjusted the curve of the drive.

Stokowski

I cannot remember a time when I didn't know Leopold Stokowski.

I hardly distinguished myself, however, at my first children's concert. Stokowski, avuncular, asked to have me brought backstage afterward. "And what did you like most about the concert?" he asked me. "My new shoes," I replied.

I played the piano indifferently and at fifteen had taken up the harp, for which I seemed to have a certain facility. Stokowski, who had a genius for publicity, invented a series called Youth Concerts—no one younger than thirteen or older than twenty-one was admitted. As a stunt, he had a few instrumentalists within those age limits sit in with the orchestra for the first concert. At the last moment someone thought of the harp—where was there a harpist of the required age? The Curtis Institute was telephoned—the harpists were all too old. Finally, they thought of the Philadelphia Conservatory and found the only person who qualified for the age limits—me!

So the night before the concert, never having played in an orchestra—or even a duet—I was sent for, handed copies of the harp parts, and told to show up the next evening.

Luckily, the pieces to be performed were all in the familiar orchestral repertoire—*Scheherazade*, *The Firebird*, *La Grande Pâque Russe*, and so on—and we had recordings of them all. I listened to them carefully, marking the score where the harp could really be heard. My technique was not sufficient to play out all the notes, so I learned the passages where the harp sounded clearly and simply placed my fingers on the correct strings in the other sections, where the harp would be drowned out by the orchestra.

Stokowski had his own way of seating the orchestra—first violins on the left, second violins on the right, then the cellos. He placed the harps in front of the cellos, in full profile to the audience, horribly exposed for the novice. Fortunately, I had friends in the cello section next to me, and they would prompt me: "Four, three, two, one, here you go . . ."

I apparently didn't make too many gaffes, because none of the other young instrumentalists got asked back while I played in six more concerts, even in Stokowski's orchestration of "The Internationale" that had a grateful harp part.

Through Stokowski's keen interest in new music I got an early immersion in works far from the standard symphonic or operatic repertoire of the time. I heard Alban Berg's *Wozzeck*, Schoenberg's *Gurrelieder*, Shostakovich's *Lady Macbeth of Mtsensk*, Prokofiev's *Pas d'Acier*, to name a few.

Stokowski conducted the first performance in America of Ravel's *Boléro*. Afterward, a dear old lady came backstage to enthuse, "Oh, Mr. Stokowski, I so enjoyed your *Bordello*."

He was alive to the technical possibilities of his times. When others scoffed at radio as a venue for classical music, he was working with engineers, twiddling the dials himself, to produce a richer, truer sound.

Stokowski was a fixture in my pantheon. He was the height of glamour, not only to me, but to most of female Philadelphia. He was a skillful showman with a great sense of theater. Careful lighting emphasized his blond mane and his expressive fingers (he was the first conductor, I believe, who gave up the baton).

He had a seductive, caressing accent, entirely self-invented. He was born in London.

And his personal life was delightfully thrilling. How could you get better copy than by going off to India with Greta Garbo? And marrying the young and ravishing Gloria Vanderbilt kept up the excitement.

However, Stoki (as we called him) took quite a shine to me. Occasional presents would show up especially made for me: a silver bracelet and ring with my monogram he designed, a set of luggage with my monogram. Pretty heady for a teenager.

One evening when my father was taking me to hear *Rosenkava-*

lier for the first time, Stoki asked me to come around to his apartment before the performance. My father drove me to the apartment but stayed in the car. "If you're not down in ten minutes, I'll be up to get you," he warned. Stoki was a notorious lothario. My father needn't have worried. Stoki was waiting at his door and gallantly handed me a beautiful rose to hold during the performance.

One can only admire Stokowski's curiosity. He enlisted Carlos Chávez as his guide to hunt out authentic indigenous music in Mexican villages.

To thank him and, to quote him, "as an expression of his admiration for Mexican culture," Stokowski waived his fee for a performance with the Philadelphia Orchestra of Chávez's ballet called *HP*, with décor and costumes by Diego Rivera.

I must have been about fifteen at the time, but I still remember it well. The dancers were transformed into fruits and vegetables, and at the climax they all disappeared into a giant refrigerator.

One can only admire Stoki's zest for the unexpected. He had accepted to conduct a benefit concert in the Mexican town of Morelia. (I was living in Mexico by that time.) The orchestra was barely above the amateur level, but that didn't faze him. The crux of the evening was to be a performance of Tchaikovsky's *1812 Overture*, with real guns blazing away at the finale.

Stoki arrived to find that one of the strikes endemic to Mexico had cut off the town's electricity. He was always extremely conscious of his appearance: catastrophe! He only used an electric razor and was not going to try anything else. He stormed. No electric razor, no concert.

The organizers were appalled. The concert was sold out. Total impasse.

I had somehow struck up a conversation in the hotel bar with some engineers overseeing the building of a new highway. I told them about the problem. After a few tequilas they gallantly offered to help me out—and they did. They installed a portable generator outside the hotel, and it was turned on just long enough to produce the current to feed Stoki's razor.

The concert was a wild success, with the roar of the guns eliciting great whoops of appreciation.

At ninety-five, Stokowski signed a five-year contract with Columbia Records. But unfortunately, he died that year, when he was about to record Rachmaninoff's Second Symphony.

His legacy lasted a long time: the glorious, rich, unique sound of the Philadelphia Orchestra.

Postscript:

This was written before the sad news of the Philadelphia Orchestra's financial difficulties.

In the 1940s, Arnold Schoenberg's music was still considered impossibly difficult to play and/or to listen to.

Stokowski had heard a private performance of the Piano Concerto (op. 42) and, never daunted, decided to program it for one of the NBC Symphony radio broadcasts that he conducted. Although the performance—on January 6, 1944—went off without incident, it created such a furor that NBC didn't renew Stokowski's contract.

Recently, on January 26, 2010, I heard Daniel Barenboim play Schoenberg's concerto at Carnegie Hall with the Vienna Philharmonic to rapturous, almost frenetic applause.

Now we come to the two glowing strands that illuminated my life for half a century. They were inextricably woven into each other's lives too: Aaron Copland and Leonard Bernstein.

Aaron Copland

I met Aaron Copland during the summer holidays after my sophomore year at Sarah Lawrence. I had gone to Mexico with a few friends. The conductor of the Sinfónica de México, Carlos Chávez, was one of the musicians who had come to our house several times while he was guest conductor of the Philadelphia Orchestra. My father wrote to him that I was arriving in Mexico, and I found a note from him at my hotel, inviting me to come to a rehearsal.

Typically for the times, a strike had closed the usual concert hall, the pompous Bellas Artes, a wedding cake of a building with the famous Tiffany glass curtain, so the rehearsal was taking place in a disaffected church.

I arrived to a wave of jazzy syncopations; Chávez was rehearsing Aaron Copland's early 1926 Piano Concerto, with the composer himself at the piano, a rangy figure with a splendid beak of a nose. He was grinning with delight as he bounced up and down on the piano stool.

The Indian musicians responded instinctively to his made-in-America rhythms. Chávez was obviously completely at home with Copland's idiom.

During a break in the rehearsal, Chávez introduced me. It was love at first sight, at least on my part. I always thought Aaron looked more like a scientist than a musician. He was tall, gangling, engagingly toothy. He gazed out at the world with blue-gray eyes, through clear-rimmed glasses, with an expression of benevolent curiosity.

This turned out to be an epic occasion for me. The only other people sitting in on the rehearsal were Diego Rivera and Frida Kahlo. We were introduced, we chatted, and to my delighted surprise they invited me to go with them in their box that evening to the concert.

After the concert we all went out to supper with Chávez. I sat next to Aaron. He told me he was living in a small house in a provincial town called Tlaxcala, about a four-hour drive from Mexico City. This was 1936, and Aaron was very hard up. "I've rented a piano; it's very quiet there. The electricity goes off now and then, but you get used to candles." Later in the conversation he said, "Only trouble is, there is no marmalade there, and I miss marmalade with my breakfast."

So the next day I enlisted an obliging boyfriend to drive me to Tlaxcala with a whole carton of marmalade. "The girl's crazy!" Aaron said, with a characteristic giggle.

Aaron was working on an opera for high school kids called *The Second Hurricane*. The manuscript sheets were on the battered upright piano, and he sat down and played it through for me, singing all the parts in that way composers with no singing voice manage to do.

I particularly loved a haunting melody called "Gyp's Song." The words were by Edwin Denby, the poet and superlative dance critic who wrote for the old *Herald Tribune*.

After that it was back to Sarah Lawrence for me, and back to his fourth-floor walk-up loft for Aaron. He was a pioneer loft dweller. It was in what was then a seedy part of town, now transformed by Lincoln Center. It was cheap and practical because there were no residents in the floors below to complain about noise, only workshops of one kind or another.

It was strictly utilitarian—no attempt at softening the bleak space with memorabilia of any kind. Aaron's taste was always austere. He never even noticed the accumulation of dust, but finally I couldn't stand it any longer, and I spent a whole week's pocket money to get it cleaned up.

Even later, when Aaron had money and a good-sized house up the Hudson (now brought back to life as Copland House), his surroundings were modest and sparsely furnished. Only music and books mattered to him. He cared little about food—he never learned to cook, and he practically never took an alcoholic drink. His clothes were nondescript—neat but anonymous.

Leonard Bernstein once said to me about his beloved Aaron: "Plain, plain, plain! Can you imagine Aaron wearing a ring or jeweled cuff links?"

Our friendship blossomed. Aaron would take the train to Bronxville to visit me at Sarah Lawrence; I came into New York whenever a work of his was performed. I was always Aaron's "date," and I would carefully collect programs after the concert for his archives.

Through Aaron, I met a number of young composers: Marc Blitzstein, David Diamond, Israel Citkowitz, Arthur Berger, and Paul Bowles (this was before Paul became known as a writer) and his wife, Jane. And Clifford Odets, Harold Clurman and the Group Theatre people, John Houseman.

Aaron took me to my first New York glamorous evening party, given by the Kirk Askews. Kirk was a fashionable art dealer; Constance was a well-known hostess and an occasional patron of Aaron's.

There I met such people as Salvador Dalí and his formidable wife, Gala; Pavel Tchelitchew, who painted Mrs. Askew's portrait with her mink coat as background; and Alice B. Toklas and other celebrities of the time.

Aaron himself cared absolutely nothing about "society" or "celebrities"—his friends were usually young musicians, writers, and artists.

In the months after I returned from Mexico, the obliging young man who had driven me to Tlaxcala was pressing me to marry him. I finally agreed. Aaron wrote to a friend, "My girl has gotten herself engaged—the only girl I could have married." Then he added (I can almost hear the giggle), "This will confuse the biographers."

Lewis A. Riley Jr. and I were married in my family's rose garden in Philadelphia. Aaron came, bringing a wonderful present. He had written out all the words to my favorite song from *The Second Hurricane* and orchestrated it; it was inscribed:

> all written out for Peggy and Lew's wedding
> for sole performance on Peggy's Harp and Lew's Guitar
> from their composer friend Copland.

My handsome new husband was a young American who lived in Mexico. He had properties there and had an interest in the polyglot firm (Mexican, German, American) that was developing Acapulco—and eventually ruining the idyllic coastline. He was completely at home in Mexico, spoke perfect Spanish, and even played the guitar.

A new friend from Mexico, the caricaturist and ethnologist Miguel Covarrubias, came up to be best man.

A string ensemble from the Philadelphia Orchestra played a favorite of mine: Mozart's *Eine Kleine Nachtmusik*.

I always kept in touch with Aaron, and in the summer of 1941 he invited me for the weekend at his rented house at Tanglewood, where he was teaching. This was unusual, because Copland, though affable, did not like to have guests under his roof. In fact, he would say darkly "There are guests in the house" the way someone else might say "There are mice in the house." And I was a female. A first.

When I came down for breakfast the first morning in a very discreet dressing gown, Aaron looked at me, somewhat bemused, and asked, "Is that what girls wear?"

He had invited some students to come by that afternoon. A young whirlwind with a shock of black hair and a strong nose burst through the door and settled down at the piano—it was Leonard Bernstein. He played and played and played, until, exhausted, he flung himself, perspiring freely, full length onto the ground.

Lenny, having graduated from Harvard and studied piano at the Curtis Institute in Philadelphia, was one of the chosen few pupils studying conducting with the great Serge Koussevitzky at Tanglewood. He had met Aaron a few years before and adopted him as idol and loved mentor. As Aaron said to me in an aside, after introducing the prodigiously gifted young man, "We don't have to worry about *that* one." It was clear that he already was a star.

How right he was! "That one" in short order was conducting summer concerts. Then, in 1943, as the assistant conductor of the New York Philharmonic, he rocketed to fame when, without a rehearsal, he took over the podium when Bruno Walter fell ill.

A close, even at times romantic friendship linked the two—Aaron the older by eighteen years—that survived all the turbulence of Lenny's personal life and professional career.

But Aaron the teacher was never blinded by the brilliance of his protégé. On being shown some early compositions by Lenny (all of his life, in spite of the conducting triumphs, Lenny longed to make his major mark as a composer), Aaron cautioned him, "Stop writing warmed-over Scriabin and write something that's really your own." And Lenny, not known for his reticence, didn't hesitate on more than one occasion to write to Aaron that portions of a Copland score were "dull" and "needed re-working."

That same weekend Aaron took me swimming to a nearby lake. Rather, I went swimming, and Aaron stood upright, fully dressed, on the shore, leaning against an overturned lifeboat, pages of musical manuscript in his hands. He was orchestrating a piano score—he always composed at the piano and orchestrated later. "Sometimes it's very tedious. I prefer to do it while something else is going on," he said.

I came back to New York from Paris, where I was working, as Aaron's date to go to the gala concert celebrating the New York Philharmonic's 125th anniversary (in 1967). It was an extraordinary event: some two hundred musicians—performers who had appeared with the Philharmonic and composers who had had their works performed by the orchestra—were seated alphabetically by rows.

There was a photograph in a subsequent program of me in a one-shoulder evening dress by Grès, and long white gloves, walking proudly down the aisle on Aaron's arm.

By then, Lenny had become conductor and music director of the Philharmonic.

Although I had moved to Mexico, in 1940 I was in New York, where I suddenly fell ill and ended up in the hospital. It was my birthday, October 1, and Aaron came to visit with the most precious gift he could give me. He was always a voracious reader, and two of his favorites were the sixteenth-century French essayist Montaigne and André Gide. He brought me his own limited-edition copy of Gide's essay on Montaigne, signed by Gide and inscribed to me by Aaron.

I was also in town for Aaron's seventieth birthday, on November 14, 1970. He wrote me the following on receiving my note in which I tried to say something of what he had meant to me:

Dearest Peggy,
  That was a beauty of a letter you sent me, such as only you could write. I loved it!

Can it possibly be more than thirty years since we first met? (Seems like yesterday.) Anyhow, it warms me just to think of you and I love you dearly . . .

Aaron

In the 1970s, Aaron gradually stopped composing; the muse was being elusive. But he threw himself into conducting with what I can only qualify as jubilation. He simply adored conducting, and he received engagements from all over the world (highly lucrative, incidentally). Technically, he was not the best of conductors, and players sometimes complained his beat was uncertain, but most orchestras did their best for him out of respect and affection.

The physical exertion kept him lean and supple, the new challenges were stimulating. But gradually the increasing loss of memory could no longer be ignored.

Lenny and I grieved to see our beloved Aaron's shining intellect dimmed by Alzheimer's. He didn't recognize most people, but he still recognized us. We wanted to be with him for his birthday, so Lenny and I drove up the Hudson to where Aaron had a house, and helpers. Incidentally, driving with Lenny sent one's pulse soaring.

Friends had organized a little event in the local movie house to celebrate the birthday, with performances of Copland's music. We collected Aaron and seated him between us. He sat quietly, showing no particular interest in the proceedings. But at the end, when there were exuberant bursts of applause, with the instincts of the old trouper, Aaron rose to his feet and acknowledged the ovation.

A combination of circumstances in the previous years had brought Aaron and me together in a number of places. Something inaugurated by the State Department called the Good Neighbor Policy sent Aaron to several Latin American countries as a musical ambassador.

Aaron was the perfect choice to represent American musical life: he was tactful, he spoke adequate Spanish, he had unquenchable curiosity about the local composers, and he promoted American composers as a whole, not just presenting his own work.

Our routes sometimes coincided. In Havana we used to go to an enormous popular dance hall, just to listen. Two orchestras played at opposite ends of the room. We sat somewhere in the middle, and Aaron could listen to both orchestras at once. He particularly liked the *danzón* with the bright flute line riding above the violin, trumpet, and piano, and he enjoyed the endlessly inventive rhythmic patterns.

Eventually, *Danzón Cubano* was the result of these evenings. Incidentally, Aaron was never known to dance.

The next month I was back in Mexico, and Aaron was in California writing for the movies. He wrote to me on Thanksgiving Day:

Darling Peggley:

Victor [Aaron's companion at that time] seems to be having difficulties getting this letter started so here I am to the rescue. If I didn't know you were in Mexico I could read it on his face. He keeps urging me to write a symphony in Chapala, so if there weren't a war on that would be the thing to do. Write a symphony with you as inspiration. As it is, life runs along very quietly at Oakland and now I'm more sorry than ever that you never did get up here to see how very nice it is . . . Well, anyway, the thing for you to do is to rest up, and come back soon, and continue to be an inspiration to everybody as usual.

Love, A.

Aaron often came to Mexico. He had a particular affinity for Mexico, its people, its landscape, and he had a collegial friendship with the Mexican composer and conductor Carlos Chávez. Chávez performed Copland's music regularly with his Sinfónica de México. Copland dedicated several works to Chávez.

In Mexico, Aaron and I used to go to a sprawling lower-class dance hall called El Salón México. There were three separate spaces, each with a different admission fee. The very cheapest had a sign requesting patrons not to throw their lit cigarettes on the floor because they would burn the ladies' feet. The ladies in question were of course barefoot. Aaron's popular *El Salón México* came out of these evenings.

The gifted photographer Irving Penn took my favorite photograph of Aaron for me, sitting at the piano, in profile, the curve of the sheet music propped on the piano echoed by that beak of a nose. I was pleased that in a recent profile about Aaron (it was his centenary) in *The New Yorker*, "my" photo was used full page.

Leonard Bernstein

After meeting Leonard Bernstein at Aaron Copland's house in Tanglewood, I was to be based in Europe for the next twenty-and-some years (1948–70), mostly in Paris. He had gone on to glory.

Our paths crossed on many occasions, Lenny usually accompanied by his sister, Shirley. He conducted in Paris in 1948, starting modestly with the Radio Orchestra and rapidly building to engagements with the top French orchestras. At first he was dismayed by the undisciplined orchestra musicians, who did not always come to rehearsals but would send substitutes. (Jerome Robbins had the same problem when he started to work with the ballet company of the Paris Opéra.) But by sheer force of personality, and his dazzling talents as conductor and pianist, he soon had them playing their hearts out for him.

The doyenne of Paris society, the aged and very musical Baronne Edouard de Rothschild, gave a supper party in his honor, after one of the concerts. Her invitations were prized. Guests arrived, most unusual in Paris, on the nose.

That evening Lenny had a particularly frenzied triumph. Shirley was not there to ride herd. In his dressing room backstage, admirers of various sexes were pressing one more scotch on him, gratefully received. In my role as sheepdog, I did my best to extract him; it was slow going. Finally, embarrassingly late, we arrived at the grand town house. I will never forget the tones of the butler as he announced in a stentorian voice, "La Baronne Edouard ATTEND."

Of course the usual Bernstein charm righted the situation after a few Bernstein kisses.

Lenny and I were both friends of the French composer Francis Poulenc's. On an unforgettable occasion, Poulenc invited us to a dress rehearsal at the Opéra Comique of his latest work, a spirited musical setting, full of fun, of a farce by the poet Guillaume Apollinaire, *Les Mamelles de Tirésias.*

Poulenc, Lenny, and I sat huddled in the darkened house—it was freezing cold, as there was still very little heating in postwar Paris—while the ravishing Denise Duval, in transparent veiling—how she avoided pneumonia is a mystery—sang from a Folies Bergère–type runway that she was not going to be a housewife anymore. She was going to lead a man's life.

We both loved Poulenc's lilting music, and Lenny was to conduct *Les Mamelles* later in New York. David Hockney designed the engagingly witty sets.

That same year, Lenny was conducting in Holland, and I was in Holland writing some features for *Vogue.* Lenny and his sister were staying at a nearby beach resort, Scheveningen. I was at a hotel in The Hague. I went out to join the Bernsteins for lunch.

It was a glorious day, one of those days when the Dutch light lived up to all those marine landscapes. "Let's go riding" was Lenny's sudden inspiration.

I had arrived in a town outfit; this was long before the ubiquitous blue jeans. "I'll fix you up," Shirley offered. We went to her room, and I got into a pair of her slacks and one of Lenny's shirts, and we were off.

Our rented horses responded to the great stretch of open beach and Lenny's urging and galloped *presto con fuoco.* Lenny started shouting poetry into the wind, Auden mostly. "Don't you know any poetry?" he shouted to me. I was too out of breath from holding my plunging horse to respond.

A few days later we went to Amsterdam for a concert, at the Concertgebouw, conducted by Herbert von Karajan. "You *know* I'm a better conductor than von Karajan," Lenny whispered all too audibly.

By now it is 1950. I was living and working in Paris, and Lenny and Shirley were in town. Lenny had come to conduct the Radio Orchestra. It so happened he had a gap in his schedule and I had accumulated a month's vacation time. We were having dinner in one of those little upstairs rooms at Lapérouse and had finished off a diaphanous soufflé. "Let's go somewhere, anywhere, you choose," said Lenny. "All right, let's make it Spain" was my contribution.

So we went. Those were still the Franco days, and Spain was very puritanical. They were dismayed at the Ritz in Barcelona that Lenny and Shirley wanted to sleep in the same room. They were also dismayed by the dachshund puppy the two had picked up en route that was far from housebroken.

Lenny was delighted by the *sardana* that was danced in the public square in front of the cathedral on Sundays. It is the most democratic dance in the world. Anyone can join in. You just step into the circle and grab the hand of your neighbor. The women place their handbags and the cake for Sunday lunch in the middle of the circle, and everything is safe.

Lenny being Lenny, he had to be part of the action. He pulled me in, and being a *músico*, he immediately grasped the structure and when we should stop—the music had a way of suddenly stopping, leaving me with one foot in the air.

He liked best the little bars of the *barrio chino* with its flamenco singers and children dancing outside entranced by the music. There was an old man who sang as if his heart were broken, eyes closed, stretching out his hand. We went to hear him night after night while Shirley sensibly went to bed. We loved his lament for his love who had entered a convent, "She who was most loved has become a nun" ("La Hija de Don Juan Alba," it was called).

From Barcelona we went to Majorca, to a little fishing village a Spanish friend had recommend, Cala d'Or. We settled down happily to the swimming routine, but Lenny missed having a piano. The hotel management owned a little shack across the road we could use, and I managed to arrange for an old upright piano to be sent out to us from Palma, the capital.

So every day we went to what Lenny called "a mansion grand in a foreign land"—(courtesy of Auden?). Lenny played everything from musical comedy to grand opera, with Shirley a worthy singing partner, both of them remembering every word of every lyric, including numbers by our friends Adolph Green and Betty Comden—such as "I Can Cook Too."

Both Bernsteins were confirmed hypochondriacs and traveled with a bulging satchel of potions and remedies. Inevitably, Shirley fell ill. A doctor from the nearest village was called in. He arrived in his little horse-drawn buggy. His name was Don Virgilio.

He examined Shirley. "What did he say?" Lenny asked me anxiously (at that point I was the only one who knew Spanish). "He says, 'Either she will get better, or she won't.'"

Some time later Lenny stepped on a bee, and his foot swelled alarmingly. Don Virgilio came back on the double. By this time, he was completely under the Bernstein charm and invited us all to his little house, where he gave us small glasses of sweet Málaga wine and danced and sang to a song called "Mi Jaca," with us providing a clapping accompaniment. Then we all danced.

Our month's holiday over, we headed for the airport, with a few tears. Lenny went on to Israel to conduct; I returned to my Paris office. He took off a heavy gold link bracelet I always wore and put it on.

It was not as usual then as now for men to wear jewelry. A conductor's wrist is very visible. The gold bracelet was the subject of comment. Later, when Lenny married Felicia, she sent the bracelet back to me. I still wear it.

I had not met Felicia Montealegre, the beautiful Chilean girl who had come to New York to study piano with Claudio Arrau. But Lenny talked to me about her often, and the pros and cons of marrying her. Twice he had been officially engaged, but twice he couldn't go through with it.

Felicia hung on resolutely, in spite of what must have been humiliating public rejections (nothing was kept under wraps with Lenny).

He wanted to be a good Jewish family man, but he had an unquenchable, as he called it, "dark" side.

Finally, they did marry in what was the best possible move for him but not all plain sailing for her. I became extremely fond of Felicia. She was charming and talented—both musically and as an actress. She gave him three splendid children. Lenny adored them. She made their apartment in the Dakota a center of lighthearted multilingual hospitality. I owe many happy evenings and stimulating encounters to her.

At one such evening, a fellow guest was the Russian poet Yev-geny Yevtushenko. He spoke no English or French but had picked up a bit of Spanish while in Cuba. He rather stuck to me as, aside from our Chilean hostess, no one else spoke Spanish. We left at the same time, and in the elevator he asked me, "What did you think of the dinner?" Somewhat surprised, I answered I thought it delicious. "But so short . . ." I understood he meant so few courses. He con-tinued as we exited, "When you come to my house, there will be *platos y platos y platos*"—"course after course after course." I gath-ered Russian hospitality involved a steady succession of dishes.

Sadly, Felicia died far too soon, in 1978. I was deeply touched when Lenny and the children asked me to speak at her memorial.

On a happier note, Jamie, Lenny's eldest daughter, had a baby boy. We were all in the Bernstein box to hear and watch Lenny con-duct the Philharmonic. After the concert we rushed to the Dakota, where the baby was left in the care of their faithful Julia. Lenny, bursting with pride, pointed to the baby: "There goes the first Jew-ish president of the United States."

Lenny was as generous as he was expansive. Soloists who per-formed with him have told me that no conductor could be more supportive. When I started my lecturing career at the Metropolitan Museum in 1971, he sent me, unsolicited, this little text to be used for my publicity: "Madame Bernier has the gift of instant communi-cation to a degree I have rarely encountered, and in a field where it is not easy to be communicative without being glib. Indeed, her lectures are richly informed, full of fresh surprise, and delivered with elegance and simple charm."

And the night after my lecturing debut at the Met, Lenny and Felicia gave me a large party. If it had not been for that, I think only a handful of people might have come to the auditorium. I had been away from New York for twenty years and so was an almost un-known quantity.

Lenny immediately took to my husband, John Russell, when he arrived from England. Typically, he wrote an eloquent paragraph for John's book *The Meanings of Modern Art*. When John Russell and I were married, on May 24, 1975, Lenny was John's witness; Aaron Copland gave me away; Philip Johnson gave the wedding. He had arranged a little concert following the ceremony in his new sculpture gallery. And who led me in on his arm? My new husband? Not at all—Lenny Bernstein.

Afterward, Lenny asked me, "Why didn't you ask me to write a piece of music for your wedding?" "It never occurred to me; I wouldn't have had the pretension," I answered. A few days later a music manuscript arrived from Lenny.

> For the Russells, R. + J.
>   Meditations on a Wedding
>   With love from Lenny, May 1975
>   (Marked *Andante con tenerezza* [tenderness] followed by *dolce . . .*)

So I own an unpublished Bernstein work.

Whenever something important happened in my life, I always wanted Lenny around, and he was always there.

I was given a French decoration in 1980 (Officier de l'Ordre des Arts et des Lettres). I was told that I could have a few guests but that the ceremony had to start on time. I told Lenny, "I'm inviting you, but don't come if you are going to be late." He was notoriously late everywhere. When John and I arrived at the French consulate, there was Lenny, walking up and down in front of the entrance, cape flapping in the wind, pointing to his watch when he saw us to indicate he had arrived not only on time but ahead of us.

When John's book of essays *Reading Russell* was published some years ago, his publisher gave him a lunch in a private room at Le Cirque. Lenny was invited. We sat at the bar together before the tables were seated. "Do you remember 'La Hija de Don Juan Alba'?" he asked me. More than thirty years had passed since we had heard it in Barcelona, and he remembered every word, in Spanish, and conducted me for a duet in his cigarette rasp and my feeble contralto.

I was lecturing in Turkey for an American organization in 1990. John and I were cut off from the outside world for some time, so we did not get news of Lenny's alarming deteriorating health.

The day I got back to New York came the unbelievable headline:

Leonard Bernstein was dead (October 14). A heartbreaking note was that I found a telegram from Lenny apologizing for being late with my birthday greetings—my birthday is October 1—and sending love. It must have been one of the last things he did.

We had a cloudless friendship. He inscribed one of his books to me with the affectionate nickname he had for me and added, "who has never given me anything but joy." I could say the same about him.

Early Mexican Moments

When I had met Diego Rivera and Frida Kahlo at the Sinfónica rehearsal in Mexico City, they had invited me to go with them to the concert that night. I was to collect them at their house in a suburb called San Ángel.

The house to which I went later that day in high expectation was two houses in one.

There was a big blue cube for Diego and a rather smaller dark pink one for Frida, with a connecting bridge between them.

It was designed and built by a young architect and painter called Juan O'Gorman. It was remarkably daring for its date.

At that time, San Ángel was a countrified suburb in which sedate family houses stood in large leafy gardens. People who walked by the O'Gorman house must have said to themselves, "What on earth is it? Is it a factory? A ship that never went to sea? Why aren't the stairs indoors, as they are everywhere else?"

But to me the house seemed like a wonderland, and not least for the flamboyant welcome that I got from my hostess.

Although I had done my best with my limited student's wardrobe, Frida took a quick look at me and would have none of it. "Come on, kid, I'll fix you up," she said.

Next thing I knew, I had been transformed from an anonymous college girl to a transplant from a Tehuantepec market. Multicolored swaying skirt, embroidered *huipil*, pre-Columbian necklaces galore, and her masterpiece: my hair became a bright tapestry of flowers and ribbons.

Frida laughed a great belly laugh of satisfaction at her work (she could laugh like a trombone in rut), tossed down one more little shot of tequila, and called Diego over to admire me, and off we went to sit in their usual box for the Chávez concert.

You couldn't mistake Diego Rivera. He was well over six feet tall. He had been known to weigh more than three hundred pounds. And, as he himself admitted, he had a face like a gargantuan frog.

Frida, by contrast, stood five feet three and was delicately built. An attack of polio in childhood had left her with a withered right leg, and she was never to recover completely from a horrendous traffic accident in 1925 that had left her more dead than alive. Surgical and other painful treatments went on most of her life.

But she did not strike me as an object of pity who shrank from being looked at too closely. On the contrary, she drew attention to herself by adopting the spectacular costume of the women of Tehuantepec, of which she had made me a pale reflection—full-length swaying skirts ruffled at the hem and the embroidered overblouse called a *huipil*. Usually a big shawl went along with it, a rebozo. I still own a deep blue rebozo Frida gave me, and I have worn it onstage at the Met. Sometimes, as can be seen in some of the self-portraits, she added a face-framing extravaganza of ruffles and pleats that was the traditional Tehuana headdress. And she usually wore her hair entwined in a thicket of flowers and ribbons improvised every time. This was often topped off by garlands of heavy pre-Columbian necklaces. She didn't stint on the rings, either, on both hands.

She often painted her nails—orange, purple, green, whatever went best with the outfit of the day. Incidentally, Frida had never been to Tehuantepec; she just liked the becoming costume, it played to Diego's *mexicanidad*, and it made her the most noticeable kid on the block.

I was to discover she had a great sense of mischief. No one was more fun to be around. Her vocabulary in both Spanish and English would have made a truck driver blush.

Rare was the man or woman who was not seduced by her, and seduction was her specialty.

After such a beginning, how could I not fail to fall in love with Mexico?

Some Animals I Have Known

After my marriage to Lew, my new life in Mexico began.

As a child, I didn't have any pets. No dog, no cat. I'm not counting two personable pink-eyed white mice that my Francophile father named Aglavaine and Selysette (these were characters out of a Maeterlinck play, I believe). The pet shop had guaranteed both were male, but one day Aglavaine or Selysette, I'm not sure which, produced sixteen offspring. That strained my schoolroom capacities. I think they were banished. (I had lessons at home tutored by a French governess.)

My first real pet came into my life in Acapulco in 1938. My young husband and I (we were respectively twenty-one and twenty-three) were staying in a small hotel in the town while our house was being built. This was long before the painful tourist boom that defaced a once-tranquil little port.

There was a knock on the door. An Indian boy, holding something, said to me, "Buy this, señora, and I will kill it and give you its skin." It was a baby ocelot. I was horrified and without another thought said, "Don't kill it. I'll buy it."

So I found myself in a small hotel room with a little snarling, hissing creature. My husband was out at the time.

By the next day, the ocelot was following me around and arching its neck to be petted. Not a snarl. It turned out that I was an animal tamer.

When the house was finally built, there were also quarters for the various local animals I accumulated. (There was a large garden.) It got around that there was an American señora who would buy animals, so as time went by, I ruled over a large menagerie.

The ocelot was a favorite, and I dignified it by calling it Tigre (Tiger). I used to brush it with Yardley's brilliantine. It had its box— it was meticulous—in the spare bathroom next to my bedroom. When the door was opened in the morning, it would come bounding out across the room and leap onto my bed to reach me, licking and purring. The purr was louder than a cat's. I found it very soothing when I had a migraine to use the ocelot as a pillow under my head.

Although I tried to compensate for what might be lacking in its diet (raw meat) with limewater, the ocelot developed what I took to be a form of rickets. Its back paws were painful when it jumped onto my lap.

There was no vet in Acapulco, so I took the ocelot to the one doctor in town who treated babies and presented my patient. The doctor was indignant. But I said to him, "Just treat him like a baby, weigh him, and give him the appropriate medication." So he did. A first: an ocelot on the baby scales.

I always took the favorite animal to Mexico City with me, where I had an apartment, although it was forbidden by the fledgling airline. I ignored this and rigged up a basket with a loose burlap covering the top for the ocelot. All went well until a sudden dip of the plane sent the ocelot springing through the burlap and out of its basket, to the terror of the other passengers. But in Mexico a discreet exchange of pesos arranges everything. I went right on transporting my favorites by air.

At one point I had left Tigre in the Mexico City apartment under the care of my Indian maid while I made a trip to New York. At that time, 1940, the Museum of Modern Art was organizing a vast Mexican exhibition: *Twenty Centuries of Mexican Art*.

I had become very friendly with the brilliant and combustible Mexican painter José Clemente Orozco. While Diego Rivera was a master of self-publicity and the center of spectacular news of one kind or another, José Clemente, although equally talented, was often overlooked. In fact, he was somewhat forgotten in his own country. He had a wife and several children and was very hard up. Seeing this, I hired a space, had my maid sweep it out, and put on the first Orozco exhibition in Mexico since 1916. We did quite well.

So I was anxious that José Clemente get equal booking with the flamboyant Diego in New York. I went to see Nelson Rockefeller, who was president of the Museum of Modern Art at that time. I knew him slightly. He listened good-naturedly while I held forth on the importance of giving Orozco his proper position in the upcoming exhibition. He made me the following offer: if I could persuade Orozco to come to the museum and paint a panel in front of spectators, he would pay the expenses. José Clemente had no telephone, so I cabled him to come to my Mexico City apartment at a certain date and hour to receive an important call from me.

Long-distance calls were a big deal in those days, so I went to Nelson's office to telephone. I hadn't realized that Nelson understood Spanish, but when I shouted down the telephone (Orozco was very deaf) that there was a very rich man—"un hombre muy rico"—who would pay for him to come to New York, I saw Nelson chuckling behind his desk.

But Orozco immediately made objections: "*Me parece un circo*"— "It sounds like a circus to me." "*Además tu tigre me está molestando*"— "What's more, your tiger is bothering me." My ocelot was apparently nipping at his ankles.

In spite of this, Orozco did come up to New York and did paint the panels in the Museum of Modern Art called *Dive Bomber and Tank*, while some members of the public were allowed to watch, at a distance. It is still there.

This was so long ago that when Nelson and his wife gave a party for the visiting Mexican artists, it was black-tie. We rented a suitable outfit for José Clemente, but then the problem arose of his black tie. I have failed to explain that Orozco had only one hand, having blown off the other in some chemical experiment. It is difficult to tie a bow on someone else frontally, so I stood on a chair behind José Clemente and reached around and tied the tie.

Back to my menagerie. The most intelligent and crafty animals I ever knew were the coatimundis. They are furry creatures, perhaps related to the raccoon, with a pointed snout and a bushy tail like a Christmas tree. They scamper on all fours and can climb trees or, if visiting me in Mexico City, curtains.

What distinguishes them from other animals, aside from their superior wits, is their love of perfume. Most animals have very limited tastes as to what smells agreeable, but the coatis went in trances when confronted by a vase of tuberoses or would delightedly sniff at my wrists if there was a trace of eau de cologne.

They would keep an eye out for the bottle of Tabac Blond that was on my dressing table. I would observe them, glancing at me to see if I noticed, approaching warily, then pouncing on the bottle to try to push it over.

They are shrewd. In Acapulco, there was a swinging screen door between the kitchen and the open-air dining room. They figured out how to push the door open and rush in before it closed.

They would watch the kitchen to see if the cook might be out. If she was, they made a dash for it and made a meal of whatever was within reach, a bowl of raw eggs, for instance, munching them down, shells and all.

In Mexico the coatimundi is called a *tejón*. As we might say of someone crafty that he or she is "foxy," in Mexico they say such a person is *muy tejón*.

Over the years I had a number of coatimundis. As was my habit, I would take the favorite up to Mexico City with me. The coatis live in tropical forests, and Mexico City is at a high altitude. The favored coati felt the cold and found the most comfortable spot was in my bed, next to me.

At one point I had some minor ailment, and a Mexican doctor was called into service. He said, "Señora, I must examine you," and pulled up the covers. He was astonished to find a coati in the American señora's bed.

Once an Indian brought me an anteater, not the most prepossessing of animals, but I added it to my menagerie. There were no spare cages or spaces for a new acquisition. My husband was away on a hunting trip, so I put the anteater on a temporary basis in his bathroom. Although limited in intelligence, the anteater, no fool, heaved itself into the cool depths of the toilet and with its little paws pulled down the lid on top of it.

My husband rushed back from his hunting trip and headed for his bathroom. He was in such a hurry that I had no time to say to him, "Don't look now, but there is an anteater in your toilet."

Monkeys were an important contingent in my menagerie. It

started with a pair of long-legged and long-armed spider monkeys from Veracruz, named Canuto and Titina. Frida Kahlo had similar monkeys and took a lively interest in mine, asking if they were behaving well. In fact, I think it was because of my menagerie that Frida took to me, although she said most "North Americans," as we are called south of the border, had faces like unbaked muffins.

Like many pairs, Canuto and Titina did not get along. Canuto took to seizing her by one leg and flinging her away from him. So they had to be kept apart and had separate cage-residences.

Titina was all affection, and we would go for walks together, her tail around my waist, holding my hand. She was so well brought up that I could take her out to luncheon, where she would sit on my lap facing me and not touch any of the food until her own plate was placed on the floor.

Then there was a minute wizened little monkey from Brazil, a marmoset, named by me Don Changuillo, because in spite of his small size he commanded respect. Don Changuillo accompanied me on my archaeological digs, perched on top of the turban I wore to protect myself from the dust of excavations. From that vantage point he could spot a grasshopper from a distance and with a flying leap capture it in one paw.

The only trouble with the monkeys was that they had a great fondness for eating hibiscus flowers and plucked them with glee as if they were ice cream cones. Ruin for the garden.

I had one problem animal, a kinkajou. It drank. It was nocturnal and spent its days in the darkened quarters I had provided for the night shift. At the cocktail hour, it would come swinging along the beams above the terrace bar by its long prehensile tail, drop onto the bar, to the dismay of the human customers, and grab a glass.

I am not making this up: it would then head for town and find its way to the Siete Mares Bar. I would get an angry telephone call from the bar's improbably named owner, Jorge Hardy, to please come and get it because it was annoying the customers.

Like many drunks, it ended badly. It hurled itself out of a moving car. That did it.

Then there were the birds. Most Mexican village houses had a few birdcages hanging from the porch rafters, with canaries and the like. I followed the custom, but my favorite was an inconspicuous little gray bird called a *cenzontle*. It had an uncanny ability to briefly follow a tune sung to it, before breaking out into its own cadenzas.

One time in New York an aged and wealthy admirer took me to a concert of the NBC Symphony Orchestra led by Arturo Toscanini. It was a hot ticket. The excitement of the evening was the world premiere of Shostakovich's Seventh Symphony. It has a simple, repetitive opening theme.

I was back in Mexico City the next day, and on to Acapulco. I sang the little theme to the *cenzontle*, which adopted it easily. When Carlos Chávez, conductor of the Sinfónica de México, came for lunch soon after this, he almost fell into his guacamole when he heard, for the first time, the Shostakovich theme trilled by a local bird.

The stars of the bird collection were two brilliantly colored macaws. They perched in a palm tree just outside my dining terrace, their wings slightly clipped so they would not stray into the neighboring property. They had raucous voices, but this was forgiven because of their spectacular coloring.

They had a great fondness for butter. When I came out on the terrace for my breakfast, they would sidle down the palm fronds in their pigeon-toed progress and perch, one on each of my shoulders, to be rewarded by nibbles of buttered toast.

The most unexpected addition to my menagerie was a small penguin from Antarctica, brought to me by some sailors. I made it a little collar, attached a length of thin rope, and put it in my station wagon.

I drove to a secluded beach (they still existed then) to avoid intrusive attention. My new acquisition took to the water, and seemed to take to me. The penguin became my favorite swimming companion.

Unfortunately, my delightful new animal friend had arrived with what I thought to be a case of bronchitis. There was no one around who could advise me. In spite of my ministrations, I no longer had a penguin.

Up, Up, and Away

There was no plane service from Mexico City to Acapulco in those early days. I am talking about the late 1930s, early 1940s.

To get to Acapulco from Mexico City, you had to take the winding, climbing, dipping main road—not yet an autoroute—down from Mexico City's seventy-five hundred feet to balmy Cuernavaca at fifty-five hundred, on to Taxco, avoiding Bill Spratling's silver shops, up again to the chilly peaks of Tres Marías—Lew thought it advisable to stop for a tequila for good luck—keep going through Chilpancingo and its fly-specked café, finally, several weary hours later, down to the tropical vegetation of Acapulco.

There was a rudimentary airstrip, just a flat stretch of baked mud, and a tin shanty. There might be a few small planes parked there belonging to Chante Obregón Santacilla, who took people on excursions, or to Ángel Zárate, who was game—not always advisably—to take passengers on longer hops. Service was casual. Zárate asked me once if I would mind holding the door.

We put ourselves in Zárate's hands to get us to Morelia. There was one other passenger, an aged French miner. Somewhere between Acapulco and Morelia there was engine trouble, and we crash-landed in a cornfield.

Somewhat shaken, I got out, not failing to take the book I was reading, Céline's *Voyage au Bout de la Nuit*, and an unopened bottle of red wine.

The three of us trudged toward a nearby village while Zárate fiddled with the engine. It was a small village, with just a few palm-thatched huts. The Indian ladies kindly offered me the hospitality of a hammock.

It was getting late, and a chicken was brought out to be cooked on a charcoal brazier. On an impulse, to improve the flavor, I poured in a good slug of red wine. This provoked much surprise and merriment.

The ladies huddled around me. I spoke very little Spanish then, but understood they wanted to know which one was my *marido* (husband): *el viejo* (the old French miner) or *el joven* (my husband). "*El joven*," I answered.

They seemed relieved. "How long have you been married?" they asked. "Two years," I told them. "How many children do you have?" was the next question. "None," I answered.

This caused quite some agitation. They obviously talked it over and came back to me. "We want to know how you do it," they asked me.

My limited Spanish was not up to that one.

I spent the night in the one hammock, and by the next day Ángel Zárate had fixed the crippled engine. Hoping for the best, we climbed back in and actually made it to Morelia.

On another flight he crashed, badly, landing at Acapulco. We were not on that flight, but went out to the airstrip to try to help the wounded. We heard later that Zárate's luck had run out. He had crashed again. This time was his last.

We acquired our first plane; it was a little Piper Cub. Later, there was a larger Beechcraft. Chante Obregón gave Lew flying lessons and some sort of paper that purported to be a license. And Lew taught me.

To this day I have a very poor sense of direction, but here I couldn't go wrong. All I had to do was to follow the coastline until I came across an inviting uninhabited beach. We went on delightful flying and swimming picnics.

One time we realized we were very short of petrol for the return. I remembered there was a naval station at Icacos, halfway back to Acapulco. We landed there; I climbed out in my bathing suit, brandishing a beach towel, and talked the astonished sailors into selling me a little *gasolina*. I filtered the gasoline through my beach towel, not being too confident of its purity.

It had begun to get dark, and our friends were worrying about us. There were no lights on the landing strip, so they gathered their cars around it and put on their lights so that we could see to land.

Landing there was always tricky; there was the bay on one side and a mountain range on the other. You had to sideslip in. We made it.

Under the Volcano
(*pace* Malcolm Lowry)

I am the only white woman in the world who has witnessed the birth of a volcano. The only other woman who was there was the wife of a poor Tarascan farmer, Dionisio Pulido, who had a small cornfield in the village of Paricutín, in the state of Michoacán.

Pulido was working his plot when there was a sudden fissure in the earth. He tried to cover it. It widened and let out a spout of sulfurous vapor. It opened up further with a great roar and a flinging skyward of a torrent of molten lava.

Terrified, Pulido called out for his wife. They fled in frantic haste.

I was living in Mexico at that time. The day of the eruption, February 20, 1943, a friend and I had decided we would try the famous hot water springs at the Balneario de Agua Blanca of San José Purúa, Michoacán. We left Mexico City and drove due west.

Before we had a chance to test the curative powers of the vaunted hot springs, we picked up a whispered rumor that something extraordinary was happening at a hamlet called Paricutín.

We decided to investigate. There was no road to Paricutín, only a mule track. So we rented mules and were off.

Even before we arrived, the sky was livid with great gusts of flames. Once nearer, we saw a cone rising above rivers of molten rocks. It was dark by then and bitterly cold. A few Indians arrived wrapped in their serapes.

We lay down on the ground, all close together like sardines, for warmth. We watched all night, overcome by the awesome spectacle and the noise. There were earth-shattering roars as the volcano shot up streams of flaming lava. As the molten rocks hit the cold earth, they split in furious explosions.

We were there all night, small human beings in the face of a gigantic cataclysm. Nobody spoke. I had brought a bottle of tequila, and we passed it up and down the line until it was empty.

By daylight, we saw that our faces were black from the falling ash. What trees had been there before were stripped bare of foliage—blackened trunks, twisted branches in a Dantean landscape.

More Indians arrived to stare silently at the devastation. Then there were *abrazos* all around with our new friends from that extraordinary night, and we went our separate ways.

Soon after this, the whole area was cordoned off; no one was allowed anywhere near the still-active volcano.

We learned later that the eruption had completely wiped out Paricutín and the neighboring hamlet of Parangaricutiro. The inhabitants were relocated. The eruption continued until 1952, and the volcano grew to well over 1,345 feet aboveground.

I do not imagine that it was of much comfort to the villagers who had lost all their crops and farm animals to learn that this epochal calamity was a onetime thing.

Malcolm Lowry

There was one real hotel at the time, the Mirador, run by fat Don Carlos Barnard and his fat family. Boys were already earning pesos diving off the high rocks below the hotel dining room.

There was one bar in town—we are in Acapulco in 1938—called the Siete Mares, run by a reedy Mexican. The one waiter was a broken-down former boxer known to everyone as Champ.

The one place to have a drink and dance was the open courtyard of the local brothel called, inevitably, El Foco Rojo (The Red Light).

The tourist invasion had not begun. Lew and I were the only English speakers around.

We were building a house. This involved a slow-beat progress in keeping with the tropical heat. And it was hot. Meanwhile, we lived in rented rooms above the town.

It was there that a boy—the *mozo*—came up with a message from the bar. A foreigner, ragged and bleeding, had been thrown off the Cuernavaca bus, with no money, speaking no Spanish. He had been dumped there. Would we come down?

We went. There was a chunky fellow of about thirty, matted blond hair, unshaven, clothes indeed torn and bloodstained, ranting incoherently.

The verdict of the Siete Mares was clear: "*borracho, borracho*"—drunk. I knew enough Spanish to recognize the next word *cárcel*—prison. But in spite of the haze of alcohol, the words he was mumbling had an unmistakable echo of a literate English background.

There was something about him, despite his unpromising appearance, that made me feel he was worth helping.

Impulsively, I said, "We'll take him home and clean him up."

This is how we became the temporary guardians of the highly gifted and spectacularly drunken English writer Malcolm Lowry. I had never heard of him. This was some years before he finally had his tortured semiautobiographical novel *Under the Volcano* published—it was to be widely admired—and long before John Huston made it even better known by his highly fantasized film treatment, with Albert Finney as the doomed dipsomaniac.

I had had no experience whatsoever with drunks. I thought that with care, a systematic hiding of bottles—even a regimen of exercise—he would shape up. I would take him to the beach and supervise his swimming. He loved the water. He used to talk about having served on a Norwegian freighter.

Of course I was wrong. But once sober, he was so articulate, so amusing, so totally original, that I persevered in spite of constant lapses. Because however ingenious I was in doing away with the bottles, he always outwitted me. There would be tearful promises of reform, secret slipping of pesos to the maid for more bottles, then plunges via his favorite mescal with what he called his demons.

It was hard to piece his story together. Bits and strands would emerge, then tangle and twist. The American writer Conrad Aiken, a serious drinker himself, was a boozing father figure. Lowry mentioned Cambridge. There were constant references to sinister forces bent on trapping him. The avenging angels of fate were after him. He seemed to be on the run because of unpaid bills and overstaying his Mexican visa. He was terrified of the police and convinced he was being spied upon. He apparently had been living in Cuernavaca. What was he doing, penniless, on that bus? A wife was mentioned vaguely; she seemed to have disappeared from the scene. He alluded to his family sending him money, but evildoers took it away from him.

He was adept at wordplay and vastly entertaining when he was not in the grip of whisky, tequila, and/or mescal. Not surprisingly, he was obsessed by the nightmare world of German Expressionist cinema. He loved American jazz, particularly Bix Beiderbecke. He said he had owned a ukulele, and said he played it very well.

He invented a little dance to the tune of Grieg's "Death of Aase"; we would stomp around in a circle singing, "All we need is capital, capital, capital."

He had DTs and would storm terrified into my room in the middle of the night. In Mexico, the cocks often make their raucous serenades at an ungodly hour instead of waiting until dawn. This would bring on further terrors, horrors. I became so aware of his fears that I started to absorb them myself.

In the classic mold, he fell in love with his nurse. The situation became untenable. Finally, we had to send him on his way, in clean clothes, with money in his pocket, back to the Cuernavaca bus.

A few years ago Malcolm Lowry's biographer Gordon Bowker tracked me down in London and came to interview me. He told me about an unpublished novella by Lowry called *La Mordida*—*The Payback*—which included a fictionalized account of his time with us.

The events he wrote about never happened. One described how he had beaten my husband in a swimming race, which very much impressed me. In fact, Lew was an expert swimmer and had taught Malcolm the crawl.

More poignant was his tormented mea culpa of having raped me while my husband was away. Nothing of the sort ever happened.

To quote from his *La Mordida*:

Certainly he had not been able to help falling in love with Peggy. [This was a childhood family nickname, long since discarded] . . . The anguish of the Riley incident, and writing that poem here:

> Love which comes too late is like that black storm
> That breaks out of its season, when you stand
> Huddled yet with upturned tentative hand
> To the strange rain.

What a bestial thing that had been of him to do! Drunk or not he could find no forgiveness in his heart for it, even if he never knew precisely—and alas!—what he had done. But to have betrayed someone who had befriended him as unselfishly as had Riley and Peggy, finding him drunk and penniless there writing poems in the Siete Mares, and then buying him clothes, . . . succouring him as well as they could for the reason which above all others should have secured his loyalty, that they believed in his talent, . . . feeding him, . . . offering him their car, even at the very end, their car—the warm-hearted, generous kindliness of these two people who could have been friends all his life: and who were indeed as husband and wife so well matched, . . . singing on their guitar to-gether, swimming together, celebrating their anniversary every month: where were they now? Had he done, he wondered, any permanent damage—to say the least—to that relation-ship? . . . There had not been excuse for, when R's back was turned, trying to rape her—though had he? He would never know.

Malcolm disappeared from our life with that bus to Cuernavaca. Many years later, in 1947, when I was living in Europe, I read about the publication of a tormented novel, *Under the Volcano.*

Only then did I learn more about him. He had begun drinking at fifteen. He confided in his diary, "Secretly I had decided that I would be a drunkard when I grew up." He came from a substantial English family who sent him money regularly via bankers who rationed the handouts, but nevertheless it invariably was spent on drink. He was in and out of jails and mental institutions on three continents and was constantly being evicted for drunkenness. He managed to get into Cambridge—probably through family pull—but did poorly.

Out of all this turmoil emerged a splendid if flawed novel, *Under the Volcano.*

Malcolm died in 1957 at a cottage in Ripe, East Sussex. He was not yet fifty. Mystery always surrounded his death. Two causes were reported: one was that he had committed suicide; the other, acute alcoholism. A broken gin bottle was near the body sprawled on the bedroom floor.

Paul and Jane Bowles

Aaron Copland introduced me to Paul and Janie Bowles in 1937. Lew and I were newlyweds; so were the Bowleses.

Janie was a small sprite, crop-haired, snub-nosed. "What's it like being married, for you?" she asked me. Since Janie was a lesbian and Paul a homosexual, their marriage was not exactly a mirror image of ours. She called Paul, most inappropriately, Fluffy or Bubbles.

She limped. As an adolescent, she had had tuberculosis of the knee. Her mother took her to a Swiss sanatorium, where she was put in traction for many months. She then went to school in Switzerland. As a result, she spoke fluent French and knew some bawdy French songs.

She never wanted people to know she was lame. She always put a small Band-Aid on her knee, as if she had just had an accident.

Paul was short, compact, very blond. At that time he was known as a composer to a small group that included Virgil Thomson. Writing and *The Sheltering Sky* came later. He wore a truss, an object of great shame. It was to be ignored. Once Janie picked it up. "You touched it," he accused her. Never again.

Paul was involved in helping a theater group from an all-black YMCA in New York. We are in the late 1930s; there would not have been an integrated group in those days. One of the members had written a play that involved two white lynchers.

This presented a bit of a problem. They appealed to Paul. He appealed to Lew and me. Of course we agreed to participate.

We showed up for rehearsal. Our part consisted of rushing onstage looking menacing and rushing off.

We did this on the great night, to great acclaim.

We were feted at a dinner given after the performance; with Paul we were the only whites.

This was my first and only experience in the theater.

Paul and Janie thought of going to Mexico. We were building a house in Acapulco. "Come along," we said. They came.

Our house wasn't finished. We rented a house on a point over the sea belonging to Bill Spratling, the American who made Taxco famous again (in colonial times it had been the source for silver) for its silver jewelry, and for its relaxed sexual mores.

The staff consisted of one copper-colored youth, whose usual uniform was a wisp of chiffon draped around his neck.

Paul's room was on the upper floor, where all around there was silence, except for the sound of waves lapping at the rocks. He slept with great balls of wax in his ears and a black mask.

Swimming and the beach were the main attractions and occupations. By midday, in the blazing sun, Paul would get a particular glint in his eye and say urgently, "I just have to have some *hot soup, hot soup now*." Even the most resourceful hostess would find this a difficult request.

Paul's father was a dentist who had perfect occlusion. Paul had a comic turn, imitating his father, explosive with rage, his occlusion threatened by a grain of sand in the spinach.

It seemed a good idea to rent them their own house. We found one in town that belonged to a good-looking American beachcomber who had been married to a silent-screen star (Nancy Carroll), had taught Shakespeare at Princeton, and had settled in Acapulco to enjoy the obliging female population and to start a pearl-diving business. The equipment for the pearl diving lay in a disorderly heap in one corner of the courtyard, nestled under some dusty palm fronds.

Janie adopted an armadillo and named it Mary Schuster, after a friend of hers. The armadillo has a very small head and a correspondingly small brain. After lunch, Janie would call out, "Now, Mary Schuster, come for your French lesson."

Eventually, Janie moved inland to another rented house. Paul went off to Tangier. Janie enjoyed playing the role of a conventional housewife and inviting the local ladies in for tea. The genteel facade was apt to be interrupted by the Indian maid bursting in and screeching, "Is it now time to kill the chicken?"

Janie enjoyed seducing conventional middle-aged women and producing them like fairground trophies. One who looked like the chairwoman of the local Republican Party was named Helvetia Perkins. Janie brought Mrs. Perkins to our Mexico City apartment.

I used to bring the favorite animal of my Acapulco menagerie up to Mexico City with me. At this time it was a wily, well-behaved coatimundi. The coati was thoroughly at home in the apartment. But when we went onto the landing to say goodbye to our guests, the coati rushed out. Feeling lost in unfamiliar surroundings, it scrambled up Mrs. Perkins's skirts, thereby putting its rescuers in an uncomfortable situation.

On another occasion, in Paris, Janie produced a nicely suited gray-haired lady named Rose who ran a tearoom in Connecticut. "She's a volcano in bed," Janie confided.

Rose was duly introduced to Diana Cooper and various other highlights of the Parisian scene. "Don't understand your friends," Rose complained. "They don't talk about anything."

"What do your friends talk about?" I asked.

"Business and sports," Rose answered.

By this time, the early 1960s, both Janie and Paul had moved to Tangier, but Janie showed up in Paris now and then, where she was a conscientious explorer of lesbian bars. I was in Paris then running my art magazine, *L'ŒIL*. She sent a message to my office: "I must see you."

We went out to a café. "You are a businesswoman," Janie said. "Tell me what you think of this business letter." She had been cabling her bank in Tangier to send her money, but could never get an answer. Her letter:

Dear Mr. Vivanco [he was the bank manager]
    If I do not receive my money by Tuesday, I will shoot myself.

Yours sincerely,
Jane Bowles

I said it was an excellent business letter.

Janie was a highly gifted writer with an outsized writer's block. John Ashbery and Tennessee Williams prized her work. She wrote in all a novel, *Two Serious Ladies*, a few short stories—a wonderful one was called "Camp Cataract"—and a play, *In the Summer House*. At her request, I read the play aloud to Oliver Smith. He loved it and produced it on Broadway to a somewhat bemused audience.

Writing was a titanic struggle for her. A severe stroke put an end to the struggle. Alcohol and drugs continued the destruction of this brilliant, witty, adorable, impossible person.

The Good Neighbors

Before Pearl Harbor plunged us into World War II, the State Department initiated something called the Good Neighbor Policy. The idea was to send out the word that we North Americans are civilized people (much nicer than the Germans) and interested in Latin American culture.

The Museum of Modern Art was an active partner in this program. This is how I, a twentysomething who hadn't even graduated from Sarah Lawrence (I got married instead), and my husband, Lewis Riley, of approximately the same age, were entrusted with a cargo of North American paintings. We were to shepherd them in turn to Colombia, Venezuela, and Cuba. In each country we were to put on an exhibition, arrange for the publicity, and scout the local scene for interesting artists.

The talent, as they say in showbiz, were contemporary American artists such as Eugene Speicher, Bernard Karfiol, Yasuo Kuniyoshi, Thomas Hart Benton, and other WPA-era stalwarts.

Two other similar exhibitions were to travel to other South American countries in the care of representatives of the Modern.

My qualifications were that I had been unofficially connected with the Modern and its curators, particularly when the museum was planning the mammoth *Twenty Centuries of Mexican Art* exhibition for 1940. I knew the leading artists well—Diego Rivera, Frida Kahlo, José Clemente Orozco in particular—and so was able to help out.

Lew was indispensable in that he spoke Spanish like a native Latin American (Spanish Spanish has a different ring to it) and played the guitar.

Our first stop was Bogotá. In the course of our duties we got to know Eduardo Santos and his elegant wife, Doña Lorencita. Don Eduardo was the president of Colombia. Previously, he had been editor of the leading newspaper, *El Tiempo*, which was owned by his family. The Santoses very hospitably invited us to what was billed as a tea.

We arrived to find a large group of people, and to Lew's relief cocktails were served. We chatted and we sipped; these diplomatic novices were somewhat shy about total immersion in diplomatic circles. My Spanish was only passable. French helped. On this trip I was to meet several ladies of a certain age who had studied in Paris with André Lhote. Time passed, and we were mentally edging to the door, when Doña Lorencita announced that tea will now be served and led us into an ornate dining room with a large table set as if for a substantial meal.

The very solid cakes were served like courses. There was no escape. As we choked down what we counted on being the last bites, Doña Lorencita announced, "And now the North Americans will sing for us." To our dismay, a guitar was produced; somehow it had been leaked that Lew played the guitar. But he only played to accompany Mexican ranchero songs, and sometimes we sang together in somewhat discordant thirds.

So there we were, faced with the cake remains and a large attentive audience. We did our best for our country.

When we had finished exhibiting our wares and made the rounds of local studios, the problem arose as to how to transport the exhibition to Caracas, Venezuela. The local facilities were not reassuring. So I had the entire show packed under my supervision in a truck. I hit lucky with an obliging taxi driver and said to him, "Follow that truck. Don't let it out of our sight."

For ten days we weaved up and around and down the Andes. At the border with Venezuela, Cúcuta, the Colombian authorities had failed to send the release papers to allow the paintings to exit the country. We waited two days at Cúcuta, and you can be sure those days seemed very long.

By then the taxi driver had become a family friend. He invented a little song called "Peggy la güera de Nueva York" (Peggy the Blonde from New York). He had heard Lew speak to me as Peggy. And I am not blond, but then everything is relative.

We finally made it to Caracas and were met by the director of the local museum, Luis Alfredo López Méndez. He seemed very nervous and was perspiring freely. It was ten in the morning, so we were a bit taken aback when he suggested a scotch. Anything for the job, we accepted.

Very soon he blurted out, "I will tell you, someone is sure to tell you, I am the man that 'Latins Are Lousy Lovers' was written about." We remembered that an article by someone called Helen Gurley Brown had appeared in a well-known American magazine. She had been married to the subject. We expressed our sympathy at this poignant admission.

Eventually, we actually moved into Luis Alfredo's ramshackle house. We were offering our services for the Latin American venture without a fee; as a contribution to the war effort, the Modern was to provide a per diem for expenses. This was so small, and the cost of living in Venezuela was so high, that the only way to survive was to accept his hospitality.

What I most remember about our stay as his guest was that he had a maid with a harelip who bellowed an idiotic local song called "Aurora" all day as she dusted absentmindedly.

I also remember the bus signs to a neighborhood called Paraíso: "Paraíso Directo."

We were in charge of publicity and sent a selection of photographs to the local newspaper. This included Speicher's magisterial portrait of Katharine Cornell as Candida and a lush nude by Bernard Karfiol. The newspaper printed the nude with the caption "Katharine Cornell as Candida." Very naughty. The reactions we heard were usually a highly amused *"Ay, qué cándida!"*

It became evident to us that the most interesting artist was an eccentric figure who lived on a beach off Macuto. We saw his work in the Caracas Museum: mainly white landscapes, delicate yet firm. His name was Armando Reverón. So we drove off to find him.

We found him at work on the beach, an emaciated figure painting at an easel propped in the sand. There was a second easel and a second figure busily painting away: his pet monkey. This was accepted by all as the most natural thing in the world.

We were invited to lunch in his tent with his companion, a shy, dusky native woman. He explained to us that there were no knives, he didn't believe in them, so we used objects carved in wood by our host. He didn't believe in tea or coffee either, but offered a drink I remembered from my childhood: Postum. The food consisted of vegetables and fruits. No meat—so who needs knives? The only other guests were some life-sized dolls Reverón had sculpted.

I reported my impression of Reverón's work to the Modern. This was in 1941. The museum put on a Reverón exhibition in 2007. No one remembered that it was my idea. (And no one at MoMA remembers that they have Orozco's *Dive Bomber and Tank* because of me.)

We reached our last stop, Cuba, in December 1941. Days were already short. It was quite dark when we were met by a distinguished Cuban intellectual, José María Chacón y Calvo—round of person and serious of mien. He took us on a motorized tour of Havana, pointing out the important landmarks, such as the National Capitol, a Washington Monument (D.C.) look-alike. The only trouble was that by then it was pitch-dark and the Cubans had only a halfhearted interest in illumination.

Much was made of the arcane fact that a diamond was buried under the floor of the National Capitol, at the precise point from which all roads in Havana were centered. I was disappointed to learn later that the diamond was synthetic.

When we were leaving Havana some time later, Chacón y Calvo sent a formal letter of thanks to Lew (to the man, not the woman, mind you) ending (it sounds better in Spanish): "Will you do me the favor of throwing me at the feet of your wife?" Since he was distinctly chubby, I wondered if he might bounce.

It was symphony orchestra season, and for the chic women of the capital this was the cue to bring out their furs—regardless of the tropical temperature. And the family diamonds (real, these). The orchestra's conductor at that time was a personable Italian, much favored by the ladies.

But the real music came from the streets. There seemed to be literally music in the air, with rumba rhythms pulsating from every café and street corner. A favorite number described a hearse being pushed along a street with its burden, but when a rumba is heard, the corpse springs out of its coffin and gets up and dances.

No one appreciated the uninhibited rhythmic vitality more than

Aaron Copland. He was in Havana for a Good Neighbor Policy tour similar to ours—to my good fortune, we had coincided in Bogotá, Caracas, and now Cuba.

For economy, I had rented an apartment to avoid hotel bills. I took over the kitchen and bravely entertained. "Everybody" came, including the American ambassador, Spruille Braden. I served an orange ice cream of my own invention. It had a somewhat unusual texture. "How amusing, fur ice cream," one of the guests was heard to remark.

I acquired, briefly, a taste for Cuban cigars: Romeo y Julieta, Partagás, and Bolívar were the best, I thought. I had gone to watch them being rolled into shape by young women at long tables. They were being read to aloud by a person on a high stool.

These were still the days of the reprehensible dictator Fulgencio Batista, much admired by the State Department as a bulwark against Communism. Fidel Castro would emerge a few years later.

Of course I visited studios. Unfortunately, the most interesting Cuban artist, Wifredo Lam, was not back in Cuba from Europe. I did like the work of Amelia Peláez, elements of Cuban architecture, and decorative arts peering from a strong black grid. I know there is a vibrant art scene now, and I hope to return to see what is going on with a whole new, talented generation today.

The Cuban visit was cut short by the horrific news of Pearl Harbor. I had been walking along the famous Varadero Beach outside Havana with Aaron Copland when we heard a broadcast from a beach shack.

As soon as possible, we packed up the exhibition and headed for home.

More Mexican Moments

When I returned to Mexico after my marriage, I found that because of the war in Europe, whole new groups had arrived to diversify and enliven the scene. There were gifted émigrés from France—particularly the Surrealists, who found what the imperious Surrealist leader André Breton called "a country in which myth is still alive." Breton was followed by the poet Benjamin Péret and his wife, the painter Remedios Varo; the Austrian painter Wolfgang Paalen and his French wife, Alice Rahon, who wrote poems and developed into a painter; and the scene designer Esteban Francés.

There were Spaniards escaping from Franco and central Europeans fleeing the Nazis. There were brilliant people and, as always at such times, dubious people escaping responsibilities or the law (or both).

I did a stint at a canteen benefiting the Red Cross. I followed the red-haired mistress of the ex-king Carol II of Romania, Magda Lupescu. She warned me, "Always be sure to weigh the sugar before you leave." It took a Romanian to think of that one.

By this time Diego and Frida had left the double-cube house. Home was now the Casa Azul in Coyoacán—at least for Frida. This house was built by her father; she was born there in 1907, although she always fudged on her birth date and pretended she was born in 1910, the year of the Mexican Revolution.

Since 1958, it has been the Frida Kahlo Museum, and as such it has also soaked up a certain amount of amiable nonsense along with the Mexican sunshine, as Hayden Herrera pointed out in her pioneering biography of Frida.

Many a visitor has gone away believing what we read in the inscription at the entrance to the museum—that Frida and Diego lived together here from the day of their marriage in 1929 until her death in 1954.

Not mentioned is the year of great upheaval in which they separated, divorced, and remarried. Or the many stays in New York and Paris, San Francisco and Detroit. Or the long periods when Diego found it more convenient to live in his studio, or elsewhere.

Frida did not on the whole care for "gringos," as we are called in Latin America. If I was exempt from that, it may have been because of our shared love of animals.

Frida's garden in Coyoacán had thickets of trees and splashes of flowers and hanging vines, populated by a cherished cast of monkeys, parrots, little Mexican dogs (*escuincles*), and even a small deer.

Living in the tropics with plenty of room, I too collected animals. I had a large and varied menagerie. She would ask me for news of my boarders as if they were family members.

Diego had lent the Blue House, rent free, to Leon Trotsky (Diego and Frida were still in the O'Gorman double house at the time) when Trotsky and his wife arrived in Mexico in 1937, very much thanks to Diego having interceded for them with the Mexican president, Lázaro Cárdenas.

Trotsky at that time was the world's most unwanted man. As an agitator in the service of worldwide revolution he had no equal. But when Diego was thoroughly roused, there was no limit to his generosity.

Diego and Trotsky were the best of friends, and when Diego was away, as he often was, Trotsky enjoyed the attentions of the brilliantly costumed Frida.

Trotsky's enemies seemed for a time to leave him alone. In fact, he led "a normal life," and as part of that normal life he went to bed with Frida Kahlo. That came naturally to both of them.

Frida was never in love with Trotsky, but undoubtedly she saw him as a considerable catch. Once it was over and done with, life went on as before, minus the love letters that Trotsky had slipped into her hand and the assignations in a house nearby.

The affair had been brief. "I have got sick of the old man," Frida wrote to a friend.

But in April 1939, Trotsky broke with Diego Rivera on political grounds. The visitors moved out, just down the street, as it were.

The new villa was turned into a fortress: windows blocked up and lookout posts overhead. But to no avail. In August 1940 a trusted associate who doubled as an agent for Stalin came into Trotsky's study, took out an ice pick, and thrust it deep into the back of Trotsky's skull.

I visited the house recently. Nothing has been moved. His heavy bulletproof vest still hangs in the closet; the old-fashioned Dictaphone is still on his desk. Trotsky was buried in the garden in which he enjoyed taking little walks, his only diversion.

When I lived in Mexico in the early 1940s, we became bona fide members of the Rivera-Covarrubias circle. There was Diego's old friend Roberto Montenegro, who had lived in Europe and spoke nostalgically of Juan Gris and Jean Cocteau. Roberto was an early enthusiast for Mexico's endlessly varied and inventive folk art.

Roberto's contemporary Adolfo Best Maugard, Fito to us, was another pioneer in the reassessment of *mexicanidad*. He was an elegant dancer; I can still see his narrow brown suede shoes moving through a *danzón*. (In those days there was a big nightclub with a permanent band. Agustín Lara reigned supreme. I can also still hear his sepulchral voice crooning "Noche de Ronda.")

Roberto Montenegro was also about the only artist who had painted Frida. Surprising as it seems, Diego had never painted a proper portrait of her, although he included her in several frescoes.

Diego did paint a portrait of Miguel Covarrubias's wife, a dark-haired exotic woman who called herself Rosa Rolando, but was plain Rose from Brooklyn. She was a spirited cook, and there were memorable meals at Tizapán, where the Covarrubiases lived.

On one occasion when we went to lunch at the Covarrubiases', besides the usual cast there was the utterly beautiful Dolores del Río, who had left Hollywood to star in a long series of Mexican filmed revolutionary romances. Another guest was a dashing, handsome key figure in the Mexican movie industry, Emilio Fernández, always known as El Indio. He and Dolores had never met.

This was a society in which instinctual drives were promptly acted upon. There were a lot of people at table, the food was delicious, and there was a tumult of lively talk. Nobody noticed that El Indio and Dolores had slipped away from the table. But then, after lunch, Rosa showed us around the house. When she opened the door to one of the guest rooms, there were Dolores and El Indio in bed together.

(Some years later, Lew Riley and Dolores del Río were married.)

I was in Mexico for my first wedding anniversary. In Mexico, the best man at a wedding, the *padrino*, has a special relationship with the new couple. Living up to this, Miguel Covarrubias gave us joint caricatures in a double frame made of shells—my husband was a devil, I was an angel.

I asked Frida, who—withered leg or not—would climb up the several flights of my Mexico City apartment to visit me, what I could give him to thank him. She thought for a moment, then said, "I'll tell you exactly what to do. Get a shoe box. Fill it with earth. Bury an *idolito* [a little figurine] in it. Tie a toy shovel on top of the box and write on a card: 'Dig here, you old archaeologist.'" So this is what I did, although what I buried did not live up to the Covarrubias standard.

Miguel Covarrubias was already renowned at nineteen as a caricaturist. The original *Vanity Fair* magazine invited him to come to New York, where he made witty, wicked drawings of the celebrities of the moment. One was a series called Impossible Interviews: Sally Rand (the fan dancer) with Martha Graham, for instance, or Jean Harlow being analyzed by Sigmund Freud.

But his remarkable eye led him to explore completely new fields. He became an expert ethnologist, recording in texts and drawings the civilization and folkways of peoples as varied as the Balinese and the women of Tehuantepec.

We went with him to the Veracruz region, where in steamy tropical heat we hunted up remnants of the Olmec civilization. It was almost inevitable in Mexico at that time to become interested in pre-Columbian archaeology; it was part of the rediscovery of Mexico's extraordinary heritage. I had found some little clay figurines when ground was broken for our Acapulco swimming pool. To learn something about them, I went to Mexico City to follow the classes of Alfonso Caso, the father of Mexican archaeological studies.

When a highway was being carved out of the surrounding mountains, I used to go out with my little geologist pick and look for traces of shellfish in the cut. Any remnants indicated that people had once been living there.

Frida told me that Miguel and Diego were fierce rivals as collectors of pre-Columbian art. She described their going on expeditions together to hunt for *idolitos*, each trying to get up earlier in the morning than the other to be first on the chase.

Another great interest at that time was architecture. Mexican architects were boldly striking out in new ways. They were not hesitant about color. Foremost was the elegant Luis Barragán, then quite unknown outside of Mexico. He was forging his unique blend of pared-down rigorous garden design at the Pedregal and creating luminous spaces.

Luis was a devout Catholic. He had a crucifix hung over his bed. An attractive young woman I knew told me that when she went to bed with him, he would turn the crucifix around to face the wall.

A much-talked-about event in the spring of 1940 were the lectures given by a distinguished Spanish *refugiado* philosopher, José Gaos. He had translated Heidegger, and Heidegger of course was his subject.

Several young men I knew, perhaps more familiar with the bridge table than with existentialism, valiantly tried to follow. I am not sure how much of Gaos's Filosofía de la Angustia permeated—but how can you resist a title like that?

Neither Diego nor Frida was interested in classical music. She loved the pulse-raising blare of the mariachis and had the mariachis come over to play at the slightest provocation—or without any. But both were fond of the composer-conductor Carlos Chávez. They cherished him for his championship of Mexican composers and his role in building up the Sinfónica de México—which incidentally, at that time, played more contemporary music than could be heard in New York. They had a warm friendship with Aaron Copland, who lived quite some time in Mexico and was completely at home there. He wrote his *Salón México* based on those experiences.

Diego was monstrously ugly, but his girth was matched by his charm, his overwhelming vitality, and the gusto he brought not only to his work but also to eating, talking, flirting, collecting, and rather amateurish political activity. He took it for granted that he ought to sleep with every attractive woman he met, and most often he did. Sex for him was natural, inevitable, and if ever a woman refused to share his bed, he couldn't understand what all the fuss was about.

Naturally, Frida suffered from his constant infidelities, in spite of her own. When they were passing affairs, she tried to overlook them. One of his more public attachments was to María Félix, the sultry ruling Mexican movie star of the period. When a reporter asked if he was in love with her, he said, "All of Mexico is." When he tried to marry her, she was flattered and amused but unresponsive. The publicity didn't hurt, though.

In her memoirs, she had a lot to say about his well-known and highly inventive mythomania. There were the long conversations with Stalin (whom actually he had never met). There was the human flesh that he had eaten with African cannibals. Better yet, there was the story of how he had been born as a pair of Siamese twins and had hidden his sister under an enormous cape. He claimed that when he fell in love with her, they had to be separated without anesthetic.

In the matrimonial tit for tat, Frida kept up her side. When she found out that Diego was having an affair with her beloved younger sister, Cristina, it came as a hideous shock. She retaliated by leaving the house and beginning an affair with the Japanese-American sculptor Isamu Noguchi, then a young man. A secret apartment had been taken for the purpose.

Although Diego didn't care about her many lesbian affairs, he was violently jealous of any male intruder. He came after Isamu with a loaded pistol. A scene out of a French farce occurred when Isamu got away over the roof. Unluckily, Frida's dog came trotting up with one of Isamu's discarded socks, thereby giving the show away. Eventually, Frida managed to forgive her sister and broke off her affair with Noguchi. Order of a kind was restored.

There was an international flavor to the entertainment on offer at that time because of touring foreign companies and performers, cut off by the war from their home base. There was an admirable season of French theater when Louis Jouvet brought his company to

Mexico. Jouvet himself in Molière's *Tartuffe*, for instance, was unforgettable. It was poignant hearing the French, knowing the conditions in Paris under the occupation.

The Mexican scene was wonderfully varied. Sometimes, I went to the bullfights: *"el domingo en la tarde"* (García Lorca), the women dressed to kill, the men with their obligatory big cigars. I knew of all the bullfighters: Armilla with the skinny bandy legs and the big hooked nose; the handsome El Soldado, who always had a pretty girl in the president's box. I enjoyed reading the newspaper write-ups of the bullfights, with their highly colorful vocabulary.

There were amusements: meeting friends before lunch at the Ritz Bar, with the mural by Covarrubias of Xochimilco. One day it snowed, and customers and barmen alike rushed out into the street to see this unique spectacle.

Going to the Tenampa at three in the morning after a party to drink *caldo de pollo* and hear the mariachis. The fun of being serenaded, with a group of mariachis singing "Las Mañanitas" under one's window.

There were fascinating discoveries: the remarkable photographs of Manuel Álvarez Bravo (he photographed me up on his roof with the vast Mexican sky as background).

Rufino Tamayo was not living in Mexico at the time. I got to know him later in New York, and in Paris, which he heartily disliked. His ambitious wife, Olga, wanted him to have a Paris exhibition on his résumé, so, very much against his will, Rufino spent a winter in Paris. He found the light depressingly dark compared with Mexico. There were no compensating elements from his point of view, but Olga did get that exhibition catalog to show around. David Alfaro Siqueiros was not in Mexico at that time, either.

The artist whom I got to know well was the splendidly cantankerous José Clemente Orozco, whose life was entirely and willfully apart from the Rivera-Covarrubias circle and the current artistic scene. It seemed appropriate that he had blown himself up at sixteen making a chemical experiment. Particles remained in his eyes—he wore very thick spectacles—and he had lost a hand. He used the remaining stump to spread pigments on his canvas.

We became friends, in spite of his total lack of English and my still rudimentary Spanish. I visited him often, despite another hurdle: his conviction that chewing raw garlic was the best way to preserve one's health. He painted three portraits of me. I never knew what happened to them.

Mexican muralists were rediscovering the art of fresco painting on a large scale. José Clemente used to talk to me about early tempera techniques and his own discovering of Giotto's follower Cennino Cennini. He himself had covered vast walls both in Mexico and in the United States (at Dartmouth College and in Pomona, California), but he was virtually ignored at that time in Mexico. He was quite unable, in fact unwilling, to attract the kind of limelight that bathed Rivera and Siqueiros. Frida was still an unknown quantity.

Another favorite, of Frida's and mine, was José Guadalupe Posada, the nineteenth-century printmaker. His point of view was all that was most Mexican. Skull and skeleton ranked high in his cast of characters. He also specialized in freaks, assassins, and suicides. Posada's world was one in which skeletons went to confession, attended the funerals of other skeletons, took part in bicycle rallies, and doubled as frisky waitresses.

Of course there was a Never Never Land quality to this parallel life to the grim realities of wartime Europe. My husband, as a foreign resident, was not drafted, but once the United States entered the war, he volunteered and left for America. Bette Davis had fallen in love with him and followed him from army camp to army camp, causing quite some ink to flow. I stayed behind for a while to look after his interests. If I had not, Mexico being Mexico at that time, he would not have found much on his return.

We had divorced in a very Mexican offhand way. There had been no venom; we simply agreed that having married very young, we had grown in different directions.

A lawyer friend drove us to a small neighboring town, where an ordinary house doubled as a town hall. We gave our names and thumbprints, there was a fine-looking stamp affixed with a flourish to a document, and that was that. We were divorced. I presumed it was legitimate; I didn't look at it too closely.

Vogue—First Job

I didn't go to school until I was ten years old. Instead, a French governess was imported to teach me at home, in what came to be called "the schoolroom."

She ruled over me, abetted by two correspondence courses. One from France, the Cours Boutet de Monvel, came in the kind of purple ink that was then used for French bistro menus. The other, from Baltimore, was the Calvert Correspondence School.

The latter was a favorite because, along with the pages for regular lessons, there came small sepia photographs of famous monuments: the Sphinx, the Parthenon, the Lion Gate of Mycenae.

I awaited their arrival in high anticipation. I would pin them up on the board in my schoolroom, arranged with care. New arrivals would require new arrangements.

Little did I know that in one form or another, I would be doing the same thing the rest of my life. The fact is, I remained fascinated by images, and not only from high art. Traveling, I invariably acquired postcards and would stack them up in my hotel room in an improvised layout.

Eventually, this led me, a young American, to starting and editing an art review in Paris, in French. I founded *L'ŒIL* in 1955 and continued until 1970, when a divorce from a French partner ended that phase of my life.

The events leading up to the creation of *L'ŒIL*, in retrospect, seem improbable. I had been living in Mexico and had not been back to the United States for several years.

In Mexico—we are in 1945—I befriended a tall, elegant, neurotic woman, Nada Patcevitch, British born, the wife of the stylish guiding spirit at Condé Nast, Iva Patcevitch. She was recovering from a shipwrecked love affair.

I offered her my small guest beach house in Acapulco, where I lived at that time.

Some time later I came up to New York for some personal business, intending to stay two weeks. Nada had already returned to New York. She was about the only person I knew there; my family was scattered elsewhere. I called her up. She invited me to come for drinks.

That is how I met the Condé Nast high command in one swoop. There were Iva Patcevitch, Russian, and wife; Alexander Liberman and Tatiana, his wife, both Russian; Edna Chase, who would be editor in chief of *Vogue* for nearly forty years. I was wearing a Mexican skirt and white blouse. Tatiana growled at me in French, "You ought to wear a black blouse with that skirt."

In spite of that vestmental gaffe, Pat, as he was known, invited me to go with him to a birthday party for Mrs. Chase the following evening, Nada being away. During the evening, he took me aside and offered me a job on *Vogue*. During the same evening, Mrs. Chase invited me for lunch the next day.

She took me to Voisin, the restaurant in vogue (not the magazine) at the time. I was enjoying the chocolate soufflé with its accompanying whipped cream when she surprised me by suggesting I come to *Vogue* as a fashion editor. I explained that I had been on a beach in Acapulco for the last five years and knew absolutely nothing about fashion. She answered tartly, "My child, I know a fashion editor when I see one."

A few days later, I had somehow met the features editor, a bustling know-it-all named Allene Talmey. She offered me a job in the features department.

I was completely free at that time, unencumbered by attachments. I was so struck by the three offers coming one on top of the other that out of sheer superstition I accepted. I also hoped that an assignment might take me back to France. Incidentally, the fact that I spoke French had a good deal to do with all this.

My sister, Heather, who was in Mexico, obligingly packed up my things and closed the Mexico City apartment. I didn't go back to Mexico for thirty years.

I had my first business talk with Mr. Patcevitch. He offered me the usual starting salary of forty-five dollars a week. I burst out laughing, "Why, Mr. Patcevitch, my ignorance is worth more than that." He looked surprised and offered me seventy-five dollars. I accepted. It was just enough to buy a hat by Tatiana du Plessix at Saks Fifth Avenue. If you knew what was good for you at *Vogue*, you bought a Tatiana hat, her husband being the all-powerful Alexander Liberman.

Apparently, it was routine in those circles that *Vogue* and *Harper's Bazaar* poached on each other's territory. Sure enough, I got an invitation for lunch with the top editors at *Harper's Bazaar*. I was met by several well-hatted and well-suited women, then we were joined by the inimitable Diana Vreeland, who came loping in, announcing, "I've just been to the most *di-vine* funeral." A job was offered, this time—of all improbable possibilities—as managing editor.

When I loyally reported this to Mrs. Chase, she literally wept out of fury.

Although I wanted to write features connected with my own interests, I was slotted as a fashion editor and placed in an office with the top fashion editor, Babs Rawlings, along with her two black-and-white spaniels, which were in permanent attendance. Winter and summer alike, she wore open-toed sandals that showed off her brilliantly painted toenails.

So my professional life began. With some apprehension, every morning I walked down the long corridor to what was now my office, past the copywriters bent over their typewriters, wearing elaborate hats (Tatiana strikes again)—large up-swooping brims and veils pulled tightly across their faces. Substantial rhinestone chokers seemed to be de rigueur for the daily uniform.

Incidentally, all the typewriters had a French acute accent so that "Condé Nast" could be spelled correctly.

Soon I was taking what were called sittings, although this meant standing up, in the big photographic studio *Vogue* used at the time. No makeup artists or hairdressers hovered. The editors, I discovered with dismay, were expected to wreak transformations on the compliant models, so I plunged in with brush, hairpins, and that old-fashioned lacquer, like glue, that had to be coaxed out of the bottle. Nothing remotely sexy was tolerated. Not even a breast outlined discreetly. Beware of the nipple suggested by wool jersey. One editor in chief, Jessica Daves, once axed a summer shot of a girl in a short beach coat "because people might think she had nothing on underneath."

I was eventually able to swerve from the fashion beat and got to work with top photographers, including the invaluable Irving Penn, to photograph such subjects as John Cage (almost disappearing into an open grand piano) and the unlikely duo—neither spoke the other's language—of Arshile Gorky and Wifredo Lam.

Chick Austin

It was probably in the first week of my first job, at *Vogue*. We are in 1945. To my surprise, I had been acquired by the Condé Nast Publications network and invented as a fashion editor, a distinction for which I was totally unqualified.

I was sitting in the office I shared with the head fashion editor, Babs Rawlings. "Go to Knize and take a look," she said vaguely.

All I knew about Knize was that several European men friends used a delicious cologne made by Knize. But Knize was a famous tailor in Vienna before the war, I learned. And a branch had opened in New York when the Vienna store had to close.

Off I went and met Mr. Wolf, director of the shop. We chatted, and I told him I had just arrived from Mexico. It turned out that he was a collector of pre-Columbian objects. He was highly interested to learn that I had not only taken courses on the subject at the University of Mexico but also worked on some minor excavations myself.

"I have some good pieces at home," he told me. "A few people are coming for drinks next week to see them, won't you join us?"

Of course I went. I didn't know anybody, but was delighted to see some characteristic Colima pottery, a good Teotihuacán mask, and some *idolitos* from Guerrero, the region where I had lived.

Soon I was joined by an elegant man, about forty, who was equally interested in Mr. Wolf's collection. We talked. There was a compelling gaiety and charm about him. As usual at a cocktail party, there had been only cursory introductions. I hadn't caught his name. But when he asked me to come to Hartford for the weekend to look at paintings, I immediately accepted.

When I thanked Mr. Wolf for the evening, I asked him, "By the way, who was that nice man I was talking to over by your Guerrero pieces?"

He was not the Pied Piper, although there was some common ground there, but he turned out to be A. Everett Austin Jr., known to everyone as Chick. He had been the director of the Wadsworth Atheneum of Hartford from 1927 through 1944.

Off I went to Hartford. Chick met me at the station platform. He was an unmistakable figure: in magnificent Mandarin costume, with the embroidered Chinese hat that went with it, and a long pigtail. Completely impervious to the astonished stares from the regular commuters crowding the platform, he explained breezily he was on his way to give a magic show at a local high school.

"My wife expects you; I'll drop you at the house and come back later to take you to dinner."

The house was as unlike its neighbors on Scarborough Street as its owner. It had a small-scale Palladian facade with slender central columns and a triangular pediment. Once inside, I discovered it was only one room deep. As Chick commented cheerfully, "Like me, all facade."

Downstairs was rococo fantasy and floating colors. Upstairs, my room and bathroom were strict Bauhaus modern. Mrs. Austin, Helen, a charming woman, seemed totally unfazed that her husband had brought home a new acquaintance for the night.

She explained that Chick had invented an alter ego, "the Great Osram," and as a magician did magic performances. This seemed perfectly in character.

The Great Osram returned and, dressed like a soigné Westerner, escorted me to an Italian restaurant. No Mrs. Austin.

The conversation flowed seamlessly. The wine flowed too. Soon Chick was telling me the heartbreaking account of his struggles with his board: how he had built the Atheneum's collection from nearly nothing to an extraordinary group of Italian baroque and modern masterpieces only to be unappreciated by the trustees. With great emotion, he evoked some of the exhibitions that had broken new ground: Surrealism (1931), the first comprehensive Picasso exhibition in the United States (1934), the concerts of new music, the costume balls, the theatrical performances with him, the impresario, often on-stage, having painted most of the scenery. The cinema department was the first in a museum—seven years before MoMA, he said.

Then, with tears rolling down his cheeks, he told me he had been fired.

I was moved to tears too. Impulsively, I reached into my hand-bag, pulled out a little pre-Columbian bronze of a small man in a conical hat that was my good-luck charm, and handed it to him. "Keep this." He took it.

It was close to midnight, but he said, "Let me show you the museum." He still had the keys to the building.

The night watchman of course recognized him and stepped aside. Chick led me into the galleries, turning on the lights as we went from one to another.

He showed me scores of pictures that he had bought, from Fra Angelico's *Angel* to Dalí's *Apparition*; masterpieces by Piero di Cosimo, Cranach, Caravaggio (a great ecstasy of Saint Francis), Poussin, Le Nain, Tiepolo, Goya, Degas. He had bought the first important Max Ernst for America, *Europe After the Rain*, the painting that Max had rolled up in wartime Europe and mailed to the Museum of Modern Art—it was there when he arrived as an émigré. Few people had heard of Balthus at that time. Chick bought the only Miró sold of the splendid 1933 series shown by Pierre Matisse. And there was a Mondrian. The Picasso exhibition opened the same night that he presented Gertrude Stein's *Four Saints in Three Acts* with Virgil Thomson's music. What a night that must have been!

These were not just canvases to him but his own flesh and blood—his children. Seeing them with him was the most extraordinary experience.

Years later, in 1957, I was in Paris editing the art review I founded, *L'ŒIL*. I had heard that Chick had taken over the Ringling Museum in Sarasota, Florida. I wrote to him and asked if he would write an article about it for me. He answered promptly that he would.

There was a delay, then came an ominous letter from a secretary saying I would have to wait for the article because Mr. Austin was going into the hospital for an operation.

Next thing I knew, he was dead.

In 1969, I had left Paris for personal reasons. Before I even had time to catch my breath in New York, my friend Michael Mahoney launched me on a new, totally unexpected career. He was the head of the art department at Trinity College in Hartford, Connecticut. He announced that I was giving a series of fourteen lectures on the background of twentieth-century art.

I learned from the printed program that my talks were called the "A. Everett Austin Fine Arts Lectures." Michael knew nothing of my connection with Chick.

In 1972, I was invited to the Wadsworth Atheneum to give a lecture on Diaghilev and the Ballets Russes. It was in conjunction with an exhibition of costume designs by Léon Bakst.

Along with the Russian material, there was a display in memory of Chick, with objects and papers that had belonged to him.

And what did I discover? My little pre-Columbian figure was right there among the memorabilia. The curator told me that Chick had always kept it with him, right by his bed.

Virgil, Aaron, and Nadia Boulanger

I was sent to Paris by *Vogue* in 1947 to report on what had been happening in the arts since the isolation of the war years.

I knew Virgil Thomson, who had lived many years in Paris but was now installed in New York at the Chelsea Hotel. I went to see him to get his advice. Virgil was small, rotund, cherubic of cheek, and acerbic of tongue. He had always been nice to me, although he would say with a slight edge, "Oh, she's *Aaron's* girl."

At that time Virgil was writing brilliant music reviews for the old *New York Herald Tribune*. The mystery was that no sooner had he settled in his seat for a concert than he fell soundly asleep. To all appearances, he only woke up at the end of the performance, at the noise of the applause. Yet the most lucid, perspicacious account of the concert would appear the next day.

Equally mysterious was how he managed to produce the most memorable food in what was literally a small hotel closet transformed into a kitchen. Luckily, he didn't take up much room himself, and his organization was a marvel of ingenuity.

Thanks to Virgil, I had an introduction to Olivier Messiaen, who allowed me to sit in on some of his music analysis classes at the Paris Conservatoire. This composer of rhapsodic works of religious inspiration, with an assist from birdsongs, was dissecting Bach's counterpoint like a surgeon. And I got lost backstage at the Paris Opéra with Eric (*Vogue*'s *dessinateur*) looking for Roger Désormière (another Virgil Thomson connection), the conductor of an unforgettable *Pélleas et Mélisande* (we finally found him).

But the introduction that was the most precious and rewarding for me was to the twenty-one-year-old Aaron Copland's composition teacher, Nadia Boulanger. She had remained a touchstone for excellence in his life. He was to be followed by a procession of young American composers: Virgil Thomson, Walter Piston, even Elliott Carter at one point. It became a "must" to have had some contact with the illustrious Mademoiselle, as we always called her. Only Aaron had earned the right to address her as Nadia.

Because I came from Aaron, on my arrival in Paris she immediately asked me to her studio walk-up apartment—36, rue Ballu—where Aaron had studied so many years before. It was a freezing cold February day, and her apartment—like most places in these immediate postwar years—was unheated. An erect, fine-featured woman, she seemed completely impervious to the cold. "But she was always like that," Aaron said with a chortle when I reported this. I didn't dare shiver.

She allowed me to listen to some of her classes. Her pupils were drilled in orchestration, analysis, sight-reading of orchestral scores at the piano. She was indefatigable, teaching all day, every day. In summer she ran a music school in Fontainebleau. Her musical enthusiasms ran from Renaissance madrigals to twelve-tone serial composers (referred to by Francis Poulenc, deprecatingly, as "les dodécas").

Just before I was to return to New York (I was to come back to Paris on an almost permanent basis a little later), Mademoiselle came by my hotel to leave a goodbye present: it was a box of Kleenex and a bar of soap, the most precious objects, unobtainable in Paris at that time.

Long after that first visit I went back to 36, rue Ballu with Aaron for one of Nadia Boulanger's ritual weekly teas. Without even realizing it, Aaron automatically reached out in the dark to switch on the light over the staircase—years of habit. It was cold in the apartment, and the cakes were stale. "They always were," Aaron whispered.

Paris Again

When the French fashion houses began to open again in 1946–47 after World War II and the occupation, American magazines thought it worthwhile to send people over to report on them.

I was one of them. I edged into the fashion world almost sideways. I thought I was going to write art features when I was recruited by *Vogue*. But Mrs. Chase thought otherwise, and her word was law.

I found myself on one of those first transatlantic flights that stopped over for the night at Gander, Newfoundland, to refuel. You rested, fully dressed, in one of a line of cots in a kind of barracks.

My immediate neighbors were a group of Dominican monks—Italian, no English. I had studied Italian a long time ago in college but had had no opportunity to practice. I could only remember a few lines of Dante, about returning from hell, not much of a conversational opener. I tried it out, anyhow, and got a gratifying response.

My traveling companion was a small, angelic, and gifted artist who was the magazine's *dessinateur*. He went under the name of Eric. There was much use of fashion drawings to illustrate magazines in those days. My entire professional training was a hissed injunction as I left for the airport: "Keep Eric sober."

Keeping Eric sober turned out to be a major project, but if his gait was sometimes unsteady, his line never wavered.

The *Vogue* team was lodged at the Crillon, the only hotel that had any heating. It included the star photographer Horst, who had photographed all the famous prewar beauties, including Chanel, and was still at it.

Our life in Paris was of an almost embarrassing ease compared with the lot of most Parisians. Bitter cold, shortages of all kinds, a telephone system with a freakish life of its own, electricity unreliable in the extreme. And everywhere recriminations and evening of scores about who had, and who had not, behaved decently during the occupation.

Breakfast in bed was served by tailcoated waiters bearing beat-up metal trays, with paper handouts rallying the population to de Gaulle, instead of linen. Had we been up to it, we could have had champagne and foie gras, but no fruit.

I enjoyed my sorties with Eric. They went something like this. He would call for me in the morning at the Crillon, natty in bow tie and bowler hat, slightly unsteady already. Then he thought a pit stop for a dozen oysters and a bottle of white wine advisable before our first appointment. A seraphic vagueness enveloped him throughout the day. After several hours at Schiaparelli's he would ask in a loud stage whisper, "Where are we?"

Confronted with the model, he always started with the eyes. Then mysteriously, the very essence, the spirit of the outfit, would come to life on his page.

That first season in Paris, there were very few professional models to pose for our photographs and illustrations. I rounded up my more personable acquaintances and, when really hard up, would pose myself, face averted, because at that time *Vogue* did not want its editors to appear in its pages.

Eric drew me in a Paulette creation, looking as though I were just waiting for the next glass of champagne at Maxim's. In reality, due to the intense cold, I was in bed, warmly dressed, fur coat on top, covers pulled up to my chin.

The first party for the fashion press was given by Edward Molyneux, an Englishman who had had a successful career in the Paris couture before the war and had just reopened. He lived in a large apartment on the other side of the Seine from the Crillon. Guests crunched through heavy snow on foot across the Place de la Concorde, in evening clothes. There was still no automobile traffic at all.

The room was full of French women, incongruously wearing towering plumes of birds of paradise in their hair. Someone had discovered a cache of them. There were few new clothes available, and even fewer opportunities to dress up. So they made the most of it.

The setting was Molyneux's long, pale beige living room in pure 1930s style, heated with the makeshift elements of the times. It was banked with superb Impressionist and post-Impressionist paintings. A number of them are now in Washington's National Gallery, donated by Ailsa Mellon Bruce, who had acquired them from Molyneux.

The first important couture show I went to on my first Paris visit was presented by the house of Lucien Lelong (incidentally, Lelong, as head of the Chambre Syndicale de la Couture during the war, saved French skilled workers from being shipped to Germany). It will be remembered, if for nothing else, because the clothes were designed by a shy, cherubic unknown young man, the future couture star Christian Dior. The man Cecil Beaton described as looking like "a bland country curate made out of pink marzipan" was to blow the fashion landscape sky-high two years later with the New Look.

I somehow struck up a cozy relationship with Lelong, who favored me with generous prices and invited me for an amusing lunch at his apartment. He told me about the high life in the 1930s and spoke wistfully about his failed marriage to the beautiful princess Natalie Paley. "If only she had been a little less *folle* and I had been a little more patient."

He was proud of his elegantly designed bathroom and showed off his latest acquisition: an electric toothbrush. I was suitably impressed; I had never seen one before.

I negotiated with my employers to lend me Horst and Eric after the collections, so that I could record some of the interesting figures in the postwar art world and in the world in general. UNESCO had just been created, and the first director general was a peppery and illustrious British scientist, Sir Julian Huxley. Getting an appointment was not easy; he clearly thought anything as frivolous as *Vogue* was a complete waste of time.

I managed finally, and brought Horst along. Huxley bustled in, his eyebrows angry thickets. Horst put on his lights and was about to start shooting when there was a loud bang. The frail electricity system was not up to the challenge. "Fellow can't even manage his bulbs," Huxley roared, and stamped out.

Our next project, to photograph Gertrude Stein and her poodle, Basket, in Pierre Balmain's salon, was clear sailing, with all concerned well pleased. In fact, it resulted in one of Horst's most famous, often reproduced images. It shows a massive Gertrude Stein, an obviously unmovable monument (Alice B. Toklas never referred to her as Miss Stein or Gertrude: always Gertrude Stein, so I will follow Alice's lead). She is looking up at the opposite of her mirror image: a willowy model in evening finery, beruffed and beplumed.

Off in the distance are two very small figures: they are Eric and myself. We are often cut off when this image is reproduced, so I make my claim to be seen here.

Balmain's salon was the choice of venue because the Stein-Toklas ménage spent the occupation years in the country and the young little known Pierre Balmain was a near neighbor. They exchanged visits and vegetables. Incidentally, how two elderly Jewish ladies remained very visibly in occupied France unharmed is somewhat cloudy.

When Pierre opened his salon at the liberation, they wanted to be on hand to cheer him on. Alice even wrote a text to be handed out to visitors. I still have it. Or did Alice really write it? Remember, *The Autobiography of Alice B. Toklas* was written by Gertrude Stein.

Balmain made them clothes. Alice, who never lost her practical sense, said, "For heaven's sake, Gertrude, don't let anyone know Pierre dresses us. We look like gypsies."

Gertrude Stein died before I came back to live in Paris, but during my Paris years I often saw Alice; in fact, my office for *L'ŒIL*, my magazine, was just down the street from the rue Christine, where Alice lived. I would, on invitation, drop in for tea. There was no nonsense about a biscuit or two; there would always be a delicious selection of just-baked cakes. Alice would sit in her rocking chair, so little that her feet in their hand-knitted socks and sandals hardly reached the floor. There she rocked like a little old owl—hooded eyes, just the trace of a mustache.

Whenever she had come to some little festivity at my place, or I had done some small favor, a thank-you letter would arrive promptly, written in such a minute script that a magnifying glass was the best weapon.

While Gertrude Stein was alive, people came because of Gertrude, to listen to Gertrude. Alice was somewhere in the background. Now people came to see Alice, to listen to Alice. And she was a very good talker with quite a sharp tongue.

Alice not only was a superb cook but also wrote a cookbook, both useful and highly idiosyncratic. She didn't hesitate to include our mutual friend Brion Gysin's recipe for hashish fudge.

In another key, I went to see André Gide. He very sensibly was all muffled up against the cold and was wearing a black stocking cap that made him look like an ancient Chinese sage.

He told me he had just finished translating *Hamlet* for Jean-Louis Barrault. He talked about the different tonalities of English and French and very kindly offered to give me an introduction to Barrault.

Barrault arranged for me to have tickets for *Hamlet*. I took along another *Vogue* contributor, the illustrator Marcel Vertès. Vertès was a bulky Hungarian who apparently didn't appreciate Shakespeare. About half an hour into the performance he said to me in a highly audible voice, "I'm bored, and it is very bad for me to be bored." I managed to steer him out between acts. Between acts I went backstage, to see Barrault. I told him how much I admired his memorable *Les Enfants du Paradis*. He spoke about mime and the great mime Marcel Marceau. Then it was time to get back to the hall. Jean-Louis gallantly escorted me and took my hand so I could climb down directly from the stage back to my seat.

I had an appointment to photograph Le Corbusier and the writer Jules Romains, who had some sort of joint project at the time. We were to meet at the Galerie Charpentier, a large combination art gallery and auction house. As a novice interviewer, I was quite intimidated by these luminaries. Everything started out smoothly, but suddenly Romains became absolutely odious and said he was leaving. To my shame, I burst into tears. Whereupon, most unexpectedly, Le Corbusier put his arm around me and said to Romains, "I've never seen such rude manners, and to a charming young person." I had always heard that Le Corbusier was extremely difficult, but I keep a fond memory of him.

A highlight of that first Paris fashion foray was to go to a Balenciaga collection. The master couturier had an almost mythical aura. No one got to see him. He never went out. He hated the press. He would slip out the back door to avoid customers. He was so austere, he didn't even wear a wristwatch.

Balenciaga's salon at 10, avenue George V was run with the discipline of a convent by the intimidating Mademoiselle Renée. It was not large. There were five white *canapés* for the important people; lesser souls had to make do with little gold chairs with red cushions. No music for the presentations. Silence. No flood lights.

The mannequins held up a card with a number as they stomped by. Balenciaga's models were often really plain. One was distractingly walleyed, I remember. The master had instructed them to never smile, never make eye contact, just to look haughtily over the heads of clients.

But the clothes were fabulous!

I was lucky because the word had been passed down to be kind to me, and the kindnesses were extraordinary. When I was back in Paris in the 1950s and 1960s, I had my own vendeuse, the motherly Madame Maria. She knew I longed for several numbers from the collection. She could imagine my finances. After she consulted with Mademoiselle Renée, I was made a startling offer: they would give me the references for the material needed to make the five numbers I coveted so that I could buy the necessary fabric from the French cloth houses. Thus armed, I should go to the Madrid branch of the house—"They don't have decent fabrics," said Mademoiselle deprecatingly—where they would make the models I wanted at a fraction of the Paris price.

This was done, and I got a suit, an overcoat, and several dresses. Mademoiselle Renée asked to see them. "They don't even know how to fit properly," she sniffed, and had a house seamstress make the adjustments.

On several occasions I was lent a dress or an outfit. I was going to Fort Worth for the opening of an exhibition of the School of Fontainebleau. I was guest of honor because I had advised the organizers. A full-length gold evening dress and matching coat—borrowed finery—made quite a splash. The invitation for this event suggested that the ladies' dress should be inspired by the School of Fontainebleau. Since the women in these paintings were invariably bare breasted, I rather wondered what the results would be.

I flew off to Fort Worth and was rushed straight to a television studio. A young person instructed me hastily, "Tell the folks about the School of Fountenblue, where it was, who did it . . . you've got two minutes, hon."

I had barely caught my breath when there was a cut for the commercial. A voice intoned, "When the Russian aristocrats fled the revolution, they took with them their most precious possessions— [a spotlight flashed on a heap of jewels] their jewels [great rolling of drums] *and* the recipe for noodles Romanoff. Now back to lovely Madame Burniay."

Now back to Paris: there was a superb tailor at Balenciaga, the courtly Monsieur Denis. I actually splurged for several made-for-me suits. At the sales, thanks to prompt warning by my vendeuse, I acquired a full-length orange coat; it looked terrific over a black suit.

When Matisse saw me in it, he suggested, "Wear a yellow scarf with it." I did.

On hearing about this, some friends of mine, Bob and Mimi Schwartz, who are professional daylily breeders, created a bright clear-yellow lily. They named it "Rosamond's Yellow Scarf."

The other reclusive designer, a total original both professionally and in her private life, was a woman known as Madame Grès. What she did she did extremely well; and she did it alone, with no assistant toiling away in the wings, nor were there any preliminary sketches. Her way of working was peculiar to herself. With a single piece of material, which could measure eighteen to twenty feet across, she created directly on an individual living body. Coaxing the fabric with her fingers, she pleated, molded, manipulated. Working with headless pins and then basting, she took the ephemeral and made it lasting. For more than forty years she created seductive dresses inspired by Greek architecture and sculpture, but ringing subtle changes every time.

She was also versatile. She made me a scarlet-and-brown tunic and trousers costume to wear lecturing on Queen Christina, that art-loving Swedish sovereign who preferred to dress like a man.

Grès's passion for privacy, almost anonymity, led her to avoid parties, openings, public events. She never went to restaurants. I met Madame Grès in the 1960s, when I was running my art review, *L'ŒIL*. Uncharacteristically, she had gone to a reception at which I also was a guest. When we were introduced, she told me in her gentle sotto voce way how much she admired *L'ŒIL*, then she said, "I like the way you look. Come to the salon."

I remember my first impression on walking up the flight of stairs to her salon at 1, rue de la Paix. It had none of the generic bustle of a couture house. It was more like the antechamber of an aristocratic nunnery. Cream-colored walls, light-wood furniture, no vitrines of glittering accessories. Voices were never raised.

Mademoiselle, as she was always known in the salon, was a slight dark-eyed figure, every strand of hair hidden in a tightly wrapped turban, no makeup. She wore monochromatic jersey dresses and matching cardigans. She must have known that I could not afford couture, but whenever I went to the salon, several outfits had been set aside for me. Were they models or samples? I never knew, but they were impeccably fresh, and whenever necessary they were adjusted to my measurements for no extra charge.

As I wrote elsewhere, she made me a suitably glamorous yellow evening dress to wear as Aaron Copland's date to the gala concert celebrating the New York Philharmonic's 125th anniversary.

Over the next year or so I acquired seven outfits on very generous terms. Later, I gave most of them to the Costume Institute of the Metropolitan Museum.

Her personal life was inviolate; even her death was kept a mystery. When the Costume Institute of the Metropolitan Museum put on a Madame Grès retrospective in 1994, her daughter let it be known that Grès was following the event with keen interest. "Thank you for not forgetting me" was her message to her American admirers. Only after the exhibition closed was it revealed, in the Paris newspaper *Le Monde*, that Madame Grès had died the year before.

However odd, this was in line with her discretion and her solitary ways.

Now It's London

I returned from Paris fascinated by the new stirrings in all the arts, so much to look at, to listen to, to read about. However seductive, the fashion world, I felt, was not the be-all and end-all of possibilities.

I communicated my misgivings to my employers. I had serious thoughts about returning to Mexico. Then the Condé Nast high command—that is to say, Patcevitch and Liberman—came up with a generous proposition. A new position would be created for me, European features editor. "We've never had one before," I was told (in fact they have never had one since). "We'll see if you are worth it; otherwise we'll bring you back in six months." I didn't come back for years.

I left for my newly created post as *Vogue*'s European features editor, for which I had absolutely no qualifications beyond curiosity, in the spring of 1947.

I started out in Paris as already described, then went on to London. I knew nobody. There were a few scattered members of my mother's English family. Uncle Guy came up from the country to take me to lunch. We discussed the fate of the unfortunate Aunt Olive—she who was dissolved in a vat of acid. As Uncle Guy commented jovially, it was difficult to find the appropriate words for the condolence letter.

The New York office had asked my opposite number in the London office to give me a cocktail party to introduce me to people of interest. The hostess was Clarissa Churchill, later to marry Anthony Eden. She gave the party but, in what I learned was typical English fashion, didn't introduce me to a single soul.

I was picked up by Cyril Connolly, whose *Unquiet Grave* I admired, so that was a good start. Cyril in turn, perhaps sniffing some dollars in the offing, took me to dinner more than once and introduced me to some of his *Horizon* contributors, including Stephen Spender and Dylan Thomas. Cyril, on hearing I had rented a château in the Dordogne—his favorite region of France—immediately invited himself for the weekend. To his chagrin he discovered it wasn't a real château at all, but a bungalow next to some imposing ruins. Nevertheless, that summer he stayed for a month.

Dylan Thomas attached himself to me and accompanied me on my rounds. One time I had to cover the movie *Odd Man Out* with James Mason. Dylan came along and came back with me to the *Vogue* office. It created somewhat of a stir, Dylan sitting patiently by my side as I typed out my report.

Life in London was still very difficult for Londoners, with shortages and discomforts on every side. I was very popular because I practically ran a contraband operation, regularly bringing suitcases bulging with legs of lamb, cheese, butter, and cake from France.

I was living in luxury at the Dorchester, thanks to Condé Nast, and had abundant hot water. After a while, I had a queue of English men of letters lining up outside my bathroom for a hot tub.

There were spectacular kindnesses in return. I was asked to write an account for *Vogue* of the London theaters that were only lit by gaslights and candles—no electricity yet. I came down with the flu and couldn't move. Stephen Spender came to my bedside and offered to go and cover the story for me—"and you sign it," he said. Of course I didn't sign his account.

I simply looked up people I admired. I had the nerve to walk into Faber and Faber's offices, having made an appointment with T. S. Eliot. He received me courteously and signed my copy of his *Four Quartets*.

I had met Elizabeth Bowen, whose *Death of the Heart* I had been reading. It was getting near Christmastime. She asked what plans I had for the holiday. I had none. "You'll spend Christmas with us," she said. So I had a splendid Christmas dinner with Elizabeth Bowen and her husband, Alan Cameron.

Later, Cameron very kindly took me to lunch at the Reform Club so that I could see what a traditional British club was like.

In Search of Proust

When I was sent to France by *Vogue* in 1947 with an open-ended assignment, to provide feature material, the first thing I wanted to do, as a passionate Proustian, was look up the surviving people and places connected with Marcel Proust.

I was given the well-known photographer Erwin Blumenfeld. "He is rereading Proust in preparation," the features department asserted. That was news to Blumenfeld, who had never opened a page.

It is a tourist circuit today, but at that time I don't believe anyone had done anything like it.

We started at Illiers (Combray in the novel), some sixty-five miles from Paris, an anonymous little town in the Beauce region. Proust's father, Dr. Adrien Proust, came from Illiers, and Proust as a child spent the Easter holidays there with his family. The parish church, Saint-Jacques, looks very much the same as described in the novel, with its asymmetric church spire.

"Humble yet majestic," according to Proust, who had Tante Amiot say, "If it played the piano, I'm sure it would play with real feeling." She became Tante Léonie in the novel, and her house on the rue du Saint-Esprit with its two entrances is still (or was in 1947) right there, the back door opening onto a tiny garden.

In the novel, Gilberte has an impressive garden called Tansonville. It had two models, and I saw them both. One, on a much more modest scale, belonged to Proust's uncle Amiot, who had made a little pleasure garden at Illiers with winding paths and flower beds and hawthorn hedges and a small pond. I saw it as an overgrown thicket of greenery. Monet provided the other model at Giverny, where he had dammed a stream and made a water garden that has now been brought back to its original state and is almost alarmingly popular.

The Hôtel de la Gare still existed on the main square with its advertisements painted on the side for Chevaux et Voitures, Salons et Cabinets, and its Café et Billiards.

The War of the Madeleines had not yet started; only one bakery claimed to provide the authentic madeleines prized by Proust. I am told there is fierce competition today from challengers to the title.

The survivors of Proust's world were aged parties, so I had to be quick on my feet to catch them. For instance, I had a date for tea with Reynaldo Hahn, Proust's great friend, and to my dismay he died two days before our appointment.

I met the aged aristocrat with my favorite title, the Duchesse de Clermont-Tonnerre, who as a young girl, Elisabeth de Gramont, had entertained Proust at her family's property in Normandy. She brandished an ear trumpet and rustled with innumerable chains as she peered down my bosom, while I queried her about summer holidays with Proust at her family's château.

I was too late with the Comtesse Greffulhe, the famous once-great beauty who had been one of the models for the Duchesse de Guermantes; she died shortly after I arrived in Paris. But I went around to her fine town house on the rue d'Astorg, where her possessions were about to be auctioned off. It was strangely lugubrious to see the piles of porcelain, the candelabra, the tarnished silver, the endless accoutrements of vanished festivities.

On a livelier note, thanks to introductions from the American-born Roman princess Marguerite Caetani (founder of two admirable literary magazines, *Commerce* and *Botteghe Oscure*), I went to see two very much alive relics. Prince Antoine Bibesco lived in a splendid apartment on the tip of the Ile Saint-Louis, with walls glowing with paintings by Vuillard. On a table in the anteroom was a stack of postcards with, in facsimile, a fragment of a letter from Proust to Anna de Noailles saying, "The only friend who really understands me is Antoine Bibesco."

Hearing the click of my heels on the parquet, even before I entered the salon, he called out, "Will we make love before or after lunch?" "After," I answered, to gain a little time. I got out of that one unscathed.

The next appointment was with a distinguished minister who will remain unnamed. He opened the front door himself, in a long dressing gown. Once I was inside, he opened the dressing gown to reveal he was naked. Being young and agile in those days, I leaped over a sofa and from a safe distance fired a few questions at him, before darting out the door.

I went to see another witness of the Proustian past, the Romanian-born princess Marthe Bibesco (a cousin of Antoine's). She had written a little book, *Au Bal avec Marcel Proust* (*Marcel Proust at the Ball*), and I had hoped to pick up some firsthand material. She had recently returned to Paris from sitting out the war elsewhere and was temporarily living at the Ritz.

She duly received me, wearing a trailing tea gown. It was four in the afternoon. When I explained my interest in her impressions of Proust, she waved a languid hand and said, "Before we go any further, ten thousand dollars please." I thanked her politely and said the equivalent of "not today."

The best-known portrait of Proust is by his friend Jacques-Émile Blanche, as a bland young man with an orchid in his buttonhole. It is bad luck for us that Proust was never painted by a major artist. We know what he looked like, but the portraits that turn up over and over again are always the same ones, and none has that extra dimension which would make us know more about Proust than he cared to tell himself.

I first saw the Blanche portrait on an easel in the conventionally luxurious Paris living room of his niece Madame Mante-Proust in the late 1940s. It was quite uncanny because the niece, sitting in her pale blue damask salon chatting about the social season, looked so much like the portrait. She had the handsome, melancholy eyes, heavy lidded, darkly circled. She talked about "cher Marcel" as she gestured at a pile of manuscripts by the window. This was before the manuscripts had been donated to the Bibliothèque Nationale. I spent fascinated hours going over narrow notebooks, many with additional pages attached in long accordion-like strips, almost illegible with corrections, paragraphs added, lines suppressed—a proofreader's nightmare. The pages still exuded the faint musty smell of the medicinal powders Proust would burn for his asthma.

I was so new in France that when I set out for Normandy with Blumenfeld, I did not know that August 15 was a national holiday and that not a single hotel room would be available on the coast. Blumenfeld was equally oblivious. The office manager at the time did not care for me, and I think he kept this dark on purpose. He did say, keeping in mind the pennies, "Keep away from the auberge Guillaume le Conquérant, and above all don't have a meal there." The auberge Guillaume le Conquérant was a favorite of Proust's, and I was determined to reconnoiter there. I went in with my colleague, and we lingered over a delicious lunch.

Somehow the manager heard our conversation in which we were wondering where we should spend the night. He came over and broke the bad news: there would be no question of a hotel room, let alone two, in the entire region. Seeing my dismay, to my surprise he made an astonishing offer: the upper floor of the auberge had been transformed into a little Madame de Sévigné museum, because she had stayed there. "Her bed is on display. If you promise to be out by six in the morning, I will have it made up for you, and your companion can sleep in the car." We agreed, and to thank him had another meal at the auberge.

At six in the morning Blumenfeld arrived to wake me up and take my photograph amid the grand drapery. I was just in my underwear; there had been no question of bringing in a suitcase. He made me a splendid print of the photograph as a memento.

Since childhood, Proust, like his narrator, had been going to Cabourg, by the sea in Normandy. In his novel Cabourg becomes Balbec. It was our next stop. The Grand Hôtel was still closed; it had been severely damaged by the bombardments that preceded the Normandy landings. I managed to wangle my way in to see the shattered glass, the boarded-up windows, the elevator suspended between two floors, and the unstrung strands of the crystal chandeliers trailing like streams of tears. It was from the large windows of the Grand Hôtel dining room that the narrator first sees the group of the "*jeunes filles en fleur*" and falls in love with Albertine.

The star performer of my cast of Proustian characters was Jean

Cocteau. Cocteau and Proust were longtime friends. Cocteau was eighteen years younger than Proust. They came from similar backgrounds, well-off Parisian bourgeois families. Both were closely attached to their mothers. Both were homosexual. Proust kept his inclinations secret, Cocteau most certainly did not.

Cocteau used to live over the gardens of the Palais Royal, near Colette. In my early days in Paris we sometimes met for lunch at an excellent restaurant nearby, Véfour. We both enjoyed the Regency décor and the champagne served in carafes.

Jean was a spellbinder and he knew it. The fantasy, the gossamer verbal constructions, the reminiscences, the theories, the new activities—films, ballets. At four in the afternoon we were often still at table, Jean weaving a story with those legendary hands of his—"like articulated jewels," someone said—making me a drawing on the back of the Véfour menu, his elegantly sharp features framed by carefully haloed hair (we both got our permanents at Alexandre's).

Of course I used to ask him about Proust. It might have been a set piece, but it was brilliant.

"I listened to him with the ears of my heart," Jean began. "When he started to talk, his moaned parentheses became so beautiful that people who had meant to go simply couldn't leave. Proust's way of talking followed the convoluted lines of his writing, with sentences spun out, interwoven, superimposed, with threads lost and picked up again—punctuated with great bursts of laughter."

A further description of Proust by Cocteau comes from Francis Steegmuller's *Cocteau*: "He would receive fully clothed—collar, tie, gloves—lying on the brass bed, which was a carryover from his childhood. There were tables littered with medicine bottles, piles of school notebooks, and, on an ebony table in the corner, an accumulation of photographs: duchesses, cocottes, dukes, doormen of great houses. There were slipcovers everywhere, the chandeliers were wrapped in muslin—there was an opalescent coating of dust over everything. He never allowed Celeste [his housekeeper] to dust, thinking this made his asthma worse. The whole place reeked of the anti-asthmatic powder he used to burn.

"Proust's rooms were always ordinary, if not bleak; he paid no attention to their décor, but simply accumulated bits and pieces from his family—everything disappeared under the sea of manuscript pages that billowed everywhere, overflowing from bed tables, chairs, and mantelpieces. The only personal note: his portrait by Jacques-Émile Blanche was on the right wall.

"There, in his cork-lined room, at some advanced hour of the night—the only hours Proust received his friends—he would read to them from *Swann's Way*."

Cocteau said he would start reading at any place, mistake a page, jump one, interrupt himself, lose his place in all the extra pieces he tacked on, splutter with laughter behind his gloved hand. "His modesty was legendary. He would repeat, 'It's too silly . . . I really can't go on,' and apologize for making them listen to such foolish stuff."

Visits to Matisse

One of the few times I saw Henri Matisse out of bed was when I went to call on him in the spring of 1948. I was new in Paris on my *Vogue* assignment. I had made friends with Pierre Matisse, the distinguished dealer, in New York, and he gave me an introduction to his father.

The great man was in his Paris apartment, 132, boulevard du Montparnasse, which he had taken over after the war. He received me kindly, with French formality, calling me Madame (I was a young person at the time). I had chosen my dress carefully, thinking of what might please him: it had pink and blue intertwined stripes against black. I was rewarded. He admired it. He was conservatively assembled himself, a blue tie and blue sweater bringing out the blue of his eyes; white beard neatly trimmed, every scanty hair in place.

I brought family news from New York. Communications were still difficult. He explained that he was not staying in Paris for long; he was about to go back to the south of France. He had left his regular apartment in a large wedding cake of a building at Cimiez, above Nice, called the Hôtel Régina, after Queen Victoria, who had stayed there when one only went to the south of France in winter. During the war Cimiez was thought to be too exposed to Allied bombing before the landings, so he had moved inland to Vence, where he had rented a villa called Le Rêve.

I had brought along a recent publication, a magnificent album about him with loose color plates and a text by Louis Aragon, published by the famous Swiss publisher Albert Skira, who was to play an important part in my professional life. Rather timidly, I asked Matisse if he would sign it.

"Leave it here with me," he said, "and come back for it tomorrow." I followed his instructions. When I went to pick it up the next day, I found he had added a quizzical little self-portrait and inscribed it *"Hommages respectueux."*

The combination of the friendliness of the informal drawing and the formality of the inscription—"Respectful homages"—for a young person was typically Matisse.

That summer I was in Antibes, visiting Picasso (a great throwaway line, but it happened to be true). An appointment was arranged for me to see Matisse at Vence. I had not realized what a nightmare it would be to get there. There was no public transportation, I didn't drive. I finally came upon a very ancient taxicab driver who just happened to be there on holiday with his equally ancient cab. My appointment was for noon; we left in what should have been plenty of time.

Soon, to my dismay, I realized we were hopelessly lost. My driver was from Avignon and didn't know the region. What under other circumstances would have looked like idyllic landscapes—many made familiar from early Matisse paintings—began to look like visions from Dante's *Inferno* to me.

It was one o'clock before we finally got to Vence, then we had to find the house itself, which was outside the village. To keep a distinguished old gentleman waiting is bad enough, but to keep a Frenchman from his lunch!

We finally found it, and with beating heart I walked up the little path to the front door and rang. It was opened by an extremely handsome but clearly very angry woman. It was Madame Lydia, as we always called her, Lydia Delectorskaya, who had been Matisse's model and assistant for many years. "You're late," she practically hissed at me. I was ready to flee. But then I saw a stocky figure approaching: it was Matisse himself. "You're late," he echoed Madame Lydia. Then, mellowing, he said, "Well, as long as you are here, you might as well come in for a moment."

At my first visit, he had made the connection with his son Pierre; there had been no mention of *Vogue.* But now the *Vogue* connection surfaced alarmingly. "I believe you write for *Vogue* magazine?" he said. I said indeed I did. "Then you owe me thirty-eight dollars please." I was dumbfounded. There had been no correspondence about this. I was mystified. "*Vogue* published a work of mine before the war and never paid me the rights. Thirty-eight dollars please."

I mumbled that I had just come from the beach and didn't have any dollars in my beach bag. "A check will do," he said. "But I don't have a checkbook with me." I was quite distraught. "But I have one," he said, and went to get it.

He came back. I was so new in France I had no idea how to make out a check in French. So it was under the dictation of one of the greatest twentieth-century masters that I wrote out that I owed him thirty-eight dollars.

I noticed that he was watching my pen. It was a new-model Parker that had not yet reached France. "Won't you try it?" I suggested. He did and liked the way the line would flow smoothly to the left or the right. "Please keep it," I said. "Un moment." He went out to get something and came back holding his own pen. "I'll keep it if you will keep mine." Then I knew the ice was broken, and I began to breathe in a more normal rhythm. And while he was out of the room, Madame Lydia, obviously mollified by the turn of events, said kindly, "Don't worry, Monsieur Matisse likes you. I can tell. You will be able to come back."

Not wanting to press my advantages, I began backing toward the front door, with Matisse following me. He said, "The best bistro in the region is a quarter of an hour from here. The best dish they make is a *bar flambé au fenouil*. I've reserved your table for you and ordered the *bar*, so you won't have to wait when you get there."

That summer I was allowed to drop by several times to see Matisse. He would ask me to stand against a white door so that he could look at me. "What have you done for color today?" he would ask.

Not only was Matisse extremely elegant in his own person—in summer, when not bedridden, he wore loose raw-silk jackets and impeccably cut beige linen trousers—but he had a real interest in fashion. Those portraits of his daughter, Marguerite, wearing a succession of stylish hats were real portraits: of the hats. It might be in the family: Madame Matisse had worked as a milliner to help out family finances in the old days. In 1919, Matisse himself had pinned together a fantastic hat that is mostly an extravagant whirlpool of plumes. He clearly cared for his creation because it appears in some sixteen drawings and three oils.

Matisse accompanied his wife and daughter when they were choosing dresses; they were friendly with two of Paul Poiret's sisters, both couturieres, Nicole Groult and Germaine Bongard. He even went to the fittings. Incidentally, Poiret owned two Matisses.

That autumn, I was back in Paris. A telephonic invitation arrived from Vence. I hurried down, and to my surprise I found the old gentleman in bed, in the middle of the living room. The upper half of him was dressed with his usual formality, again the matching blue sweater and tie, the beard immaculately trimmed, hands manicured, gold-rimmed specs.

"I can't stand up to work anymore," he said cheerfully, "so I had my bed moved to the largest room of the house."

There was a colored rug on the bed; the foot of the bed ended in red metal arabesques; there was a red rose in a glass by his side: all very Matisse. And a typical note of convenience and order: next to the bed was a piece of furniture he had designed himself—a combination bookcase and a series of drawers on a pivot that he could swing around to reach what he wanted. Outside each drawer he had drawn in white chalk what was inside.

A whole forest of short flowers in an army of small vases covered several tables. And almost his signature: a large philodendron plant.

A board lay across his knees, and he was wielding a large pair of scissors over a heap of colored papers. Above his head was a series of bold black ink-brush drawings of his granddaughter Jackie.

Across from him, near the fireplace, was the striped red-and-white armchair that we recognize from many of his paintings.

Reflected in the mirror behind him were colored leaf shapes climbing up strips of brown paper. They were why he had summoned me. I will explain.

Obviously enjoying my surprise (he was not known to be a practicing Catholic), he told me, "I am going to design a chapel." It was thanks to his great kindness that I wrote the first story anywhere of Matisse's chapel in Vence. He told me how it had come about.

During the war he was gravely ill. Both his estranged wife and his daughter were away, in the Resistance. He was nursed with admirable devotion by a young woman named Monique Bourgeois. She put off following her vocation, to become a nun, until he was out of danger. Only then did she exchange her nurse's uniform for the Dominican veil.

A deep friendship had developed between Matisse and Sœur

Jacques-Marie, as she was now called. She came back for occasional visits. She liked to talk about her watercolors, and one time she gave him a little album of minute painted landscapes. When he showed her some of his own work, she apologized hesitantly: "Well . . . the colors are very pretty, but it is not exactly the kind of thing I like." Matisse was pleased at her frankness and said, "You are the only person who tells me the truth."

Matisse moved from the Nice apartment to Vence. By an extraordinary coincidence, Sœur Jacques-Marie also came to Vence, to a convent near her old friend. She found the nuns talking about projects for a new chapel. Aspiring to design one of the future stained-glass windows, she made a tentative watercolor. She was not happy with the results. She took her sketch over to Matisse to get his advice.

Matisse kindly made some suggestions. He sent for some sheets of colored cellophane so she could cut them out to her design and judge the effect. By the time the sheets of cellophane had arrived, the two Dominican monks in charge of planning the new chapel had also arrived—Father Couturier, a familiar figure in art circles, and Brother Rayssiguier—and Matisse's imagination had caught fire.

He had become completely fascinated with the problem of designing stained-glass windows. The two monks obviously seized a golden opportunity and encouraged him. Matisse offered to design first one, then all the windows, then the decoration of the interior, then the walls themselves. The monks happily gave up their original plans, and Matisse took over the entire project.

He had a cardboard model of the future chapel, with bands of cellophane to represent the future stained-glass windows: "The windows will run from floor to ceiling, fifteen feet high. They will be made of pure color shapes, very brilliant. No figures. Just the pattern of the shapes. Imagine when the sun pours through the glass—it will throw colored reflections on the white floor and walls. A whole orchestra of color!" He thought of the strong Midi sunlight almost as an element of building.

For the maquettes of the future windows, Matisse, in his precise professorial manner, explained his technique. First he paints sheets of paper with intense, flat color, then with a large pair of scissors he cuts out a shape. Many have a leaflike pattern. Madame Lydia, under his direction, pins them onto the strips of paper representing the future windows.

"The only decoration inside the church will be black and white. You will see how the intensity of a single black line can balance the impact of the colored windows."

He pointed out on the model: "On this side I will have a drawing of the Virgin and Child surrounded by flowers. Over here will be Stations of the Cross. Here will be Father Couturier—I mean Saint Dominic—Father Couturier posed for the drawings, so I always get confused."

Father Couturier described to me posing for the Saint Dominic figure. He sat in Matisse's studio for over an hour, chatting while the artist made sketch after sketch in charcoal. Matisse himself talked constantly while he worked. Suddenly the atmosphere changed. Matisse became tense and silent. His assistant appeared holding drawing implements with the gravity of a nurse assisting a surgeon. Almost holding his breath, Matisse made a few decisive lines on a fresh paper. This was the final drawing of the series, the accumulation of experience gathered during the hour.

Matisse had to devise a special technique to execute the wall drawings—they are huge—and he couldn't leave his bed. He explained, "I will draw on squares of white tile which have been cooked once, then coated with a special preparation. After I have drawn on them, they will be baked again, setting the line permanently.

"These squares will be small, so easy to handle. When finished, they will be spread over the walls, giving an alive surface.

"What you see here are only working sketches—I make a great many in preparation—then the final drawing will be made directly on the tiles. I draw a subject over and over again until I really feel it in my hands."

He noticed that I was looking at a large sketch of a girl's head drawn right on the living room door. "I did that blindfolded. After working from the model all morning, I wanted to see if I really had it. I was blindfolded and led to the door." It looked almost as free and sure as the other sketches.

I mentioned a documentary film I had seen with Matisse actually sketching. "There was a passage showing me drawing in slow motion," he said. "Before my pencil ever touched the paper, my hand made a strange journey of its own. I never realized before that I did this. I suddenly felt as if I were shown naked—that everyone could see this—it made me deeply ashamed. You must understand," he insisted, "this was not hesitation. I was unconsciously establishing the relationship between the subject I was about to draw and the size of my paper. I had not yet begun to sing. [*Je n'avais pas encore commencé à chanter.*]"

Matisse told me he was going to make "a church full of gaiety— a place which will make people happy." The numerous people who now crowd their way into Sainte Marie du Rosaire, as Matisse's chapel is called (be sure to make reservations: there is only room for ninety people), will undoubtedly feel he succeeded.

Matisse cared about the way the line of a drawing flowed across the page, and he also cared about how the written word flowed across the page. I was fortunate to receive several notes from him, which I cherish. They show a definite wish to establish a harmonious relationship between the space between the lines and the lines them-selves.

The envelopes are stamped with the Nice postmark: *"Nice Ses Jardins, Son Soleil, Ses Fêtes."* How appropriate for Matisse's world.

Most unexpectedly, when I married in 1948, he sent me a formal engraved visiting card (hard to imagine that Picasso would ever have such a thing), on which he wished me "complete and unlimited hap-piness." It didn't quite work out like that, but I was happy to have his good wishes.

Matisse loved reading, poetry in particular. He was a natural for marrying images with text. But he was sixty years old before anyone asked him to illustrate a book. The first time it happened was in 1930, when Albert Skira invited him to illustrate the poems of Mal-larmé, a great favorite of Matisse's.

One of the poems was about a swan. Typical of Matisse's thor-oughgoing serious approach to any task, he hired a boat at the Bois de Boulogne and went out on the lake to sketch the swans from life. A photograph records him sitting bolt upright in the boat, pad on knee, formal hat on head.

Swans are notoriously bad-tempered creatures. The great artist wasn't spared their irascibility. One of his models swiveled around, hissing alarmingly.

I learned of Matisse's thoughts about balancing an image and text from the master himself on another occasion. He had telephoned me in Paris and asked me to come down to Vence. He managed to make the sun shine steadily for his odalisques. They could loll around in the thinnest veiling without a shiver. But it was November and piercingly cold. He could stay wrapped up cozily in bed, but the visitor—me—had to rely on layers of wool jersey.

He had prepared a marvelous feast for me. He had set out all the books he had illustrated, and he pointed out one example after another to show exactly why and how he had solved certain problems in what he called the "ornamentation" of a book. As he explained it, he saw no difference between building a book and building a painting. It was a question of balancing a light page (the text) and a dark page (the illustration).

In the case of Mallarmé, the problem was to place a full-page illustration opposite a few airy lines of text without weighing them down. The answer was to make etchings done in a very thin, even line, without shading, that would leave the illustrated page almost as white as before the etching was printed. The illustration floats over the whole page, without a margin, so that the page stays light, because the design is not, as usual, massed toward the center.

The problem was exactly the opposite in illustrating Montherlant's *Pasiphaé, Chant de Minos*. What to do so that the heavy black lines used to illustrate the poem didn't pull down the rather empty page of text? His solution was to make one margin surrounding both pages, and then to accentuate the text on each page by making the top letter red. He said when he had seen the first proofs, in which red had not been used, he found the result "a little funereal." The red made the balance he was seeking. He looked at the page and held it up for me: "Red, black, white—*pas mal*."

He spent years illustrating a great edition of Ronsard, the sixteenth-century French poet who wrote so eloquently about love. Matisse worked on this, the *Florilège des Amours* (published in 1948), with a care and precision that are hard to imagine. He chose the poems himself and functioned as his own layout man. A series of albums in the Bibliothèque Nationale in Paris shows all the different stages he went through.

He tried and rejected many typefaces. He tried and rejected several kinds of paper. He modified and re-modified his own designs. Finally, 126 tender lithographs were produced. It is a glorious book. Sometimes his ornamentation would be just a grace note to the text. Sometimes he would throw an illustration over most of the page, leaving only a few lines of the poem.

I happened to be with him when Albert Skira, the publisher, delivered the first copy. His expression of delight was very moving. I own what I believe to be the only photograph of Matisse beaming. On another occasion he had said, "Can't one retain a young and ardent imagination? I feel better equipped to illustrate Ronsard's love poetry now than when I was twenty-five. Then, I didn't need imagination."

Another visitor to Le Rêve, in 1946, was Pablo Picasso. Matisse's relations with Picasso were affectionate but guarded. Matisse had been delighted when he heard that Picasso had bought his sumptuous *Still Life with Oranges*, of 1912, during the war. He wrote to his son Pierre, "Picasso is very proud of it." In a most unusual tribute from one artist to another, Picasso chose to exhibit it along with his most recent work at the first Salon d'Automne after the war. Oranges were to Matisse something like apples to Cézanne. He painted them, but also occasionally sent baskets to his friends.

Matisse recorded Picasso's 1946 visit to Vence with his new companion, Françoise Gilot, in a letter to his son (quoted from John Russell's *Matisse: Father and Son*):

Dear Pierre,

Three or four days ago, Picasso came to see me with a very pretty young woman. He could not have been more friendly, and he said he would come back and have a lot of things to tell me.

He hasn't come back. He saw what he wanted to see—my works in cut paper, my new paintings, the painted door etc. That's all that he wanted. He will put it all to good use in time. Picasso is not straightforward. Everyone has known that for the last forty years.

Picasso was far from enthusiastic about the chapel. Anything to do with the Church was off-limits as far as he was concerned. However, he did admire the chasubles, designed from cut-paper elements, and suggested that Matisse design capes for bullfighters.

When the Communist writer Louis Aragon came to call, the maquette of the chapel was on a table. Aragon resolutely ignored it. As he got up to leave, Matisse almost shouted at him, "If you don't look at my chapel, I will throw my shoe at you."

Matisse moved back to Cimiez from Vence in late 1949. His rooms at Le Rêve were too small to display the designs of the stained-glass windows. Putting his two rooms together at the Hôtel Régina gave him the exact dimensions of the chapel. In an untypically jocular vein, he said to Brother Rayssiguier, the Dominican monk in charge of the chapel construction, "I'm sleeping in the church again."

I found another personal note from Matisse, in looking over his correspondence with Brother Rayssiguier. He apologizes for a large blot of ink, then adds, "Let me try to turn it into something that will give you pleasure." And he has added flower petals around the blot. December 4, 1949.

Another nugget, this from Father Couturier's diary: "He tells me he definitely prefers El Greco to Velázquez, who is too perfect, too skillful. He's like a gorgeous fabric. A very beautiful marble. But in El Greco there is soul everywhere, even in the legs of Saint Martin's horse." July 25, 1951.

In spite of very poor health, Matisse managed to oversee all the exhausting details of the decoration of Sainte Marie du Rosaire. He even climbed up scaffolding. Begun in 1948, it took up all his time and flagging energy. It was consecrated in 1951. As he said himself: "A crowning achievement."

Henri Matisse died November 3, 1954.

René Clair and Vittorio De Sica

I met René Clair through Leonard Bernstein, in 1949. Lenny was in Paris conducting the Radio Orchestra. He had managed an introduction to the great movie director we all admired.

He reported that Clair and his wife, Bronia, were most affable. They were celebrating their dog's birthday and gave Lenny a piece of the cake.

For the young enthusiast of Dada and Surrealism that I was, René Clair's first-ever film, *Entr'acte* (1924), was heady stuff. The cast for this splendidly illogical macédoine included Marcel Duchamp playing chess with Francis Picabia, Man Ray, Erik Satie (who composed the music, which before talkies was performed by a live orchestra), and a camel pulling a hearse.

So it was with excitement that I went to meet its creator. He looked just like a Parisian in a René Clair film. He was a Parisian by birth, slight, quick, charming. His wife, Bronia, had come to Paris from her native Poland in the 1920s. She was a favorite of the habitués of the Dome and the Coupole. When I met her, she was, of course, fully dressed. But I kept remembering the famous photograph of her with Marcel Duchamp, as Adam and Eve, with the appropriate lack of costume.

The Clairs were more than affable, taking me under their respective wings. We used to go to the flea market on a Sunday afternoon. One time both René and I spied a very pretty piece of what must have been stage jewelry: a wide bracelet of black filigree sprinkled with small pink and green sparklers. Sarah Bernhardt might have worn it, we fantasized. We both wanted it. But gallantly, René insisted that I take it. I did, I still have it.

One time René telephoned to summon me: it was of utmost importance, he said, to accompany them to the premiere of a film. I joined them in the equivalent of the royal box.

It was the premiere of Vittorio De Sica's *Bicycle Thieves*. We were deeply moved by the poignant but never sentimental tale of an impoverished man and his son losing their only possession. No one cares. There is no happy ending.

René was overwhelmed. It was the greatest film since Chaplin, he said. He of course was well aware of De Sica and of his creation of a new genre of Italian realism: nonprofessional actors, natural lighting. De Sica's *Shoeshine*, made shortly after the war (I must admit I had missed out on this entirely), had made a sensation.

After the projection I was introduced. De Sica was besieged on all sides with flashbulbs popping, but with relaxed Italian charm he agreed to be interviewed.

But before I set out on a walk through Paris streets with De Sica, I went to Brussels with the Clairs for the premiere of René's latest film, *Le Silence Est d'Or* (*Silence Is Golden*, 1947). This saying had particular relevance for René. His whole career had been with silent films. I think he had reservations about the new genre.

However, he went mano a mano with the new medium and wrote and directed a musical. It was about the old music hall days, and an old-time star gave one of his last turns: Maurice Chevalier.

For the interview with Vittorio De Sica, I thought that since *Bicycle Thieves* had been filmed entirely in the open air, in the streets of Rome, by daylight, an anonymous studio setting was not indicated.

I asked him if he liked the idea of walking through the narrow streets of the Quartier Latin. We would talk as we went along. He liked the idea.

He was a handsome man, tall, well built, a strong face with a good nose, slightly uneven dark eyes. He was carefully dressed, Italian chic: a brown Prince de Galles suit and of course a hat (brown). I could well imagine that as a good-looking young man, in his native Naples, he had been what used to be called a matinee idol. He could even sing and dance. I can vouch for this: because of the miracle of Google I got Vittorio on my screen, doing exactly that.

He even sang "Parlami d'Amore, Mariù," that staple of the tenor repertoire that was a surefire encore for the Three Tenors.

A bit of research and I found out that he had made his cinema debut at sixteen. Throughout an amazingly productive career he had worked as an actor in other people's films, first to make a living, then to finance his own. He was to direct literally dozens of films. The early prewar efforts were mainly lightweight comedies, but the tone changed during and after the war with his collaboration with the screenwriter Cesare Zavattini, with *Shoeshine* (1946) and *Bicycle Thieves* (1948). The themes were the harsh conditions faced by the poor and helpless in a hostile world. There were plenty of those in postwar Italy. Incidentally, both of these films won Oscars for the Best Foreign Language film, an award especially created for them.

As we strolled along, he chatted easily in French spiced with Italian. Every now and then a few words in pure Italian twirled out happily, like the pirouettes of an accomplished ballerina. He had that peculiarly Italian gift of immediately establishing a human contact. How well it must have served him working with the nonprofessionals he chose for his films.

The film itself was shot in a month and a half, he told me, but the preparation had taken over a year. The whole thing was so clear in his mind that once he started shooting, he never even looked at the script. Lack of funds led to using nonprofessional actors, real-life locations—no building of sets—and whatever light was available.

He had asked over the radio for applicants to play the small boy in *Bicycle Thieves* to come and see him. "The man who plays the father brought his little boy; he had never intended to try out for a role for himself. His boy was too old, but the father had just the kind of face I needed—narrow and mobile—so I chose him.

"He was a metalworker in a big plant in Breda. I made him promise on his word of honor to go back to his job after the film was over. I didn't want him to have any false hopes for the future. Then I went to his employers and made them promise, too, that they would take him back."

I told De Sica that René Clair had said *Bicycle Thieves* was one of the finest pictures of the last thirty years—up to the level of the great Chaplin pictures of the early days. Naturally, he was pleased, but modest in his reaction. He asked me, "Do you think foreign audiences can understand enough without catching the dialogue? Is it clear to you?"

I asked him how he had managed to work in the streets with such crowds surging around the camera. "It was easy. We blocked off the streets; the police were very helpful. Whenever we needed people for the film, they were already planted in the crowd. You know how the artificial is often more convincing than the real? Those casual effects of people in the streets were all calculated."

I asked about the little boy who plays such an important part in the film. "He was eight years old. He came from a very poor family. His mother sold flowers in the street. He lived in a kind of cave, five people in one miserable cave. Sometimes we would go to a café together—he never asked for anything. He would eat one of the cakes I would order for him, but the second he wrapped in a napkin to take home to his mother.

"Have you noticed, as soon as the little boy comes on the screen, the whole audience is for him, he wins them right away?"

I said that the boy had great dignity.

"Yes, dignity, and a kind of responsibility too great for his years. A wonderful face, that plain little face with the big nose. Very sensitive and expressive without being maudlin. I wanted to avoid the overly pathetic quality which a prettier child might have given."

There is no sentimentality in the film, no class angle. The father is not exploited by any particular group. He is alone in the world, not responsible for his own misfortune, unable to cope with his surroundings.

De Sica watched with interest the people we crossed in the street as we walked. "The French are extraordinary, everyone an original type."

"More than the Italians?" I asked.

"Yes, more. I have never seen as many curious and interesting faces as here in Paris. I am thinking of finding some characters here for my next film."

"But what about the language problem?"

"That does not matter much, nor if they can act or not. I can make them do what I need if only I have a face to work with—that is what counts."

We walked on. I saw an agreeable little courtyard, good for our shot. There was a forlorn statue against the back wall. I wanted to photograph De Sica in front of it, but he was too tall, his head was not where I wanted it.

Without a word of direction, he sunk to his knees on the paving stones, bringing his head just in line for our picture.

A head popped out of a top-story window, and an old lady with disheveled hair looked out in amazement at the well-dressed man on his knees. He smiled up at her and said cheerfully, *"Vous voyez, madame, ce qu'il faut faire pour gagner sa vie!"*—"You see, Madame, what one must do to earn a living!" She beamed and nodded.

As we left the courtyard, the old lady waved, and we waved back. It seemed like a De Sica film. We were assembling the cast already.

On My Own for *Vogue*:
First Visit to Picasso

I came back to Paris in my new capacity of reporter writing about the arts in general. I had no training, no directives. I simply lit out toward what seemed to be of interest.

It was in this capacity that I went to Geneva to meet the hard-drinking Albert Skira, whose publications were the sensation of postwar art books circles. There followed a number of long evenings spent with Albert in Geneva nightclubs, I nursing a single scotch while Albert dove into the hard stuff.

But it was worth it. It was Albert who arranged an introduction to Picasso. And later, also invaluable, an introduction to the Swiss printers who were to print the magazine I founded, *L'ŒIL*.

"Don't wear a hat," Skira warned me, about meeting Picasso, "and don't ask any questions." I was surprised about the hat veto because Picasso had created so many fanciful, if not outrageous, hats for his favorite sitters.

At that time, 1947, Picasso had been living and working since 1937 in the top floors of a large, once-aristocratic building at 7, rue des Grands-Augustins. In earlier years the actor Jean-Louis Barrault had used these spaces for rehearsals.

By an amazing coincidence, this was the very house Balzac chose as the setting for his "Le Chef-d'Oeuvre Inconnu" (The Unknown Masterpiece), which Picasso had illustrated for Ambroise Vollard in 1931. Balzac's story is about a fictionalized seventeenth-century artist whose thirst for the absolute leads him further and further away from representation until finally nothing coherent is left.

I showed up for my appointment with Picasso looking properly inconspicuous and hatless. I walked through a large stone archway, across a cobbled courtyard, and up two flights of leg-breaking stairs, lit only by the occasional glimmer of a single bulb. A hand-lettered sign by Picasso, "ICI," was tacked to the door to identify his quarters. There was no bell. I knocked.

The door was opened reluctantly by a parchment-pale sharp-nosed apparition who peered at me through thick spectacles. It was Jaime Sabartés, Picasso's boyhood friend from Barcelona. He had come to Paris at Picasso's urgent request, in the 1930s, as companion, watchdog, and secretary and had never left. His main job was keeping people at bay who wanted to see the master. He had devoted his life to treading gingerly in Picasso's shadow, adoring him, and complaining every step of the way. Picasso teased him mercilessly but couldn't have done without him.

Sabartés led me through a small antechamber and into a barnlike studio where ancient beams held up the high ceiling. There was a large stove there that Picasso had relied upon during the terrible winters of wartime, when he chose to stay here all through the German occupation.

It was about noon when I went for the first time—the hour when he usually got up. Like many Spaniards, he lived by night.

He liked to work late at night and didn't care a hang for natural light. If anything, he preferred the strong projectors that Dora Maar, a photographer, had left behind at the end of their stormy love affair. It is thanks to Dora that we have a photographic record of the evolution of that great work, *Guernica*.

When I arrived, there were, as usual, about a dozen men standing around, waiting. I never saw a woman at these noonday receptions. There were editors, publishers, dealers, collectors, poets who hoped for illustrations, unemployed bullfighters.

Picasso finally came in, wearing an old brown dressing gown. The first thing you noticed was the extraordinary intensity of those remarkable eyes—the *mirada fuerte*. I understood what Gertrude Stein meant when she said his dark gaze was so intense he could see around corners.

Picasso went around in European fashion and shook hands with each person. He had a ritual greeting, "Please sit down," but there was no question of that. There were sagging sofas and a chair or two, but every one of them was completely covered with papers, catalogs, fragments of sculpture, portfolios, not to mention dust.

I was extremely nervous, for in spite of his simplicity of manner, one was very conscious of being in the "presence." But I was in luck, because from all those years in Mexico, I spoke Spanish, albeit with a Mexican accent, which amused him. When he heard his native tongue, he lit up with friendly incandescence.

He was so passionately attached to his native country and its language that from that moment on I felt accepted. He beamed, he asked questions, he used the familiar *tú* form, he stuck around, and before long he began to show me things.

He was immensely proud of a *Still Life with Oranges* (1912) by Matisse that he had bought during World War II. I know, because Matisse told me himself that he was very pleased Picasso had chosen it. Perhaps in its honor, Matisse would send Picasso a crate of oranges from the south of France every New Year's Day.

I got a glimpse of some other paintings that Picasso had collected (they are now in the Picasso Museum in Paris). One was a self-portrait by the Douanier, Rousseau.

Then Picasso led the way to an informal arrangement of recent work, balanced somewhat precariously on a scaffolding. One was a grim still life dominated by an ox's skull that dated from the occupation years. "I didn't paint the war," Picasso said. "I'm not that kind of a painter, but the war is right there in the work."

I was introduced to Picasso's Afghan hound, Kasbec, whose elongated snout turned up on some of Picasso's more devastating female portraits.

All around was the astounding accumulation that became part of Picasso's décor wherever he lived and worked. He could never bear to part with anything. Every book, every magazine, every catalog, every piece of wrapping, and every last length of string lay where it had fallen, together with flea-market finds, a stuffed owl, bulging portfolios of drawings and engravings. If anyone ever left anything behind, there was no hope of getting it back. It stayed on to enrich the loam.

There was no visible line between junk and treasure. Picasso's incessant compulsion to turn one thing into something else filled what he called his "museum," with such objects as former cigar boxes made into miniature theaters with pin-sized actors, pipe cleaners turned into jaunty figures. There were towers of empty cigarette boxes glued together waiting their turn for another incarnation. He smoked incessantly until late in life, when his doctors forbade it.

Sabartés gave a vivid description of Picasso as pack rat in his *Picasso: An Intimate Portrait*:

> When he finally gets out of bed, he would take the letters and papers and pile them on the buffet or a chair, or a table, or even in the dining room or bathroom. This new pile is added to another begun some other time: everything has been placed here or there in order not to mix here or there with this or that, with the intention of going over it more carefully, but he always receives new mail and never finds time to reread any of it.
>
> He has a mania for collecting everything, without rhyme or reason. His pockets testify to this: filled with papers, nails, keys, pieces of cardboard, pebbles, pieces of bone, a pocketknife, a small knife, notebooks for his literary lucubrations, matchboxes, cigarettes, cigarette lighters without fluid . . . letters and bills, very crumbled—irretrievably ruined because of his fear of losing them—seashells, a stone which suggested something to him on seeing it on the ground, pieces of string, ribbons, buttons, an eraser, pencil stump, his fountain pen, etc. Of course his coat is very heavy and his pockets bulge and split.

Then Picasso brought out a book—Aragon's translations from Petrarch—that had a frontispiece by him. He opened it and put it on the floor so that we could all take a look. On a blank page at the back, he had drawn a girl's head in colored crayons with five stars across her forehead. It was lovely and he knew it. "*Très jolie,*" he said in his rolling, Spanish-accented French. It was my first look at his new love, Françoise Gilot.

Then, with an incredibly mischievous look, he went and got out another book: poems by Tristan Tzara with black-and-white illustrations by Matisse. Picasso had colored all the illustrations. Sometimes the color accompanied the drawing. Sometimes it destroyed it, riding across the lines, creating a completely new entity. He knew that I knew Matisse. He shot me a glance: "Matisse doesn't know about this."

Not long after my first visit, I heard rumors that Picasso was working in Antibes in an old fort. No one was allowed in. Naturally, there was great curiosity everywhere about what he was doing.

Just then, I heard Picasso was back in town briefly. So I went to see him. There was the usual noonday cast, and Picasso made the usual round. After a while he came over to me and said, "You're the only one here who hasn't asked for something. What would you like?"

One had to jump fast when Picasso was in a good mood, and shut up when he wasn't. I said I was longing to know what he was up to in Antibes.

To my surprise he said, "Why not come down and see for yourself? You have all my benedictions."

Picasso and Antibes

So I went down to Antibes and got a first look at the outside of the medieval fort—the Château Grimaldi—that dominates the harbor and that guarded the secret of Picasso's new activities.

Thanks to his unpredictable generosity, I was the first person from the outside world to see what he had done there, and to publish it. But it wasn't easy.

At that time Picasso was living in very ordinary rented rooms, right over the main highway to Cannes. He never cared about décor or his surroundings. He took his meals at the café, Chez Marcel, across the street, which is where we were to meet.

I went and waited. Finally, Picasso came down the road with Françoise, looking strong and very brown, in white shorts, red-and-white T-shirt, and sandals. I could tell right away that he was in a bad mood. It turned out that an American dealer had been to his studio, and by mistake Sabartés had let him buy certain pictures that Picasso didn't want to sell.

I knew better than to even mention seeing the new work. Picasso was very polite and seemed glad to see me, but he acted as though he had no idea why I was there.

Eventually, I discovered how it had come about that he was working in the old fort. Picasso was a Mediterranean by birth and by temperament. He loved the sun, the beach, and the sea. Once Paris was liberated, he couldn't wait to get back to the south of France. Nor could he wait to get away with his new love, the beautiful twenty-six-year-old Françoise, but he had no house, no studio, no place to work except those crowded rented rooms.

At this point a local teacher of Latin and Greek who doubled as

curator of the Grimaldi fortress had a brilliant idea. (His name was
Jules-César Dor de la Souchère.) The fortress had been a somewhat
halfhearted regional museum before the war, with a scattering of
Greco-Roman remains, dolls wearing Provençal costumes, and Napoleonic souvenirs, but it had not reopened.

There were splendid empty spaces at the top. Why not, the curator reasoned, offer them as a studio to Picasso? There was always
a hope that if he went to work there, he might leave something
behind.

That is exactly what happened, after quite some hesitation on
Picasso's part (he always hated having to make up his mind). What
he left behind is to this day the great attraction of Antibes. The old
Grimaldi fortress became the Antibes Picasso Museum. But I wasn't
able to storm that fort for an agonizing week. Picasso was a specialist
in such trials, as his future biographer Roland Penrose, an old friend
of mine, knew all too well.

The day after my arrival he invited me to join him at the public
beach. In those days, he used the beach as his salon, giving appoint-
ments there. The group consisted of Françoise Gilot; two Barcelona
nephews; his thirty-year-old son, Paulo, whose main interest was
high-powered American motorcycles; his great friend the poet Paul
Eluard; and a few hangers-on. Sometimes Olga, still legally Picasso's
wife, although they had been separated for many years, would stum-
ble along too. According to French law, if they had divorced, Olga
would have been given half of his studio and its output, so he didn't
remarry (Jacqueline) until Olga died in February 1954. At the time,
Françoise referred to Olga as "my mother-in-law."

Picasso reigned over this scene in blazing sunshine, while sup-
plicants and/or dealers from Paris tried to protect themselves with
makeshift arrangements of shirts. Picasso, of course, enjoyed their
discomfort.

We would swim, eat bouillabaisse at two hundred old francs a
plate at either Chez Toutou or Chez Nounou, and hunt for interest-
ingly shaped stones on the beach. Competition was fierce for these,
with Picasso intent on the chase. Once he picked up a pebble, looked
at it, and said, "Oh, we know that one. I saw it last year." And he
threw it back.

Walking on the beach, I was astonished at the amount of gossip Picasso knew: just who was sleeping with whom, who was leaving whom. When I mentioned this to Éluard, Paul said, "But of course, everybody tells him. You can hardly expect people to talk to Picasso about art!"

This went on for about a week. It was entertaining but nerve-racking. Picasso knew very well why I had come—after all, he had invited me. I knew I should not be the first to say anything. Finally, casually, as though he had just thought about it, he asked, "Shall we go and see the paintings?" but he added quickly, "Although, bathing is much more fun." Incidentally, he claimed that he was the only man who could make love underwater. I am not in a position to verify this.

So I finally saw the Antibes paintings. At the time of my first visit to the improvised studio, there were twelve paintings on panels, none of them signed.

"Are they finished?" I asked. Picasso smiled: "As long as there is a picture around and I'm anywhere near, it's in danger."

Antibes had originally been settled by the Greeks, who called it Antipolis. In the vast spaces of his attic studio, Picasso had dreamed up a mythical population of early settlers: pipes-playing fauns, gamboling centaurs, well-endowed mermaids, and, queen of the scene, Françoise, with exuberantly flowing hair.

In their honor, and to mark his intentions, he wrote "Antipolis" on many of these paintings and drawings.

"It's a funny thing," Picasso commented. "I never see fauns and centaurs in Paris; they all seem to live around here."

Nothing ever curbed Picasso's endless powers of invention. That summer, there was no canvas to be had in Antibes and no proper paints. Picasso didn't care. Before the necessary supplies arrived from Paris, he improvised—as he always loved to do. "This is a port," he said. "They must have good marine paint, and that paint is meant for wood." So he got plywood board, housepainter's brushes, and went to work.

Naturally, the delicate question arose as to what would become of the Antibes series. Picasso's habit was to cram a place where he worked to the bursting point, then turn the key and move on. He owned a number of studios in and around Paris, and bank vaults too.

But this wasn't his property. To make up his mind about anything was always a major hurdle. He first announced his intention of "lending" the series, keeping everyone on tenterhooks. Finally, after much discreet but considerable prodding, he agreed that the works could stay where they were.

So there they are, the pride of what is now called the Antibes Picasso Museum.

So I finally saw the Antibes paintings, and wrote about them and had them photographed for *Vogue*. This was a considerable coup in art circles and publishing circles. *Vogue*'s reaction: Mrs. Chase took me to tea at the Paris Ritz and said gently, "My child, I hear you are not in the office much of the time." I answered that it was difficult to be gathering fascinating material in Antibes while sitting in the Paris office. She thought that over, then said, "But you must remember that if people are nice to you, it is only because of *Vogue*."

And from Condé Nast headquarters I had a message from the then editor of *House & Garden*: "Since you are on such good terms with Picasso, ask him to send us color suggestions for autumn decoration."

I had another world first of which I was understandably proud. Matisse himself had invited me to visit him at Vence, where he told me all about his plans to decorate the chapel that is now world famous, Sainte Marie du Rosaire. *Vogue* published my text and accompanying illustrations with no author's name up front; my name appeared in very small type in a turn at the back of the book.

I realized that I was producing too rich a fare for *Vogue* and that I should think of another outlet. It took some years to bring it about, but the first issue of my own magazine, *L'ŒIL*, hit the stands, very quietly, I admit, in January 1955.

L'ŒIL Begins with a Gift
from Picasso

In the 1950s in Paris there was not much on offer in the way of art publications at an affordable price. There was the large, sumptuous *Verve*, edited at first by a wily Greek, known always by just one name, Tériade. It had magnificent color plates and erudite articles by well-known poets and authors and was correspondingly expensive.

There was *Connaissance des Arts*, almost exclusively devoted to interior decoration, and a few trade sheets.

I had been making invaluable contacts with the leading artists of the day. I was interested in photography and had worked with talented photographers. I cared about good design and good writing.

With the enthusiasm of the innocent, I launched myself into the creation of a new art review, in French. My aim was to produce a lively publication with attractive layouts and well-written, readable texts by experts who did not pontificate, something of top quality that young people on a tight budget could buy. My dream was to see it read on the metro. Eventually, I managed it.

I had a French partner, which made fiscal arrangements feasible. Nevertheless, ingenuity and improvisation were essential.

It was through my old hard-drinking companion in Geneva, Albert Skira, that I was introduced to the Swiss printers the Imprimeries Réunies Lausanne. They had only worked with a four-color process for fine-arts reproduction. Offset, far less expensive, was the medium for advertising booklets for watches or chocolates.

After many lunches with Monsieur Lamunière and Monsieur Heng (I discovered the fine Swiss way with potatoes, the *rösti*), they rose to the challenge of printing a high-quality publication in offset.

We were able to establish a price for eight full-color pages per issue that would come in at the equivalent in today's money of forty-eight cents a copy on the newsstand.

We acquired a small office on the ground floor of a building next to the Hôtel des Saints-Pères. A window in the office gave onto the courtyard, and sometimes I would leap through, not quite up to Nijinsky in style. We had one assistant, a part-time secretary and an enthusiastic rugby player named Bob Delpire to do our layouts. (He is famous today and has his own highly successful publishing firm specializing in photography). First problem: a name.

Several possibilities, such as *Vue,* were already taken. I wanted to emphasize the visual presentation. I tried writing out *L'ŒIL,* and I liked the way the *E* backed into the *O.* We had a motto: all the arts, from all countries, from all times. It sounds better in French. That was it.

I had become friendly with Fernand Léger. Our first cover had a detail from his last great painting, *La Grande Parade.* The original is in the Guggenheim today. Léger was only one of our high-powered artist friends who gave their benediction to our venture.

That brave first issue, January 1955, presented the kind of nourishing and seductive mix that was our aim. It started out with that eminent British literary critic, Cyril Connolly, writing about the eighteenth-century Bavarian rococo. Cyril's prose was matchless, but so was his laziness. I knew that without close supervision he would spin his article in the stacks of the British Library instead of going to look firsthand.

So we took him ourselves and drove around Austria and southern Germany to see the splendors of those joyful churches and libraries. By now this circuit is high fashion, but at the time no one was interested. That summit of Bavarian rococo, the meadow church at Wies, was not even in the index of the Blue Guide to Germany.

I had always had a fondness for that life-loving sixteenth-century French king, François I, who brought Italian art to his country. This culminated in his château at Fontainebleau, where, among other things, he kept the *Mona Lisa* in his bathroom.

The leading authority on the subject was Charles Terrasse, who, incidentally, was related to Pierre Bonnard. He was director of the

Fontainebleau château that had just reopened after the war. He lived on the job, so to speak, in a little house near the entrance.

My mission was to persuade him to take the time to write an article about the School of Fontainebleau for a magazine he had never heard of, for an editor completely unknown to him.

I went out to Fontainebleau on a chilly November day. Like most people when discussing their specialty, he was fascinating. The hours slipped by. The November light was waning fast.

"But I must show you," he said. "Come with me." And he led me at a brisk pace across the cobblestoned courtyard, up the famous double staircase into a completely dark interior.

Electric light had not yet been installed, but he knew every step of the way so well that he clearly saw every statue, every stucco relief, every garlanded fresco. I didn't. "Here we have a panel painted by Il Rosso," he would say, pointing, as I strained through total darkness. Our entire tour of the château took place like that.

But we parted good friends, and he did write the article.

To round out that January 1955 number (besides an article on Giacometti), we had an interview with the venerable dealer Daniel-Henry Kahnweiler, who had been Picasso's on-and-off dealer for fifty years. He had outlived and/or outwitted the competition. Picasso never really liked his dealers. He felt he had been royally robbed when he first arrived in Paris. The exception was Ambroise Vollard, for whom Picasso made many illustrations for his editions. But Kahnweiler had created a profitable German market for Picasso, and he had staying power over the long course. Kahnweiler also became Georges Braque's first dealer and presented Braque's first exhibition in Paris.

We accompanied the interview with a photograph of Kahnweiler taken by Picasso in 1912, and in a routine way we gave Picasso his photographic credit. He was absolutely thrilled. He took back a copy of *L'ŒIL* to his quarters in the rue des Grands-Augustins and proudly showed it to every visitor. "There's an intelligent art review," he said. "They know I'm a photographer."

To commemorate the occasion of the first issue, my copy was signed by Picasso, Braque, and Kahnweiler. Braque was an early champion of *L'ŒIL*.

From then on, every month I went to Lausanne, and at 6:00 a.m., not my favorite hour, I was at the Imprimeries Réunies to see the issue through the press. Color corrections were made by hand in those days. I stood by to watch the color proofs churned out and to correct as well as I could.

Naturally, we had to accumulate material well in advance of that first issue because we had nothing waiting in the larder. It was a high-wire act.

We owe our first big publicity coup to Picasso. When he heard about the plans to start an art review, he sent a message of solidarity via Kahnweiler and said that he had "*un regalo*" for me, a present. It turned out to be the equivalent of a gold mine.

He was sending me to his sister, Doña Lola de Vilató, in Barcelona. I was the first person to be so honored. She had kept in her care a large body of his work that was totally unknown. None of it had been published. It included early sketches and family portraits and a substantial group dating from 1917.

All he asked in return is that when I got back, I would come and tell him all about my visit and show him some photographs. He had not seen his family since 1938; he had vowed he would never return to Spain while it was under Franco's rule. He had never seen his family's present apartment.

Picasso had painted the 1917 works when he had come to Barcelona with Diaghilev's Ballets Russes. He had fallen in love with one of the dancers, Olga Koklova, and was not letting her out of his famous *mirada fuerte*. Later he was to marry her, with predictably disastrous results.

As a proper Spaniard, he didn't bring his mistress home. They stayed at the Rancini, an old hotel by the port, with a view of the Christopher Columbus column. He was to make a famous painting of the column. I saw it at the time of my visit to the family. Later it became a poster for the future Picasso Museum in Barcelona.

When he was returning to Paris, he simply didn't want to bother packing up the work he had done in Barcelona. He left it all with his sister, and she had kept it gathering dust for all those years.

Apparently, I was the first person Picasso had ever sent to the family. They had been alerted about my arrival and were in a high state of excitement.

I had been somewhat surprised, on telephoning when I arrived in Barcelona, to be told, "Come right away! Come tonight! At half past eleven." Since I knew his sister, Doña Lola de Vilató, was aged and a semi-invalid, this was an unexpected hour. In true Spanish style, the family lived by night.

The family apartment, at 48, Paseo de Gracia, was in one of the solid bourgeois buildings that lined the street. There was no exterior indication that it might contain unexpected treasure. The smoothly running elevator was in sharp contrast to Picasso's ramshackle staircase.

"We're so glad to see you," they greeted me exuberantly, on opening the front door. I said I was glad to see them, but in fact I couldn't see a thing. The place was in almost total darkness. They introduced themselves: Lolita, a daughter of the house, and two sons, Javier and Pablín. "We don't know what happens to our lightbulbs," Lolita explained. "The fuses, they blow like that, for nothing."

They steered me into the salon. There too the light was dim; only one part of a lamp was functioning. I could just make out a round shape swaddled in blankets, emerging from an armchair. It was Doña Lola. She suffered from acute arthritis, and it was painful for her to dress. But she presided like an empress from her cocoon of coverings. When Picasso saw the photograph we later published in *L'ŒIL*, he said, "Isn't she splendid! She looks like a bullfighter's mother."

They thought it very dashing for a young woman to have made the journey from Paris by herself, but it had never occurred to any of them to actually go to Paris themselves. They spoke fondly of Tío Pablo, but it was clear that they had no idea of his worldwide fame.

There were no hushed tones around the invalid here. One nephew played the guitar, and the others danced and sang around Doña Lola. The merriment continued until the wee hours.

Obviously, I was burning to see the work, but Spanish hospitality and folkways had me sitting in the family circle, sipping little glasses of sweet Málaga wine, and exchanging family news. They talked about Pablo's mother, Doña María. She was very much like him, they said, short, dark, vivacious. She believed in him implicitly. After he had gone to Paris, she wrote to him once, "Now I hear you

At age six on my pony Teddy, after winning a cup in my first horse show

At sixteen with my harp

Now twenty-two years old, in my Acapulco garden with my husband, Lewis A. Riley, Jr., and assorted animals, 1938

With my sister, Heather, by my Acapulco pool, 1939 (Victor Kraft)

For *L'ŒIL* I had Giacometti's *The Chariot* photographed in the Parc Monceau, Paris; the children's bicycles echo the sculpture's wheels. 1955. (Sabine Weis for *L'ŒIL*)

Interviewing Chanel for *Vogue*; sketched by Eric, 1954

With Fernand Léger at his house in the country, 1954 (Robert Doisneau)

Picasso's sister Doña Lola de Vilató, photographed for *L'ŒIL* in her Barcelona apartment (*left*), where Picasso's boyhood portrait of her (*right*) was hanging. 1954.
(Inge Morath for *L'ŒIL*)

Gertrude Stein and her poodle, Basket; Eric and I are in the background. 1947.
(© Horst P. Horst)

Irving Penn's magnificent portrait of Aaron Copland

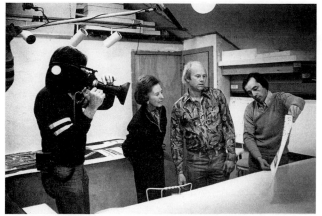

LEFT: Interviewing
James Rosenquist for
a series I did for CBS
(Photograph courtesy of CBS)

BELOW: David Hockney's
oversized card for my
ninetieth birthday

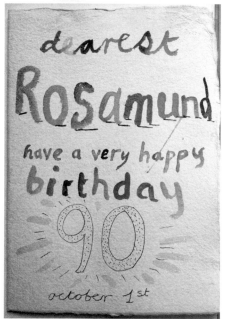

Interviewing Henry
Moore about Rodin—
in the surf at Forte
dei Marmi, 1967 (John
Hedgecoe)

Braque in his studio, where I was interviewing him about his painting *L'atelier*, 1958 (Robert Doisneau for *House and Garden*)

My photo of David Hockney in our New York apartment

Matisse in bed showing me his illustrated books, 1948 (© Clifford Coffin)

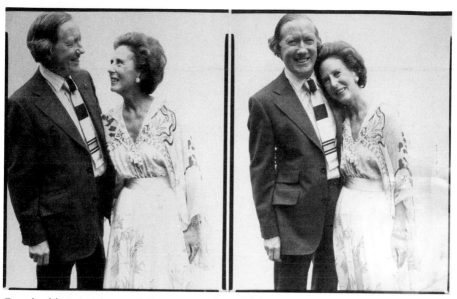

Our double portrait, a wedding present from Richard Avedon (Richard Avedon)

Our wedding at the Glass
House, 1975. The fatal
moment. (Iris Schneider)

John and his two granddaughters, Isabel and Chloe Grimshaw
(Lavinia Grimshaw)

With John and his daughter, Lady Grimshaw, at the Spanish Institute after I was given a Spanish decoration

My stepson and best friend, Olivier Bernier

With my nieces Margarita and Natalia Jimenez at the Spanish reception

are writing poetry. I'm willing to believe it. If I hear next you are saying Mass, I'll believe that too."

However, Pablo's father was Pablo's opposite in every way, tall, thin, and fair. His friends called him *"el inglés"*—the Englishman. Pablo often recorded his careworn face.

They also talked about someone Picasso had described as "a very boring old aunt, a religious maniac who was constantly telling her beads." This was Tía Pepa. The family wanted a portrait of her, but the old lady had always refused to pose.

And then, one scorching summer day when Picasso was back in Málaga for the holidays, she suddenly changed her mind and showed up despite the heat in cap and shawl, ready to be painted. Young Pablo, the family Polaroid, was out playing with his cousins. He was called in. He took out his paints and brushes and went to work.

He liked to claim that he had finished the portrait in an hour, but he was not above exaggerating in such matters. He also said, with some satisfaction, that she died the following week.

Finally, Doña Lola said kindly, "Maybe she would like to see the pictures." Lolita led me through more darkened rooms, past a case filled with plaster casts of deformed feet, a specialty of Pablín, who was a doctor. (This detail particularly delighted Picasso when I told him about it.) Sometimes the light was so dim that Lolita held up a lit match for me to get a better view.

"You can't see much, can you?" she said sympathetically. I agreed, and asked if it might be possible for me to come back by daylight. This caused consternation. The family conferred. No one stirred until midday. Since both nephews were doctors and had their offices there, I wondered about their office hours. Finally, it was agreed that I could come back at six the next afternoon.

Incidentally, everything I saw at the Vilatós' was black with grime. There were pictures all over the place, on the floor, propped against furniture, on the sofa, hanging askew from a single nail. Most of them were unframed and dim from decades of dust.

What I finally saw, and was able to photograph and publish for the first time, were early sketches and paintings of family members and friends and a whole group of paintings dating from the 1917 visit. Most of these works are now in the Picasso Museum in Barcelona.

They made a magnificent spread in the fourth issue of *L'ŒIL* and won us international acclaim. There were full pages in *Time* and *Life* and many write-ups in other publications.

Several of the large canvases by the fourteen-year-old Picasso included his father and sister. The one now known as *Science and Charity* involved an unfortunate woman dying in bed, attended by a doctor and a nun. The doctor was posed by Don José, Picasso's father, a failed academic artist who specialized in painting fur and feathers. It was he who had staged the scenario, thinking an edifying subject would make a good impression in academic circles.

Another big painting, *The First Communion*, involved a kneeling young person in white and a standing priest. Don José had modeled once again, and sister Lola posed for the first Communion candidate. Doña Lola told me about this picture: "I didn't want to pose. I didn't have a first Communion dress. But Pablo kept insisting, so I finally borrowed a dress from a friend."

There were a number of self-portraits, sketched and painted. One showed him, already displaying his love of disguises, wearing an eighteenth-century white wig, tweaking reality by the tail.

Among the 1917 crop was a figure built up in typical Cubist overlapping planes, but with the surprising addition of a hand in trompe l'oeil that seems to be bursting through the canvas. I had thought it represented a seated diner with a bowl of fruit (which is how the Picasso Museum in Barcelona has labeled it), but when I showed a photograph of it to Picasso, he corrected me: "No, it's a waiter setting the table. Can't you see he is holding a knife and fork in one hand?"

There was a painting Picasso simply identified as *Figure* (the Barcelona museum calls it *Seated Woman*) that was totally unlike anything I had seen from that period. The "figure" with its full curves evokes both human anatomy and musical instruments. It was painted in broad surfaces of chalky tones—a dusty pink, almond green, gray, white, black—painted so thinly that the bare canvas can be seen in several places.

When I talked about it to Picasso in Paris, he agreed that it was "*hors série*," as he put it—one of a kind. He said it represented certain preoccupations that he was to take up later.

There were two paintings of Spanish dancers, totally different from each other but painted, Picasso said, within a few days of each other. He could veer rapidly from one style to another. One had a straightforward approach, the features modeled, the upper part of the figure and its surrounding space highlighted by a confetti of colored dots. The other danced to a Cubist tune, in colors reminiscent of Juan Gris.

When I got back to Paris and went over to show Picasso the family photographs, as promised, and to deliver some gifts from the Vilatós, I asked him whether the seated dancer was a portrait of Olga, as the Vilatós had told me. "Absolutely not," he answered. "They are thinking of a totally different painting. I can't quite remember this dancer's real name, because we always called her *la Salchichona* [the Sausage]."

An old friend of mine, the English collector and early Picasso biographer Roland Penrose, wrote in his *Picasso Memoirs* that he had gone to visit Picasso when I was expected. Picasso had woken up in a bad mood and had told Sabartés his back hurt and he wouldn't see anyone. Penrose was disconsolate. Then I was announced. Picasso leaped out of bed and made his appearance in a white dressing gown. To quote Penrose: "Picasso welcomed Rosamond and soon forgot his pains under the combined influence of her charm and memories of the early paintings and of his sister and family. Rosamond's account of her visit amused Picasso greatly, especially the lack of light for nocturnal habits."

Picasso looked at his sister's photograph and remembered how beautiful she had been, and how often he had made her portrait. He said: "It's terrible. She should be killed, *n'est-ce pas?* My mother used to say there is nothing worse for a woman than to grow old, because that means to grow ugly." Roland remarked that his sister's eyes were as dark and sparkling as ever, but Picasso could only see the swollen formless chin, her flabby cheeks, and her tousled gray hair.

What delighted Picasso was a photograph of a bust of the Virgin that had been acquired by his father at a flea market, originally a plaster cast of a Greek goddess. He had painted it white with utmost realism, with the addition of eyelashes and golden tears and a look of sorrow.

Picasso called it a forerunner of collage. He was amused by the way two round lamps had been placed where breasts might have been.

I showed him photographs of the Vilató apartment. He looked attentively at the furnishings and exclaimed, "Ha! They live better than I do." When he spied a 1904 engraving called *The Frugal Repast*, he said, rather sharply, "I didn't remember they had that. It's worth a fortune now."

Picasso loved presents, and he lost no time in opening those I had been given to take back to him. There were heavy boxes that contained *membrillo*—a sweet gelatinous candy that only a Spanish palate can appreciate. Next came a penny bank in the form of a rooster. It rattled. The family had put in a coin for good luck. Then there was a paper bag stamped with the name of a pork butcher. It was full of sugared almonds. "That's Spain for you," Picasso said. "You buy candy at the butcher's."

Next came a carefully wrapped package with a lot of tissue paper. Rolled up inside was a handful of cotton seeds. Picasso looked around at his studio with its heaped canvases, its antediluvian papers, its portfolios, magazines, and sculptures, and said happily, "They're just what we need. Let's plant them right here."

Picasso's black moods could be annihilating. He enjoyed torturing his worshippers, keeping them waiting endlessly or not opening the door to them at all when a rendezvous had been arranged. But his kindnesses to me were memorable.

Once he sent me a photograph of himself reading *L'ŒIL* with his wife, Jacqueline Roque, looking over his shoulder. I thought, what a splendid thing it would be if he allowed us to use it to publicize the review. I wrote, asking for his permission. Writing to Picasso was like sending a message in a bottle—he never answered. But I thought I would at least try.

He didn't answer with a letter, but by return I received a strip of Leica negatives with shot after shot of Picasso holding up my magazine.

A few years later he sent me a little book he had written and illustrated himself. It was called *El Entierro del Conde de Orgaz*, after the famous painting by El Greco. It brought together an assortment of unlikely bedfellows—Velázquez and the great bullfighter Manolete, for instance—and a torrent of images, both verbal and visual.

With his usual itch to change everything he touched, Picasso had inscribed it all over the cover, making my name part of a face. He had repeated the inscription inside, possibly from affection for me, but more probably because he couldn't bear to leave a blank page alone. He misspelled my name twice, but that did not surprise me; he had a very freewheeling eighteenth-century way with spelling. In fact, he once told me he had never learned the alphabet and had no intention of ever doing so. "Why should one letter follow another in a predestined order? Ridiculous!"

He carried on his embellishments on another page inside the book and conjured up a man wearing a squashy hat. He always loved fanciful hats, and one of the happier days of his life was when Gary Cooper came to see him in the south of France and gave him his classic ten-gallon hat. For weeks after that, Picasso insisted on going around in only that hat and his shorts.

That was not the last of Picasso's "benedictions" for me.

I had been to Munich on one of my material forays for the magazine. At the great Alte Pinakothek Museum, I discovered an artist new to me, Albrecht Altdorfer, a German who worked in the early sixteenth century (about the same time as Dürer). I was struck by his jam-packed battle scene and his quirky take on the Susanna and the Elders tale, in which Susanna is not giving much away.

Back in Paris, I mentioned my new enthusiasm to Picasso. He heartily disliked travel, but he knew from books and catalogs the whereabouts of the works of art that interested him.

"Altdorfer," he said, "I had a book about Altdorfer." It turned out that once Kahnweiler had paid a call on Picasso with a book about Altdorfer under his arm. Curious as a monkey, Picasso had grabbed the book and never gave it back. "In fact," Picasso continued, "I made some drawings after Altdorfer."

"Could I see them?" I asked in great excitement. The idea of publishing unknown drawings by Picasso was thrilling. "How do you expect me to find them?" he asked, and gestured at the chaotic accumulation all around him. I agreed the possibilities looked bleak.

"You know, it had happened," he told me, "that I have promised to someone to do a drawing, and I have done it. But when they come to pick it up, I simply can't find it. Do you know what I do? I go out of the room and pretend to be looking for it, and I do another, and no one knows the difference."

I left without much hope.

But a few days later Sabartés, his gloomy factotum, telephoned me and said laconically, "Come around, he has something for you." Sabartés never referred to Picasso by name.

I was back in Picasso's studio in no time—my office was just around the corner—with a bunch of flowers that he completely ignored. (Unlike Matisse, flowers meant nothing to him.) There he was, beaming, his work trousers held up by a piece of rope. "I found them," he said triumphantly, pleased with himself, and pleased for me.

He had made drawings of the whole composition, *The Body of Saint Sebastian Recovered from the Water*, and from details of a figure praying, and he had signed them and dated them "Albrecht Altdorfer" in Gothic letters.

We published them in the May issue of our first year. Naturally, I gave back the drawings. But they were never seen again—never reproduced anywhere except in my magazine. They didn't even show up in the inventories of his estate.

We gradually built up a network of specialists, art historians, writers, but more than once I pitched in at the last minute when some long-awaited manuscript failed to materialize. Running a monthly magazine with a skeleton staff and little backlog required resource and improvisation.

That was the case with our feature on Francis Picabia. André Breton, known as the Pope of Surrealism, had promised a text. The color was already engraved at the printers—but not a word from Breton. Finally, in despair, I telephoned him.

In rolling pontifical tones of beautifully articulated French, he said, "Madame, in spite of my high regard for you, I regret to tell you that I cannot write your article."

"Why not?" I gasped.

"Parce que j'ai été envoûté par un objet maléfique"—"Because I have been bewitched by an evil object."

(How is that for an excuse for writer's block?)

"Well, get rid of it," I said.

"Impossible, madame." He spun out various arcane reasons. There was no budging him.

I did some research and found that there were two Picabia widows living in Paris. There was an Olga and a Gabrielle Buffet Picabia. I went to interview them both (not together).

Gabrielle Buffet Picabia was by far the more interesting. Finally I asked her if she would allow me to write an article based on her memoirs, as she had described her life to me, and to sign it "Gabrielle Buffet Picabia." She agreed (and incidentally got the fee).

Gabrielle Buffet Picabia's (alias RB's) article is in all the Picabia anthologies.

In the February issue of our second year, 1956, John Russell appeared for the first time. I didn't know him personally, but I would always make sure to get my copy of the London *Sunday Times* in order to read the splendid weekly article by someone called John Russell. I wrote to him and asked if he would consider writing for *L'ŒIL*. He wrote back that he would.

For two years we corresponded back and forth as editor and valued contributor. When finally he came to Paris and we met, we were both married to other people. It took fourteen years to disentangle this situation. Meanwhile, John wrote a number of brilliant articles for my magazine, and always on time.

An early one was on Oskar Kokoschka; we illustrated it with the turbulent self-portrait in a lifeboat with his great love, Alma Mahler.

I had gotten to know Kokoschka when we were both in New York. Back in Paris he wrote to me, "Be a good girl. You KNOW I am a better painter than Picasso."

Publications in France were apt to be very Gallic-centered in those days. We liked to think we had an international outlook. Early on, *L'ŒIL* was looking toward the United States. Much has been made recently of the auction of pictures collected by Robert and Ethel Scull. I went to New York with a photographer and recorded the Scull story in 1963, with the James Rosenquist mural and a Kenneth Noland target. I went to see Mark Rothko in the Bowery in 1960 and survived having to drink bourbon out of a paper cup at ten in the morning.

We showed Jackson Pollock in 1958 and during the following decade ran features on Rothko, Robert Rauschenberg (twice), Jasper Johns, Barnett Newman, and Andy Warhol.

We consistently presented articles about architects and architecture, both in France and abroad. We ran several features about Philip Johnson; he always made good copy. One was on his famous Glass House in Connecticut. Little did I know that many years later—in 1975—John Russell and I would be married there.

We wrote about Paul Rudolph. I went to talk to the great Louis Kahn a number of times. (Each time he told me, "Forget what I told you last time. Everything has changed.") He was working on that most successful of new museums, the Kimbell in Fort Worth. We did a feature on Marcel Breuer, who was designing the Whitney Museum.

I actually went with Breuer to Rotterdam to write about a department store, de Bijenkorf, that he had designed. At the time, its design and interior arrangements were the most advanced in Europe. Rotterdam had been largely destroyed by bombing in May 1940, so this inauguration had symbolic overtones. The mayor and other town worthies were on hand, and several hundred guests from foreign countries.

Center stage, as it were—immobile at the time—was a moving staircase clothed in teak. After the mayor's welcoming speech, he pressed a button, whereupon, to bursts of music—the triumphal march from *Aida*, no less—the officials took their places one by one on the staircase to be slowly lofted upward and out of sight, to loud applause.

Often I wrote these articles myself, sometimes under an assumed name. In the first decade of the magazine I traveled and wrote articles from Belgium, Finland, Italy, Denmark, New York, Los Angeles, and St. Louis, and there were a number of features from England, not only London.

By 1970, I had shed my French partner and headed for almost unknown, to me, territory: the United States.

L'ŒIL went through various convulsions. It was acquired by several publishing conglomerates. At one point a Japanese dragon lady bought it as a divorce present for her husband. For a while it disappearcd from sight. It reemerged with a capable and charming young man as editor, Jean-Christophe Castelain. When *L'ŒIL* was celebrating its five hundredth issue in October 1998, Jean-Christophe very courteously came to New York to interview me and write a generous text accompanied by my photograph.

L'ŒIL today is not what I had created, nor should it be. Times have changed.

Berthe Morisot's Daughter

We made a point at the magazine of looking up survivors who could give us firsthand accounts of past notables. There was Henri-Pierre Roché reminiscing about playing golf with Constantin Brancusi; Jacques Salomon writing about his family, which included Edouard Vuillard; Francis Jourdain, who could say in print, "I knew Lautrec, Cézanne, Monet."

In 1959, I visited a distinguished old lady (then very much alive at eighty) who was the daughter of Berthe Morisot as well as Edouard Manet's niece: Madame Ernest Rouart. Berthe had married Manet's brother, Eugène. Julie Manet Rouart still lived in Paris in the house her parents built in 1883, on what used to be called the rue de Villejust—now renamed the rue Paul Valéry because the poet too lived in the same apartment building.

I climbed the five flights to her walk-up apartment (she didn't get puffed, I did) to find a lively upright figure, snow-white hair, with a remarkable memory. She lived surrounded by family mementos that happened to be by Renoir, her mother, Berthe Morisot, her uncle Édouard Manet, Edgar Degas, and Claude Monet.

There were pictures all over the place—stacked several deep on the walls, leaning against easels, propped against the walls, over the chimney—the better to fight for their lives among the blue-and-white porcelains, the little flowers in pots, the family treasures accumulated over more than seventy years. A Delacroix watercolor perched under the famous portrait of Julie as a child holding a cat, by Renoir. Over the door, a decorative view of Bordighera that Monet painted especially for this salon. He said he had used pink tones to go with the cretonne on her walls, and if she didn't like it, she should just return it. She did like it.

And of course paintings by Berthe Morisot: portraits of Julie, her large luminous oil of girls picking cherries, her copies after Boucher and Veronese.

Julie told me that her mother as a young woman was very pretty and always elegant. When the fashion was for elaborate bustles, she ignored it. When other women wore little black boots with white dresses, she ignored that too. Even when she sprained her ankle, she went on wearing her favorite little pink silk slippers.

Berthe Morisot adored her only child and painted and drew her at every stage of her young life. Berthe was particularly fond of the Bois de Boulogne, which was near her house. Often its trees, its lake with ducks and swans, were the background for the paintings and sketches of little Julie's outings.

Incidentally, although now in the middle of Paris, in Julie's childhood the big garden was filled with fruit trees. Sometimes Mary Cassatt would come over on horseback from her ride in the Bois. She would lift up young Julie and take her for a canter.

One time when I went to visit Julie Manet, she showed me some of her mother's sketchbooks. They were full of rapid, evocative drawings, but we also came across, over and over again, the marks of a true French housewife. There were specimen menus. One consisted of *potage royal*, oysters, a stuffed turkey, *endives à la crème*, and a *bavaroise*. (One wonders how she stayed so slim on such a diet!) She loved to introduce her guests to unexpected dishes—Mexican rice, for instance, or chicken with dates.

There were also lists of silverware: "eight sets of large knives, forks and spoons, one matching knife missing."

As for the studio, I learned, it was often the extension of the drawing room or dining room or vice versa, whence many a quick change of décor resulted.

There were several of Manet's portraits of Berthe hanging in that extraordinary time capsule. I asked Julie Manet about them.

"Manet loved to paint my mother—in fact he made twelve portraits of her." Berthe met Manet when she was working at the Louvre, making a copy after Rubens. She was twenty-seven years old. There was a great camaraderie among painters who worked in the Louvre, and as Berthe Morisot was clearly a young woman of good family, it was the most natural thing in the world for Manet—who came from a similar background—to ask her and her mother to the house. Berthe was always chaperoned by her mother on such expeditions.

Manet hoped to persuade her to pose. Eventually, she did (in 1868–69) for the painting called *The Balcony.*

I asked if I might come back with a photographer. The old lady smiled and said that reminded her of when Degas used to come to dinner with his prehistoric camera. "It was perfectly terrible," she said. "There was no escaping it. Once dinner was over, we had to collect all the lamps and candles in the house (we had no electricity) and put them together under his direction. Degas would set up his camera, and we had to get in a happy heap and stay completely still. Four and a half minutes for each exposure, and we almost cried from the effort not to blink."

Berthe Morisot never ran after famous men, her daughter told me. They came to her, as if magnetized. When she took landscape painting lessons from Corot, he couldn't see her often enough. It seemed that Corot was so highly thought of in the household that he was given a special dispensation to smoke his pipe after dinner.

When she wanted to buy a piano, it was Rossini, the master of the crescendo, who went with her to the store, told her which piano to get, and autographed it for her.

Puvis de Chavannes, not a household name today, was highly regarded as a painter and thinker in the Paris of his time. As a suitor, however, he lacked élan, but Berthe Morisot preferred him to Degas in that role.

"Degas pretended to make up to me," she said once, "but he confined his courtship to a long commentary on Solomon's remark that woman is the desolation of the righteous."

Even the furniture here had associations. "You see that Empire chaise longue over there, covered in red velvet? My mother used to rest there, near the little radiator where she warmed her feet. That is where Mallarmé stood when he read his paper on Villiers de L'Isle-Adam. My father admired this text very much and asked Mallarmé to come here to read it for a few special friends. Monet was there, he only came in from Giverny for special occasions. Renoir was over there by the small sofa, he was in full dress, he looked very handsome in tails. Degas was over there. A bit bad tempered that night. Usually, he did all the talking!"

Julie Manet remembered her parents talking about the drama of Morisot's double portrait of her mother and sister. It was an unusually hefty picture for Berthe Morisot: it showed her subjects sitting side by side. Behind them, Morisot opened up the slightly claustrophobic scene by putting in a picture within a picture that suggested a whole world outside.

But there was something about it that wasn't quite Morisot—something ponderous and motionless; duty and boredom were somewhere in the air.

When she asked her friend Puvis de Chavannes what he thought of it, he said her mother's head wouldn't do at all. She took it out and did it again. Could he come over and have another look? Alas, he couldn't, though he said the rest of it was perfectly all right.

The next day, in an agitated state, Morisot went to Manet and told him she had horrible doubts about the double portrait. Generosity itself, he said he would come over as soon as he got his own picture ready to dispatch to the Salon. "Put yourself in my hands," he said. "I'll tell you what should be done."

Sure enough, he came around the following day. What happened next is best told in Morisot's own words:

> Manet came about one o'clock and said the painting was really very good, except for the lower part of the dress. He took my brushes and put in an accent or two that looked very well. Mother was in ecstasy. But there is where my misfortunes began. Once launched, there was no stopping him. From the skirt he went to the bust, from the bust to the head, from the head to the background. He cracked a thousand jokes, laughed like a maniac, handed me the palette, took it back. By five o'clock in the afternoon we were faced with the prettiest caricature you ever saw. The carter was waiting outside to take it to the Salon. Mother made me send it, whether I wanted to or not.
>
> Now I don't know what to do. My only hope is that they will turn it down.
>
> My mother thinks this is all very funny but to me it is agony.

Her mother wrote to her daughter Edma:

> Berthe will have told you about the mishaps. Yesterday she looked as if she was going to faint. Her despair and discontent were so great that they could only be described as a morbid condition.
>
> I made things worse by saying I thought Manet's "improvements" to my head were atrocious. When she kept telling me that she would rather drown herself in the river than have the picture accepted, I thought that I should ask for it to be sent back.
>
> I got it back. But now we have a new problem. Won't Manet be offended? He spent the whole of a Sunday afternoon on the picture, making a pretty mess, and consigned it himself to the carter. I cannot tell him that it did not get there in time, since [Berthe's] little painting of Lorient went with it and he will see it.
>
> As you know, even the smallest thing in this house takes on the dimensions of tragedy, because of our nervous and febrile disposition.
>
> Ah me!

Berthe Morisot had always been frail, and the privations suffered during the Franco-Prussian War further weakened her. She died in 1895; she was only fifty-four. Her husband, Eugène Manet, had died a few years before.

This left sixteen-year-old Julie an orphan. Mallarmé was appointed her guardian. He wrote the text for Berthe Morisot's memorial retrospective exhibition. Thanks to Julie's diary, we know exactly what happened when Degas, Monet, Renoir, and Mallarmé joined forces to hang that exhibition: every one of them had his opinion, and every one of them stuck to it.

> When I got to the gallery on Monday, March 2, Monsieur Monet was already there. He embraced me tenderly. And I was touched that he had come running to help us instead of getting on with his own work.

Monsieur Degas was also at work on the hanging, and Monsieur Renoir arrived soon afterward. He looked terrible. One of Monsieur Mallarmé's duties was to go and see the printers about the catalog.

Tuesday, March 3. Another full day at the gallery. The pictures look better and better. As there is more room than we had expected, we sent for Mama's copies after Boucher and Veronese.

Wednesday, March 4. We found Monsieur Degas all by himself, hanging the drawings in the room at the back. He keeps saying that he doesn't give a damn about the public, all those people who walk by pictures without really looking at them, saying isn't it beautiful. Beautiful!

By the end of the afternoon we wondered how we'd ever be ready for the following day and we agreed to meet again in the morning.

But we had to decide whether to put the big screen with the drawings and watercolors in the middle of the big room or in the smaller room at the back. Monsieur Degas is the only one who wants it in the big room, where it blocks the view and stops the visitor from standing back to see not only *The Cherry Tree Pickers* and the big Boucher copy but a lot of smaller pictures that harmonize so well when you see them from a distance and as an ensemble. But Monsieur Degas couldn't bear the word "ensemble." "There is no such thing," he said. "Only an imbecile talks that way."

Toward six o'clock it was getting so dark that only the oil paintings caught what was left of the light and the screen looked more and more like a wall that was in their way. Monsieur Monet asked Monsieur Degas if he would be kind enough, tomorrow, to try the effect of the screen in the smaller room at the back.

But Monsieur Degas swore that no one would see the drawings that were on the screen. "They are superb," he said. "I like them as much as any of those paintings." "But," Monsieur Mallarmé said, "in the roomful of drawings the screen will make an effect of intimacy. Besides, if the public sees drawings and paintings together, they won't know what to make of it."

"I don't care about the public," said Monsieur Degas. "The public never sees anything anyway. We're making this exhibition for me, for ourselves, not for the public. Don't tell me that you want to teach the public to look at pictures." "I don't agree," said Monsieur Monet. "That's exactly what we should do. If we were making the show just for ourselves, there'd be no point in hanging them on the walls. They'd look just as well on the floor."

During this discussion, Monsieur Renoir said that we really ought to put the pouf in the middle of the big room. I myself thought it might be rather nice to sit down and look. But Monsieur Degas wouldn't hear of it: "I'd stand on my feet for thirteen hours on end if I had to."

By then it was quite dark, and Monsieur Degas was stamping back and forth in his tall hat and his heavy Inverness cape. His silhouette amused me very much. Monsieur Monet was still standing up and making a lot of noise. Monsieur Mallarmé reached out with his hand and tried to straighten things out in his gentlest voice. Monsieur Renoir was slumped in a chair, exhausted. The men from the gallery were laughing among themselves. "He'll never give up," they said.

"You want to deprive me of that screen that I adore," said Monsieur Degas. "It is Berthe Morisot that we adore, not a screen," said Monsieur Monet. "And it's her exhibition that matters. Why don't I just try the screen in the other room tomorrow?"

"If you really, truly think that the big room would be better without it . . ." "Yes, I really do," said Monsieur Monet. But even then, they couldn't stop arguing. Then, suddenly, Monsieur Degas shook hands with Jeannie [her cousin] and myself and made for the door.

Monsieur Mallarmé ventured to whisper the word "pouf," only to see Monsieur Degas rush out the door like a flash of lightning. We heard him running along the little corridor. The door banged, and the jury went their separate ways, rather the worse for wear.

I'm not surprised that they were tired out. Hanging pictures can be almost as hard work as painting them. Besides, it's nervous work, and they were four highly strung people.

For Julie Manet, with her impressive memory, these happenings were as present as this morning's mail. But it had been a long inter-view. "Now let's have tea," she said, and led me to the dining room.

The table was set with two plates and two pretty blue-and-white teacups. My hostess looked at them and said with a sigh, "They are the last ones left; they belonged to Edouard Manet."

Goncharova, Larionov, and Pevsner

In November of the first year of publication of my magazine, *L'ŒIL*, 1955, we bravely presented an all-Russian issue. This was still the Soviet days, and communications with Russia were extremely difficult.

We avoided polemics and dove into the subject, starting with glorious fifteenth-century icons. We saluted the collector Tchukin's all-stars—van Gogh, Gauguin, Matisse, and others—and devoted a major article to the avant-garde with Antoine Pevsner and his brother Naum Gabo squaring off against Vladimir Tatlin and Alexander Rodchenko. We gave Kazimir Malevich his due.

At the end, there was a heavy-going (visually speaking) section of social realism with heroic soldiers and happy peasants.

A world away from this was the work of the duo Natalia Goncharova and Mikhail Larionov, first as pioneer abstract artists, then as designers for Sergei Diaghilev and his Ballets Russes. I remembered seeing color reproductions of Goncharova's festive drop curtain for the ballet *Le Coq d'Or*, given at the Paris Opéra in 1914, a vertigo of strong color and Russian peasant motifs. A favorite poet of mine, Guillaume Apollinaire, wrote the preface for the program.

I learned by chance, because they were completely forgotten by 1955, that Goncharova and Larionov were still alive and living in Paris, in extreme poverty. They were holed up in a small apartment, a fourth-floor walk-up on the rue Jacob. I went to see them.

She was small and delicately built with white hair and fine features, distinction itself. He was burly, a stocky peasant, a contrast to her unmistakably aristocratic origins. (I found out, not from her, that her great-aunt was the wife of the poet Alexander Pushkin.)

They had been together since 1900 and finally married in 1955 in order to get French citizenship and be able to stay in France.

Two small beds and a chair were the sole furniture for their one room that doubled as their salon. They sat side by side on one bed, the visitor, me, sat on the other. They were touchingly pleased and surprised at my interest. I of course was fascinated by them and the opportunity to hear firsthand about the great days of the Ballets Russes. They kept programs of the Diaghilev ballets under one of the beds. I used to bring a large cake when I visited, and I sometimes wondered if this was all they had to eat that day.

One time—I was as usual sitting on the bed opposite them—they had a conversation in Russian, which I do not understand. They clearly had a plan of some sort. Larionov fished under the bed and brought out a large early gouache by Goncharova. "For you," he said. There were great hugs all around. "You must sign," he said to her, and brought out an ordinary pen. She looked up at him like a schoolgirl for guidance. He dictated in a strong Russian accent: *"Pour Madame Bernier, très charmante."*

She carefully wrote this out and signed and handed me the gouache.

The following year I went to see the largely and unjustly forgotten Constructivist sculptor Antoine Pevsner. He and his better-known brother, Naum Gabo, designed the sets and costumes for *La Chatte*, Diaghilev's last ballet.

He was living modestly with his wife in a walk-up apartment on the rue Jean Sicard in Paris. He was a small, slight man with very firm opinions, which he was happy to impress on me.

Most of his remarks began *"Moi et Gabo."* The main point to be emphasized was that the two of them were the *only* Constructivists (forget Tatlin, Rodchenko). The important thing was to destroy the mass.

I tried to get him to tell me what other sculptors he thought, besides *"moi et Gabo,"* had made a contribution. I tried Rodin. "He brought nothing." Brancusi? "Someone I respect, but he brought nothing new." Did he feel that the Renaissance brought nothing new to sculpture? "Nothing. While Giotto and Masaccio brought new concepts to painting, sculptors continued in the same direction as Praxiteles. Always the same way of treating material, always the same block of marble, that eternal cube."

Michelangelo? "Just another Greek."

At this point Madame Pevsner brought in a very substantial cake, bolstered by a bulwark of icing. I couldn't resist asking, "May I destroy the mass?" Nobody smiled.

Wifredo Lam

I had met the Cuban artist Wifredo Lam in New York some time before I went off to Paris the first time for *Vogue* (1946). He was one of the Surrealists, along with Breton, Matta, and Tanguy, who had immigrated to America during the war.

He was beautiful: his father was Chinese; his mother Afro-Cuban. He inherited from the former his delicate build, his bronze coloration from the latter.

He never learned a word of French, although he had lived in Paris before the outbreak of World War II. He had been received as something of an exotic bird of paradise. His paintings and drawings, alive with haunted jungle spirits, interested Picasso, with whom he could speak Spanish, albeit with a strong Cuban accent. And he interested André Breton, who welcomed him as a true Surrealist.

At the outbreak of hostilities in Europe, he returned to Cuba. At the end of the war he came up to New York en route to France. He didn't speak any English.

André Breton, who also didn't speak a word of English in spite of having spent the war years in exile here, had filled him with dire warnings about the rough treatment he could expect in America for being dark skinned. He lived in a state of terror. Mutual friends, remembering that I spoke Spanish, put me in charge of him.

I was working at *Vogue* at the time and would emerge from my office in the *Vogue* uniform of silk dress and flower-laden hat (it was full summer) to take him to lunch. To my shame, I discovered he would not be accepted at any midtown restaurant. I solved that by sticking to Chinese restaurants.

We became great friends and kept in touch. By 1956, we were

both in Paris. I was sitting at my desk in the *L'ŒIL* office, snowed under with work, when Wifredo appeared, sat down, and showed no inclination to leave. He pulled out a batch of unopened letters. They were love letters from various stricken ladies, usually Scandinavian, in English. He had come to have me translate them.

Some years passed, and Wifredo was married and living in the Paris suburbs with a wife (one of the Scandinavians) and two children. "You must come and see them," he insisted. *"Son muy bonitos."*

So I went out to meet them. Wifredo asked his wife, in Spanish—he still didn't speak anything else—to bring in the children. Indeed, they were very bonny. *"¿Cómo se llaman?"*—"What are their names?" I asked. A look of total confusion came over his face. *"¿Cómo se llaman?"* he asked his wife.

No wonder. They all seemed to have been named after obscure Norse gods.

Venetian Adventures—
Venice Observed

In 1955, still the first year of *L'ŒIL*, we got the idea that we could use our experience with combining images with text for a new kind of illustrated book. There would be works of art, but it would not essentially be an art book. A profile of a city was what I had in mind. Venice would be an obvious choice.

I had not met her, but of course I had read Mary McCarthy. I thought her sharp eye and analytical mind might make her just the author we needed.

By providential good luck, Mary happened to be in Europe, in fact in Switzerland. She was looking around for an excuse to delay returning to the States and an unresolved matrimonial situation. I went to Switzerland to meet her and explain the project.

After the usual back-and-forth with such discussions, she accepted. "Don't get carried away by Titian and Veronese," I warned. "The city itself is the star."

From then on (it was 1956), I was a regular commuter to Venice. I got Mary rented rooms in a private apartment, her subscription to the library, and a few introductions. This was in February and March, not a tourist in sight, but lots of rain.

My job was to direct the small team of photographers: Inge Morath for the black-and-whites (she was not yet Mrs. Arthur Miller), the Swiss German Hans Hinz for the color transparencies, a Frenchman for the color exteriors. There was no one mutual language. The team of Italian electricians and carpenters spoke Italian and only Italian. But being Italian, they warmed to the job and would make suggestions about their favorite frescoed Virgins.

The other part of my job would have required a Talleyrand blended with a Machiavelli: getting the permits to photograph from both the patriarch's office (San Marco) and the Communist Commune (city government) directly across the plaza. They seldom agreed. A tricky case in point: I wanted to photograph Titian's *Martyrdom of San Lorenzo*, which was in the Gesuiti Church. The painting itself belonged to the Church. But the actual land on which the church stood belonged to the city. One had to get both parties to give their consent; I made many a trek between the two seats of power.

I was determined to get a color transparency of the splendidly robust thirteenth-century mosaic of the *Last Judgment* in the cathedral on the island of Torcello. This being February, there was no boat service to the island and no cozy meals at the Locanda, which was closed for the season.

This meant organizing a miniature Normandy invasion—all via boats for Torcello. We had to load up with wood for the scaffolding, to be built on the spot (the mural was high aboveground), electric equipment, even food for everyone. It was worth it: we got splendid swirling images of angels tootling on wind instruments, a resolute nude riding the waves atop a beast of the apocalypse disgorging unfortunate sinners.

On the level below, a regular ballet of blue devils tossing severed crowned heads into the flames.

Another technical challenge was getting power for the floodlights needed to photograph in the Doge's Palace. We are in 1956, and there was no electricity inside the palace. We had been given special dispensation to photograph there at night, when there would be no public. The only solution was to have generators churning away outside and a hundred meters of cables bringing the power into the palace via the windows. With my minimum Italian and minimum knowledge of technical matters, this was a stretch.

There were some tense moments negotiating with a group of a dozen black-robed Dalmatians for permission to photograph the three Carpaccio panels in the San Giorgio degli Schiavoni ("Dalmatian" in Venetian dialect), still controlled by the Dalmatian fraternity. No interpreter, no other woman. It was about how many copies at what price and when, and there was no evidence of Christian charity.

I had also come to an agreement with the patriarch's office at

San Marco about the same details. At that time, the future pope John XXIII represented the Holy See in Paris. The day of actual publication, I called the nunciature's Paris office to know where I should send the books. I was passed from one voice to another until I heard a sonorous "Ici Roncalli." It was the future pope himself. When he heard my query, he said, "Send the books directly to me, otherwise a little priest will get hold of them and I'll never see them."

My headquarters was Harry's Bar, completely empty of tourists at this season. The kind owners, besides thawing me out with cups of hot chocolate—the damp cold was piercing—knew exactly how to go about getting permits and which person should be cultivated and which avoided.

Meanwhile, Mary was working away, at first unexpectedly insecure, worrying about matters such as what she should wear to the contessa's. She had met Bernard Berenson, who held her hand and told her she should write about art. This complicated our editor-author relationship since we had very different ideas.

It ended with a compromise, but the important thing is that the end result, *Venice Observed*, is a superb book and was the best-selling art book of that season. Incidentally, no American publisher would touch it when we proposed it. "We wouldn't know how to sell it" was the usual answer. Once it was a success, everyone wanted a sequel.

Mary and I remained close friends. She was a stalwart, loyal ally in my legal problems and was an indispensable mail drop.

Many years later, when I came back to Paris to lecture at the Grand Palais, Mary was always in the front row. After the series was over, she wrote me the most glowing, generous text I could use for my publicity. I think of her with warm affection.

We went on to publish a series of books with material from the magazine translated into English, under the general title *The Selective Eye*. Our very first one got off to a flying start with an introduction by the magnificent Alfred H. Barr Jr., founding spirit of the Museum of Modern Art.

Georges Braque—
Lord of the Birds

In 1950 in Paris, I had gone to a party for the sculptor Henri Laurens, one of Georges Braque's oldest and closest of friends. Laurens had been passed over—wrongly, we thought—for a prize at the Venice Biennale.

The party was a gesture of solidarity and affection held in a bistro in Puteaux, near Paris, where the painter Jacques Villon (Marcel Duchamp's brother) used to live. We all sat at long trestle tables, and there was a very good dinner and many toasts, and finally we danced. Everyone wanted to make it a happy occasion. Everyone danced, even Braque. As a young man, he had been a great dancer, as well as bicyclist, swimmer, and boxer. I actually remembered as a schoolgirl on holiday at Cassis, on the Riviera, seeing a well-built man diving off the rocks and being told it was Georges Braque. I knew very well who he was. But after he had been gassed in World War I, he had had to take things easier.

That evening he made an exception, and I can still see him turning majestically in a waltz with his handsome features hidden under an improvised mask. In an uncharacteristically playful gesture he had torn holes in a white paper napkin that covered his face completely.

It was five years later that I had created *L'ŒIL* in Paris. Braque appeared in the first issue, January 15, 1955; that is to say, his signature, in a bold flourish, appeared above an article about Cubism by Picasso's veteran dealer, Daniel-Henry Kahnweiler. It almost edges Picasso's signature off the page to a corner, far right. Picasso, Braque, and Kahnweiler all signed my copy of this historic issue.

Braque showed a benign interest in the magazine right from the beginning. He even sent us a characteristically measured endorsement that we could use for publicity: "The first issues of *L'ŒIL* lead one to believe it will be an outstanding publication."

He promised to let me know when he had finished one of the great *Studio* paintings that were to sum up the ideas dearest to him. And sure enough, one day I got a telephone call. "*Venez,*" he said, not being a man to waste words.

Of course I hopped into a taxi in no time. Braque lived on a short no-exit street off the Parc Montsouris; it used to be called rue du Douanier but has been renamed rue Georges Braque. The house was built for him in 1925 by Auguste Perret, the father of reinforced concrete. Braque liked to say that he drew up the plans. It always surprised me that Braque lived in a house made of concrete since he disliked synthetic materials intensely and would only wear real silk, cotton, or wool. But he was very proud of the house, even down to the paulownia he had planted in the little front garden.

The door was opened for visitors by Mariette Lachaud, the tiny birdlike woman who was Braque's studio assistant for many years. It was she who led the way up a tall staircase with conspicuously easy rises and into the studio, where Braque would be waiting in his favorite oblique and slightly hooded light, filtered through semitransparent white curtains.

I was always in awe of this great old man with the commanding presence. He was strikingly handsome, with a shock of pure white hair, solidly built, but by now slightly stooped. He was courtesy itself, but he had never fully recovered from the effects of the war and found it difficult to move around. For that reason he greeted you seated on a sofa and extended his hand like a benign sovereign. He was always elegantly dressed in his own colors: dark blue, brown, black. His slippers were always burnished until they shone like horse chestnuts. He had been one of the first men in Europe to wear denim, impeccably cut.

He was a man of regular and orderly habits. Nothing could have been further from the barely penetrable jumble in which Picasso lived. He was orderly in other ways too. "Still married to the same wife?" Picasso would ask when I gave him news of Braque. He did indeed have the same wife, Marcelle, for more than half a century.

He had the same house in Paris until his death and the same house in Varangéville in Normandy. Stability was important to him.

I knew that birds real and invented had peopled his imagination for some time. He had chosen two huge birds wheeling in close formation for his design for the ceiling of the Etruscan Room in the Louvre, with stars and a crescent moon in attendance. So I was not surprised to find that his studio in the 1950s was like a well-ordered aviary in which every bird was on its best behavior.

Large birds streaked across large canvases, dive-bombing any clouds on their way. Small birds clustered on sheets of lithographs tacked to the wall. Ghostly birds lay on the floor on transparent sheets being prepared for more lithographs.

Pride of place was given to the large, majestic new *Atelier*, which had occupied several years of his time. It was like a meditation on his own studio, dominated by two red forms and a yellow rectangle, presumably a tabletop. A large white bird streaks across the canvas. Elements of the studio are crowded into a kaleidoscope at the lower third of the painting: a clutter of easels, sketchbooks, paint pots, palettes, vases, a *compotier*. The great bird is not a bird that Audubon would recognize, but a "painted bird" that has haunted Braque's imagination in various manifestations.

All around the room there was a forest of easels of varying heights. Fanned out on a sumptuous display, they made me think that I had walked into a Braque still life larger than life.

All the ingredients of his art were actually there: the plants, the bowls of fruits, the primitive masks, the shields, the standing figures, the shells and bones, and the pencils and brushes so carefully marshaled on big sheets of corrugated cardboard. There were also some unexpected souvenirs of other artists' work—a reproduction of van Gogh's painting of sunflowers for one and a reproduction of Corot's portrait of the soprano Christine Nilsson. Picasso, Braque, and Juan Gris had all admired an exhibition of Corot's figure paintings in Paris in 1909, he told me.

When I looked at what seemed to be a little child's chair that stood not far away, Braque explained that he sat there to work while Mariette Lachaud handed him the paints and brushes as he needed them, thereby saving him from all unnecessary movement.

Fired by the occasion and by the sight of Braque in his studio with all his paintings around him, I screwed up my courage and asked, aside from photographing the great *Studio* he had just finished, could we take a photograph of him in situ? He did not usually permit such juxtapositions. He hesitated—he was a man of reflection, not of spontaneity—but finally he agreed, but said, "Just a moment please." He got up and with infinite precaution went to fetch something from the other room. He came back, tucking a scarlet spectacles case into the breast pocket of his jacket. "Every picture must have a spot of bright red," he said.

Some years later, I was back in Braque's studio, this time with a mission. The distinguished American collector Joseph Pulitzer Jr. of St. Louis was a true connoisseur, scholarly and informed. He had set his heart on a noble Braque Cubist-period collage, from 1912, called *Duo Pour Flûte*. Like the works of that period by Picasso and Braque, it was not signed.

As a cautious collector, Pulitzer would not buy it unless it had Braque's signature. "I will take care of it," I said. I flagged a taxi—the collage was large but just fitted through the door—and went off to the rue du Douanier.

Braque's eyes lit up when I came in with the collage. "I haven't seen it since 1916," he said. He told me that it used to hang in his dining room. One day in 1916, Diaghilev came by and saw it and was very taken by it. "I have to show it to someone," he said, and left. He came back shortly with Léonide Massine, his new star and new love. Braque said of Massine, "He was in the full force of his youthful beauty."

Diaghilev bought the collage for Massine.

Braque was so delighted with his collage that he signed it boldly both on the front and, turning it over, on the back.

So Mr. Pulitzer got his prize. It is now in the serene new museum in St. Louis designed by Tadao Ando, as part of the Pulitzer collection on view there.

It occurred to me later that this collage undoubtedly had a particular significance for Braque. When he was a young man living in Le Havre, he took flute lessons from Raoul Dufy's brother Gaston, who was a flautist.

Braque died in 1963. He was given all the pomp of a state funeral, in the Cour Carrée of the Louvre. I went to it with Tériade, the art publisher. The funeral oration was given by André Malraux in his torrential oratorical style, practically inaudible due to faulty amplification. Massed bands played Beethoven. I think Braque would have preferred Bach.

All very well intended, but it seemed strangely at odds with his quiet, unassuming life.

The big studio upstairs is empty now, but the house downstairs was very much the same in 1967, when I went to have supper with Henri Laurens and his family. Braque had bequeathed the house to his great friend Laurens, the sculptor who did not get the prize at the Venice Biennale.

The miniature upright piano that had belonged to Erik Satie was still there, as well as the flower piece by Cézanne that Braque always kept by him.

Incidentally, for Braque's eightieth birthday a fifty-centime stamp was issued. It could not have been more appropriate: a white bird on a blue background.

Remembering Fernand Léger

I met Fernand Léger when I came to Paris in the late 1940s to write about the arts for *Vogue*. I had always admired his work in New York, but I had never met him. I had no introduction; I just wrote asking if I could come and see him. The answer came immediately, the French equivalent of "Come on over."

He was recently back from the war years as an émigré in America. He was once again in the big old studio at 86, rue Notre Dame des Champs on the Left Bank, where he had worked since 1919.

Up a narrow winding staircase to the second floor, it was typical of him that the key was always on the outside of the door, so anyone could come in. He would advance to greet you, both hands outstretched. He was a robust broad-shouldered man—just like a figure by Léger—rugged featured, freckled, the color of a good apple from his native Normandy.

He gave me a warm welcome. From then on, he never seemed too busy to show me what he was doing or to talk. He would pull out canvases for me and ask which I liked best. When, as it sometimes happened, I chose one that he considered difficult to take but that he particularly liked himself, he would clap me vigorously across the back and say, "You're a good girl; you have a strong stomach."

There were always a number of canvases turned to the wall in his studio: some were on easels, none were hung. I remember a plain plank of wood used as a palette with craters of pure color. There was a battered sofa covered with drawings and papers of various kinds, a trestle table equally littered, a few plain chairs. An interior staircase led to an alcove where he sometimes slept.

One of the paintings he showed me was called *Adieu New York*.

He had begun it at the end of a five-year stay in America during World War II and finished it in Paris. It was based on what he called "*la couleur en dehors*"—a disassociation of color and drawing. He splashed bold swaths of color across the canvas that lived quite independently of the subject matter: two separate elements in the same picture.

"I'll tell you how I got the idea," he said. "I was talking to someone in Times Square late one night. The man suddenly turned first blue, then yellow, then red—as the advertising lights swept over him. It was free color in space. So I did the same thing with my canvas. I put color on its own. I never could have invented it. I have no imagination."

Léger had been in New York a number of times before the long wartime exile, starting in 1931, when the young Americans Gerald and Sara Murphy, who lived in France, had financed his trip. He was bowled over by New York every time. He still talked about the vertical architecture, the speed, the raw energy, but also about the pretty girls: "every manicurist a beauty queen."

But he had a few suggestions: "By day, New York is too severe, why not color the houses? Fifth Avenue red, Madison blue, Park Avenue yellow—why not? And the lack of greenery. One could oblige shops to launch a run of green dresses, green suits. One could drive trees around the streets in open trucks for people who cannot go to the country.

"Since New York seems to be constantly rebuilding itself—why not build the new city in glass with blue, yellow, red floors!"

Then he confided to me a few minor complaints: "That terrible bread!" (Those were the days when only blotting-paper-like white bread was available.) "And worst of all: '*le twin bed*.' You had to get out of bed to make love, get into another bed, then get back to your own bed. *Oh là là, 'le twin bed*.'"

In New York in the 1930s and 1940s he seems to have met everyone of interest—from James Johnson Sweeney to John Dos Passos. Through the Murphys he met Archibald MacLeish, Ernest Hemingway, Scott and Zelda Fitzgerald. He told me proudly he had taught Arshile Gorky's wife, Magouche, how to make a pot-au-feu. He was an excellent country-style cook.

He lectured at Yale and all over the country. Since he never learned a word of English, valiant translators tried to keep up with his colorful, highly colloquial French.

In 1941 he joined his friend the composer Darius Milhaud at Mills College, near San Francisco, to give a summer course—crossing the entire country by Greyhound bus. Milhaud told me that with his customary generosity, Léger threw himself into student activities, painting scenery, even devising makeup for the actors. Apparently, the language barrier was no problem. When addressed in English, he would announce clearly, "I speak English, but I do not understand it."

I got to see Léger's last work for the stage (he had designed ballets in the 1930s) in 1949; in fact, I went with Léger as part of his entourage at the Paris Opéra for the opening. It was a four-act opera about Simón Bolívar, the South American liberator. The score was by Darius Milhaud, the book written by Milhaud's wife, the excellent pianist Madeleine Milhaud.

Léger had described the scenic effects he was devising with mounting excitement when I visited him at the studio. "You'll see, everything will blow up," he would say cheerfully.

I learned that the stagehands at the Paris Opéra still remembered with horror the complications demanded by Léger: not only unprecedented elaborate lighting effects for the times, but an epic crossing of the Andes during an earthquake with scenery flying all over the place.

I was able to follow step-by-step one of Léger's last adventures, combining art, architecture, and color, in 1948. When he was in New York, Léger had met the Dominican monk Father Couturier, the influential cleric who enlisted first-rate artists (Matisse, Rouault, and Bonnard among them) to decorate churches.

Back in France, Father Couturier persuaded Léger to design mosaics to cover the facade of a church high in the French Alps, at Assy. Léger, a card-carrying Communist, made no pretense of being religious. He simply saw this as an opportunity to work on a large scale in a new medium.

This was the first time Léger had worked with mosaics, and he relished the collaboration with the skilled artisans of the Bony atelier in Paris. We used to go there together to watch the men interpret the maquette, assembling small pieces of colored glass.

I monitored the process as the pieces of mosaic were assembled on some sort of heavy cardboard backing, the design in reverse.

Then I traveled to the remote spot of Assy to watch the transfer of the mosaics onto the facade of the church. The facade was covered with what looked like cement, then the sheets of cardboard were slapped on, then pulled off, leaving the mosaic embedded in the facade.

Shortly after we started to photograph the church, a heavy fog descended. The fog persisted for a week. It was impossible to see more than a foot ahead.

I had been assigned a young photographer whose company was of a unique dullness, but we were trapped together like characters in Sartre's *No Exit*. My only solace was the welcome visits of the local priest, who shared my taste for Gewürztraminer, a delicious white wine.

Léger had an open, generous nature. He enjoyed young people. He had run an academy in 1924, which attracted many foreigners. The sculptor Louise Bourgeois, then a young would-be painter, told me he was an admirable teacher—talked little, but homed right into a student's problems. When she drew a wood shaving, he told her, "Louise, you aren't a painter. You're a sculptor. You see things in the round. Go ahead, be a sculptor." She followed his advice.

He reopened his academy after World War II, and a number of Americans on the GI Bill flocked there, among them Ellsworth Kelly (who found Léger intimidating), Kenneth Noland, Jules Olitski, and Robert Colescott.

I dropped in on Léger a number of times in the next few years. He took a kindly interest in my enthusiasms and activities in Paris. Naturally, I went often to the Louvre. He approved of this, but he warned, "Keep away from the Renaissance. Watch out for that Veronese, *Marriage at Cana*—nothing but theater design—and that Monsieur Michelangelo, who couldn't paint an arm without thinking of the anatomy of the muscles."

According to Léger, the artists of the Renaissance were responsible for two fundamental errors: they imitated slavishly—in contrast to the primitives, who invented forms—and they copied beautiful subjects. "If a woman is beautiful, she is no use as raw material," he said.

"Go and look at Poussin and David. And as soon as you can, go to Barcelona and look at the Catalan Romanesque frescoes." A few years later, I did just that, guided by Miró.

He said about David, "I liked David because he is anti-Impressionist. I like the dryness in David's work. It was my direction."

By 1950, Léger had left his old studio in Paris and moved out to the country, to Gif-sur-Yvette. He had to be driven to get there because this passionate lover of the machine age never learned to drive. His friend the Catalan architect José María Sert had designed his studio there. Léger painted the doors in pure, strong Léger colors.

By then, he was a widower, and he had married a formidable Russian lady called Nadia. She had been in charge of his school and managed the studio. She was clearly out to manage everything else. She presented me with a baby, *her* grandchild, not his. "Here is the heiress," she announced.

I knew that Léger had been working for some time on a theme that had fascinated him since childhood: the circus. He used to describe the excitement of when the circus came to his small Normandy village when he was a boy. "The magic, the color, the freedom of a structure that is moved in and was built in one night, then taken away again." He spoke of the traditional parade of the circus troupe that takes place before the performance, to draw the crowd. "The gate money is tied to this parade, so it is persuasive and dynamic. The instruments are making as much noise as they can: the huge bass drum, the trombones, snare drums. The hullabaloo is projected from a small raised platform in front of the tent. It hits you right in the face. It's behind you, beside you, in front, appearing, disappearing . . . faces, limbs, dancers, clowns, pink legs, an acrobat who walks on his hands."

This is what his last great painting, *La Grande Parade*, is about (it is at the Guggenheim Museum today). The "parade" is the circus event Léger described.

I used to go out to Gif-sur-Yvette to visit Léger and to follow the development of the big painting—it was about thirteen feet long. He explained, "I've never given up the methods I learned at art school. I'm extremely slow. I don't know how to improvise. I first make preparatory sketches, many of them. Then I make gouaches, and finally I go over onto the canvas."

I was able to follow Léger juggling with ideas. There was a jungle of canvases in the studio: figures came and went, the letters "CIR" were inserted, then removed, a green landscape was tried out and rejected. One experiment was to project the entire composition in black and white forward, against a flat red background. "Too much like a ceramic wall panel." Léger decided against it.

The problem he tackled was to establish a balance between two basically unrelated elements on a large scale: an assertive dynamic play of abstract colored forms of fortissimo intensity, and the predominantly black-and-white linear composition.

During this period of struggle, I was struggling too: by 1954, I had left *Vogue* and was embarking on the perilous project of starting my own magazine, *L'ŒIL*.

It culminated in the first issue appearing on January 15, 1955, unheralded. There was no trial run, no prepublicity. It simply appeared on the stands one Tuesday morning. I had decided to use a detail of Léger's *Grande Parade* for the cover. At that point we couldn't afford four-color for the cover, so it was against a flat blue background.

Léger, a pillar of the Paris school, didn't need press coverage from a fledgling art review. But he threw himself with characteristic enthusiasm into this new venture.

He bothered to come into town for the day of the magazine's initial appearance. He came by my small office. "I've been to eleven newsstands and asked for *L'ŒIL*," he told me. "None of them had it. Get it, I told them, I'll be back." Then this staunch Communist told me, "I'm creating demand!"

He invited me out to Gif-sur-Yvette for a celebration dinner. We had a splendid Normandy feast, washed down with a respectable amount of his native calvados, a fiery apple brandy—a scene right out of a nineteenth-century French novel.

After dinner he said, "Now for the surprise," and led me into his studio. There were a number of gouaches lined up against the wall. "You choose," he said. "One is for you."

I didn't choose one of the flower forms, but an abstract composition. He was delighted and clapped me across the back with even more vigor than usual and said, "You're a good girl. I always said you have a strong stomach!"

Later he sent us a text to be used for our publicity: "What a tour de force! Never saw anything like it! Here's something really modern! Once again, BRAVO!"

I still live very happily with Léger's gouache.

Alberto Giacometti

I still remember Alberto Giacometti's address by heart: 46, rue Hippolyte-Maindron in the 14th arrondissement, a rather gloomy part of the Montrouge neighborhood of Paris. I remember it not only because of my visits there during the 1950s, and later, but because I used to send postcards to him, gathered on my frequent trips to museums and foreign parts for my magazine, of subjects that might interest him.

He had lived and worked there since 1921. He shared the crowded quarters with his brother and closest friend, Diego. Sometimes his wife, Annette, who had followed him from Geneva, was around too, although she found the place so uncomfortable that she moved to a hotel. Also, she objected to his insistence on keeping the light burning all night. He never got over his fear of the dark. But he had warned her, when very reluctantly he married her after some years of cohabitation, that he was not going to change his ways. And he didn't.

Annette was twenty years younger than Alberto. She was often treated with insulting indifference, but she will be remembered because she became one of his main models, both for paintings and for sculpture.

The studio was bleak. A single very bright lightbulb hung from the ceiling. A thick coating of dust reduced everything to a Giacometti color scheme of gray and more gray. There was always a distinctive smell of damp clay; a cluster of figures draped in wet cloth waited to be cast in plaster by Diego in his atelier just across the narrow corridor that separated the two studios. It was here that Diego made the armatures and the plaster casts from the original clay models.

There was a battered old sofa, two rickety chairs, one for Alberto, the other for whoever was posing for him, usually Annette or Diego. Red marks on the floor recorded the exact position of artist and subject. His needs were reduced to his necessary working material: clay, plaster, paper, canvas, paints. At that time Alberto was alternating, sometimes on the same day, between painting, drawing, and sculpture. No flowers. No memorabilia.

The only personal note were two little paintings in the cramped bedroom next to the studio: one of Alberto as a child painted by his father, Giovanni, a well-known Swiss post-Impressionist; the other painted by Alberto at fifteen of his brother.

Alberto himself was an impressive presence, solid of build, handsome features as rugged as if they had been hewn out of the rocks from his native Swiss mountains. He came from Stampa, a remote village high in the Italian Alps. Years of living in plaster dust seemed to have coated him permanently; even his clothes began to look like fragments of an old wall. He smoked incessantly, so a dusting of ash added to the patina.

Years before, a drunk driver had run up over a curb and crushed one of Alberto's feet. Long stays in the hospital followed. He never fully recovered, and he walked with a pronounced limp. He never bothered to sue the driver, although the negligence was clear. He simply didn't want to be bothered with mercenary transactions.

In 1950, a figure of a towering woman, as slim as only a Giacometti figure could be, rose above two giant wheels, his hospital experience recalled. Talking about this sculpture, Giacometti said, "It is usually called *The Chariot*, but I think of it as *The Pharmacy Wagon*, because this sculpture comes from the glittering wagon that was wheeled around the corridors of the Bichat hospital which astonished me in 1938.

"In 1947, I saw the sculpture before me, as if it were finished. In 1950 it became impossible for me not to make it, even though for me it was already past.

"*The Chariot* was created by the necessity to have the figure in empty space, in order to see it better and to situate it at a distance from the floor."

I wanted to photograph *The Chariot* for the first issue of *L'ŒIL*, but I didn't want to shoot against a plain wall. I got the idea of taking the sculpture out to the Parc Monceau on a Wednesday, the day French schoolchildren have the day off.

It worked just as I had hoped. The children circled around it on their bikes, their bicycle wheels echoing the giant wheels of the sculpture. Giacometti was delighted.

Giacometti was always politeness itself, even though he hated being interrupted. He would greet the visitor amiably, but then came the mantra. There were endless variations, but the gist of it was: "I don't know why you bother to come. There's nothing to see. I can't finish anything. What I have done is no good, so I'm going to destroy it and/or paint it out, and/or erase it. You can see how badly things are going."

This gloomy mood would disappear when he talked of art that was important to him. He told me that since childhood, he had made copies of works of art that he liked—from books and catalogs—sometimes just sketches with a ballpoint pen. He spoke of his favorites as if he had them in front of his eyes. He knew the walls of the Louvre as well as the walls of his cramped bedroom.

At the time I started my visits to the Hippolyte-Maindron atelier, I was preparing an illustrated book on Venice. We had commissioned the American author Mary McCarthy to write us a profile of a city. We were to illustrate it entirely with works of art that were still in Venice.

When I talked about this to Alberto, it stirred up torrents of visual memories. He had spent time in Venice in 1920, when he accompanied his father, Giovanni, who was representing the Swiss pavilion at the Venice Biennale.

Giacometti had written about his enthusiasms: "During that stay in Venice I was excited solely by Tintoretto. I spent the entire month running around the city, worried that there might be one more painting by him hidden somewhere in the corner of a church. Tintoretto was for me a marvelous discovery; he opened a curtain upon a new world. I loved him with an exclusive and fanatic love. Tintoretto was right and the others were wrong.

"The last day I ran to the Scuola di San Rocco and to San Giorgio Maggiore as if to tell him goodbye, goodbye to the greatest of friends."

However, he went on to write that that very same afternoon, "when I went into the Arena Chapel in Padua, I received a body blow right in the chest, in front of the frescoes of Giotto. I was confused and lost. The power of Giotto asserted itself irresistibly on me. I was crushed by those immutable figures, dense as basalt, with their precise and accurate gestures, heavy with expression and infinite tenderness."

Sometimes Alberto came to visit me at my Paris apartment. He was fascinated by two giant tree fern figures from the New Hebrides that I had in my salon. He thought that their great eyeless sockets carried the power of what he called *le regard* (the gaze). He used to talk about the importance of *le regard*.

"One day, when I was drawing a young girl, I suddenly noticed that the only thing that was alive was her gaze. The rest of her head meant no more to me than the skull of a dead man.

"One does not sculpt a living person, but what makes him alive is without doubt his gaze. Everything else is only a framework for the gaze."

As an example of the power of the gaze, he mentioned the gaze of the Savior in Matthias Grünewald's great altarpiece at Isenheim.

My small office on the Left Bank, rue des Saints-Pères, had walls painted a shade of blue I like very much, the color of a pack of Gauloises cigarettes (I did not smoke myself). There were no pictures on the walls yet.

Alberto dropped by. He sat down opposite me. I said, "It must seem odd to you, an art magazine where there is not a single work of art in sight."

"Not at all," he answered. "You are a *personnage sur fond bleu* [a figure against a blue background]. That's the way I will paint you one day." This never came about. It would have been difficult to pose at Giacometti's hours: all-night sessions, starting at already late hours—hard to combine with running a demanding monthly publication.

I had told him about my plan to run an article about him in the first issue. He was absolutely appalled. This was in 1954, before his worldwide celebrity, but he was hugely admired by the cognoscenti: Sartre, Genet, and Beckett had all written about him. But he was so genuinely modest that he was convinced it would harm the new magazine if I featured him.

"Come and have a drink," he said in his hoarse voice (all those cigarettes).

We went to a nearby café. He invariably drank red wine. He did his best to convince me not to show his work. "It will sink your magazine. Nobody will buy it." Naturally, I paid no attention.

Incidentally, I was rather surprised when he wanted to know if Matisse had asked me to pose. He knew I had just visited Matisse.

It was Henri Matisse's son Pierre, the distinguished New York dealer who had introduced contemporary European art to America, who organized the first Giacometti exhibition in the United States. He had been to see the then little-known sculptor in Paris in 1946. He was sufficiently impressed to present the work in an important exhibition at his gallery in 1948.

It got the best possible send-off. There was an essay about the sculptor by Jean-Paul Sartre. At that time, Sartre was high on the radar screen of intellectuals and those who wanted to be in the know.

And most important, Giacometti sent along a letter that amounted to an illustrated catalog. He had made little ideogram drawings of each piece and described it. This provided an invaluable document— a living link with the artist and his thoughts about his own work. It has often been reproduced since then, including in the Giacometti catalog of his exhibition at the Museum of Modern Art.

The exhibition was such a success that the Matisse Gallery presented a second exhibition two years later.

As I mentioned before, domesticity was not for Alberto. Meals, such as they were, were taken in neighboring bistros or cafés. His main meal, always the same, consisted of two hard-boiled eggs, two slices of ham, two cups of coffee, two glasses of Beaujolais. Four packs of cigarettes throughout the day and more coffee continued the onslaught on his health.

Nights he roamed from café to café. He never went to bed before dawn. His companion on these nocturnal forays, exasperated but devoted, was usually his brother Diego. "How do you expect to work in that condition? Nothing will come of it—maybe a little chicken?" Usually, something did come of it, although Alberto, dissatisfied with his own work, frequently destroyed it.

"Diego's head is the one I know best," Alberto said. "He posed for me over a long period of time, from 1935 to 1940, every day. When I draw or paint from memory, it always turns out to be more or less Diego's head."

Before they were closed by law, his regular rounds included a stop at one of several brothels he frequented. His favorite was called Le Sphinx.

Julien Levy, the dashing New York dealer of the postwar art world, left this affectionate description of Le Sphinx in his *Memoir of an Art Gallery*:

> The atmosphere was half nude, very carnal, pretty and amusing. The artists in the neighborhood had developed a habit of coming to the Sphinx at aperitif time . . . just for the pleasure of having a glass of wine and chatting in this rather unusual atmosphere. The girls were not at all averse to this, enjoying being treated to a drink and having a chat before their professional clients came in later in the evening.

Sadly, this easygoing oasis had to shut down in 1946, when a crusading female minister outlawed all the brothels. On October 6 of that year, the mistress of the Sphinx invited all her regular customers, including Giacometti, to celebrate the brothel's last evening.

Alberto described the origins of his *Four Figures on a Stand* as a memory of a scene at the Sphinx. His sculpture hoists four minute figures high up on a blocklike stand, which in turn is held aloft by four spindly shafts.

"Several nude women seen at the Sphinx as I was sitting at the back of the room: the distance which separated us (the shining parquet floor) and which seemed insurmountable despite my desire to cross it made as strong an impression on me as the women themselves."

Alberto's feelings toward women were violently ambivalent. They were both adored and despised. They were goddesses to be worshipped from afar, but they were also fallen women who deserved to suffer. He admitted he had fantasies of rape and murder (like Cézanne).

"Whores are the most honest girls," he said. "They present the bill right away. The others hang on and never let you go. When one lives with the problem of impotence, the prostitute is ideal. You pay, and whether or not you fail is of no importance."

His last great love was a prostitute and sometime thief who called herself Caroline. She came into his life in 1960 and remained an agonizing thorn in the side of both Annette and Diego. He painted countless portraits of her in the following years.

In contrast to his rackety Parisian lifestyle, Alberto remained deeply attached to his mother and to his native village of Stampa. He returned there several times a year to see his mother and to draw. In later years, he telephoned her frequently from Paris.

I owe the following to Giacometti's friend the late art critic Thomas B. Hess. When asked what his mother thought of his work, Alberto answered, grinning, "She can't stand it, and she gets the whole village to back her up. She'll draw out one of my new paintings and say, 'Look, isn't this terrible? Look at the dirty colors.' And the mailman will nod his head."

Alberto didn't have the slightest interest in worldly social life. In the mid-1960s I was often under pressure from Philippe de Rothschild and his wife, Pauline, owners of the wine château Mouton Rothschild, to bring Giacometti to dinner in Paris. They had started commissioning well-known artists to design the bottle labels for each vintage and were longing to have one designed by Giacometti.

It took a lot of persuasion on my part, but I finally convinced him to come with me to dinner. He was vague about the evening, and on the way in a taxi he asked me several times where we were going.

He sat politely through the dinner but nudged me to leave as soon as we could. On the way back, he agreed that the wines were superb, but he never wanted to go back again. The Rothschilds never got their label.

For years, Giacometti had never crossed the Atlantic, although his early exhibitions at the Pierre Matisse Gallery in New York (in 1947 and 1950) attracted great attention. His first reason was that boats were too slow. "You can't draw the horizon for a whole week without going crazy." His second reason: "Because I don't trust pilots. If I were in an airplane crash, I'd die of rage on the way down."

However, he did give in in 1965 and boarded the *Queen Eliza-*

beth with Annette, Pierre Matisse, and his wife, Patricia, for New York, to see his exhibition at the Museum of Modern Art.

He was delighted with the exhibition and visited it a number of times. He thoroughly enjoyed New York. He bought a plan of the city and after two days could find his way around unaided.

"It's curious that I should be the object of so much attention when I'm only a beginner. For if ever I achieve anything, it's only at present that I am beginning to glimpse what it might be.

"But then maybe it's better to get honors out of the way at the beginning so as to work in peace afterward."

Alberto died in 1966 and was buried in the Swiss Alps near his parents.

My Friend Miró

In 1954 I was in Paris preparing the first issue of *L'ŒIL*, which was to appear in January 1955. I lived near the Hôtel Pont Royal, and its dusky bar was a convivial meeting place. The venerable publishing house Gallimard was just down the street, and its authors often congregated there. (Camus, Gide, Malraux, Céline, and Proust were all on its distinguished backlist.) Sartre and Simone de Beauvoir, chased away from the Café de Flore by unwanted attention, found refuge there.

It was in the Pont Royal bar that I met Balthus, the Freudian analyst Jacques Lacan, and many other well-known characters of the times. Most notably, I met Joan Miró, who used to come to Paris to do his graphic work, with the master craftsmen Fernand Mourlot and Roger Lacourière, and he stayed at the Pont Royal. I was planning travel destinations for a future summer issue, and I asked Miró what I should show of his native city, Barcelona.

To my delighted surprise, he answered, "I'll show you. I am going back to Barcelona next week." He gave me his address—it was for an old building in the Gothic section, just off the Ramblas—but not the apartment number. Next week I left for Barcelona with that splendid photographer, Brassaï, to join Miró.

Miró was a celebrated artist in France and America by then, and I presumed he was as well-known in his own country. However, there was no one in the little conical porter's lodge at the entrance on the calle Folgueroles to give me directions. So I went from floor to floor, knocking on doors and asking for "el pintor Miró." No one had heard of the famous artist who had lived there so many years.

I finally found him, a small, benign figure (like many Catalans, he was very short), impeccably dressed as usual (he favored bow ties), white hair neatly combed, round blue eyes that seemed to look out at the world in perpetual astonishment. He couldn't wait to show me some of his favorites. High on his list was the work of the visionary architect Antoni Gaudí, a Catalan hero. Gaudí was a passion of his—the embodiment of Catalan genius in all its singularity and invention.

He detoured the well-known Sagrada Família cathedral, expressing disdain for plans to finish it. Gaudí had been knocked down by a streetcar and carried to a charity ward, where he died, unrecognized, without having finished the plans for his cathedral. He always improvised as he went along, so Miró and many others objected to contemporary architects "guessing" the master's intentions. Controversy still rages about this.

We went to the park where Miró played as a boy, the Parque Güell, commissioned by Gaudí's main patron, Count Güell. What Miró liked best about it was its technical ingeniousness combined with moments of pure improvisation, total fantasy combined with precise calculation—very much like his own work.

He pointed out that to cover the surface of the winding curved bench, which snaked around the upper terrace, would be very expensive. So Gaudí bought up odd lots of broken ceramic fragments—of teapots, plates, bathroom tiles, anything—and let the workmen invent mosaic patterns as they went along, setting the pieces into the wet concrete.

As I looked closely at the mosaic designs on the bench, I noticed circles and stars that seemed to come right out of a Miró composition. "Yes, those motifs became part of my boyhood. Circles and stars stayed with me all my life," he told me.

It was July and extremely hot. Poor Brassaï, somewhat portly, had to lug his heavy equipment around unaided, perspiring freely, his person and his camera more accustomed to Paris by night than Barcelona in July. But his alert eye captured the eccentricities and oddities of the Catalan scene in splendid photographs for my magazine.

During a very charged week in Barcelona, Miró led me up and down and all around the town. What he liked best about the famous apartment house the Casa Milà were the great ventilators on the roof like totemic presences, medieval warriors. "The splendid thing," he said enthusiastically, "is that these sculptures—because that is what they are—can't even be seen from the street. Gaudí made them purely for his personal pleasure."

Holy ground for Miró was the National Museum of Catalan Art with its rich collection of eleventh- and twelfth-century sculptures and frescoes. They were originally scattered among small rural churches in the mountains beyond Barcelona, mostly abandoned and falling into decay. Fortunately, farseeing preservers salvaged them in the 1920s and brought them to safety in the Catalan museum. "This is the art that means the most to me," Miró said. "I used to come here every Sunday morning as a boy, by myself. This painting was essential to me."

He pointed out a seraphim from the apocalypse with wings covered with eyes. "I never forgot those eyes," Miró said. Indeed, eyes appear mysteriously throughout his work where they are least expected: on a tree trunk, in the sky. In some of his *Constellation* series of 1940–41, eyes mingle with the stars.

I found that the most unexpected incidents might fill him with wonder and stir his imagination as much as the great Gothic monuments he took me to see. Once, as we were walking, he stopped suddenly and looked intently at a broken telegraph wire, lying curved in the hot asphalt of the road. "Look," he said, "*rien n'est banal ni stupide—le fantastique est partout* [nothing is banal or stupid—the fantastic is everywhere]." He carried a little notebook and sometimes jotted down a notation, of a graffito on a wall, for instance.

Although I speak Spanish, he would only speak to me in French, he so disliked Castilian Spain. "I am a Catalan," he said firmly. "The rest of Spain is as foreign to me as, say, Holland." He spoke French with that jubilant Catalan accent that rattles the French language around the tongue like so many smooth boulders being swept along in a torrent.

As he said, nothing was banal when seen in Miró's company. A stop for a midday sherry was at an eccentric bar decorated with stuffed animal heads garlanded with red peppers. A meal at a favorite restaurant, Solé, introduced me to seafood so peculiar in shape he might have invented it and a cheese shaped like a collapsed woman's breast by Claes Oldenburg. I formed a lifelong partiality for the deep red wine Priorat from Miró's favorite region, Tarragona.

When I was back in Paris from that historic, for me, Barcelona visit with Miró, I was preparing the article "Miró Shows You Barcelona" and reliving our adventures. A most unexpected treasure arrived: a large gouache dancing with emerald and black incidents on a white background. With it came a note from Miró: "Just cut out the motifs you like, and paste them in the margins of your article." Naturally, I did nothing of the sort; the gouache is with me today.

For the following quarter of a century I had the good fortune of catching up with Miró a number of times: in France, Spain, and New York. The connection was never lost. Every New Year's Day (the New Year is more important than Christmas in much of Europe) I would telephone him from wherever I happened to be, to wish him "*une bonne année.*" Once I called from Houston. *"Où est tu?"* he asked. "Where are you?" "*Au Texas,*" I answered. *"Au Texas . . . ?"* He made it sound as if I were calling from the moon.

He was known to be the most reserved and silent of artists, but he did talk to me, the old friend that I had become. I did not follow him to the remote mountain village Gallifa above Barcelona, where he tackled a completely new métier, making ceramics with an old classmate from Barcelona art school days, Josep Llorens Artigas, a master potter. But he told me about it. This was in the mid-1950s. Miró would hole up for months at a time with only Artigas and his son for company, working on an eighteenth-century kiln. No electricity, no telephone. He loved it.

"It is the unpredictability that excites me," he told me. "The accidents in the kiln. You paint a piece red, and it comes out chocolate brown. You never know what will happen. And I was so excited by the craggy vinegar-red rocks of Gallifa, they reminded me of Montroig, my family farm, that I went out and painted right on them, for pure pleasure. I was incorporating myself with the elements." These small-scale experiments led to vast ceramic murals and eventually large-scale sculptures such as the tower for a city plaza in Barcelona, named after him.

When Pierre Matisse mounted an exhibition of Miró's ceramics in his New York gallery, I was very pleased to be asked to write the catalog.

Miró came to New York for the first time in 1947. He was on his way to paint a mural in a Cincinnati hotel, and he stayed in a borrowed studio on 119th Street. His dealer, Pierre Matisse, had arranged the commission. Miró knew Alexander Calder (whom everybody called Sandy) and his wife, Louisa, extremely well. The two men had become close friends when Calder was living in Paris, in the 1920s and 1930s, although neither could speak the other's language.

Miró told me about the little circus Calder had made out of wire figures, and nothing amused him more than making the figures perform for his friends. "Once he came to my family farm in Montroig with his little circus," Miró remembered, "and he gave a performance for the farmers. Unforgettable! This huge man with the tiny figures and his incredible manual dexterity! It was very hot, and he pulled out a pair of scissors and—*crac, crac, crac*—he cut off the arms and legs of his clothes!" When the Calders went back to the United States, a lively correspondence took place, in a blend of Catalan and French and English.

Calder took over showing Miró New York. High on his list was a visit to a Harlem dance hall. Sandy and Louisa were great dancers. Miró said he couldn't dance at all. "They took me to a big place in Harlem—the Savoy Ballroom—wonderful music. Sandy told me to be very careful there, to be sure not to offend anyone by not understanding them. Louisa and Sandy danced off, leaving me alone at the table.

"An enormous black woman, superb, came up and asked me to dance. I didn't dare refuse, because I couldn't explain I couldn't understand her. So I tried." Miró stood up and demonstrated his clasping a figure towering above him.

"I met the composer Edgard Varèse when I was in New York," he told me. "I knew him very well, a very great musician. He came to Catalonia, to my farm at Montroig. There is a very rough road there, several hundred meters; at that time there were very few cars. The farmers went back to their homes in carts, drawn by mules.

These carts moved very slowly, and the wheels made a noise." Miró made a long, drawn-out sound of creaking-grinding wheels on the road. "And the hooves of the mules went *pam, pam, pam, pam.* Varèse stopped dead and was in ecstasy. This was very fascinating to me because there are such correspondences between us. The way he took from the outside world, the sounds."

There had been other visits to New York, organized by Pierre Matisse, who had been Miró's dealer since 1932. Miró liked to mention that it took until 1978 for him to receive recognition from his native land (being fervently anti-Franco, he had deliberately avoided government approval until the end of the Franco regime). However, thanks to his shrewd dealer, and texts by James Soby and James Johnson Sweeney, he was received warmly in the United States. There were two retrospective exhibitions in New York at the Museum of Modern Art, in 1941 and 1959, and exhibitions elsewhere, and in 1959 President Eisenhower presented Miró with an award at the White House.

Miró spoke no English, so direct contact with American artists was difficult unless they spoke French, as did Robert Motherwell. He was enormously touched when Robert Rauschenberg gave him a party in his studio. There was a glass skylight. Suddenly Rauschenberg picked up a pot of blue paint and flung it at the skylight, turning it blue. "This is for you," he said to Miró, referring to a famous painting of Miró's in which there is an area of blue and the notation painted by hand (in French) "This is the color of my dreams." Miró still talked about this with emotion. "He did this for me!"

I asked Miró when he had gone to Paris for the first time. He said, "It was in 1919. I went to a little hotel in the rue Notre Dame des Champs where Catalan intellectuals stayed. The owners were Catalans, they were magnificent. They rented me a room for a purely symbolic price."

He had planned to go to the Grande Chaumière, an open academy where one could draw from the model. But he told me, "I received such an enormous shock at being in Paris, I was so overwhelmed that I was completely incapable of drawing a line. The hand was as if paralyzed—it was an intellectual paralysis. I was totally unable to work for some time."

So he gave up. "In the morning I would go to the Louvre, and in the afternoon I would tour the galleries. I hardly spoke French then, but every language was spoken in Montmartre—it was full of foreigners."

I asked him if it was then that he got to know Picasso. "Oh yes, I saw Picasso right away—the day after I arrived. I hadn't met him before, but I knew his mother very well, she was *formidable*. She and my mother were friends."

"You never met in Barcelona?" I asked.

"He was twelve years older than I and already famous. I didn't dare approach him. He came to Barcelona with Diaghilev and the Russian ballet company. He was in love with Olga Koklova, one of the dancers. They stayed at a hotel together, but he came home in the morning to visit his mother and to shave.

"I used to go and see his mother, and one time she took me by the hand and said, 'Come, come,' and showed me the bathroom where he shaved. He had made a drawing on the mirror with his shaving brush, and it stayed there—she had kept it piously.

"So when I was leaving for Paris, I went to see Picasso's mother and asked if she wanted me to take anything for her. 'Yes, yes,' she said, and gave me a big Spanish cake for him. Next day, in Paris, I went and called and said, 'Monsieur Picasso, I bring this from your mother.'

"He wanted to see what I did, and from the first moment he was very interested in me, he was very generous that way. But it didn't work, the dealers; one was furious because I was staying in a shabby little room and he had to climb five flights to see me, and the place was full of cockroaches."

Miró said that he had always taken care of himself physically to be in good shape for work. "At home I swam winter and summer and walked a lot and did exercises. In Paris, I went to the Centre Américain to take boxing lessons. Ernest Hemingway went there too. It happened that sometimes we were in the ring together. He was huge, and I am very small. It made people smile."

I asked him if later he had known Klee and Kandinsky. "Klee was completely unknown in Paris when I first lived there. I used to hear about him through André Masson; in fact, Masson put me on to a German bookseller who had a large shop on the boulevard du Montparnasse where they sold German magazines. Some had reproductions of Klee. The owner used to go to Bern from time to time, and he would bring back portfolios with Klee's drawings. He would send me a note: 'I received some new Klees.'

"There was an affinity right away, which grew stronger and stronger. Klee made me feel that something more profound existed beyond *peinture-peinture*. Unfortunately, I never got to know him, for practical reasons. He lived in Bern. I was in Paris. I never had the money to make a trip.

"Much later there was a large Klee exhibition at the Galerie Georges Bernheim, and even much later there was an exhibition at the Musée d'Art Moderne—but it took a lot of time.

"Kandinsky I knew very well, much later. When Kandinsky arrived in Paris. I got in touch with him right away. Before we met, I had seen small exhibitions of his, at Jeanne Bucher's. I admired him very much. His contribution to painting was enormous. We often saw each other; we would meet and have lunch together. His work made a great impact on me, like the work of Klee. Kandinsky taught at the Bauhaus with Klee, and he said that Klee talked to him often about me. That was very moving to me to hear, very important.

"I must tell you, however, that in Paris, Kandinsky was zero. No one ever wanted to receive him. Doors were closed on him. Neither Picasso nor Braque did anything for him. Absolutely nobody wanted to have anything to do with him.

"Although I must say that André Breton, at the meetings at the Café Cyrano, Place Blanche, used to say, 'You must buy these wonderful things.' They were very cheap, but none of us had any money."

In 1960, Miró began a completely new adventure. Giving up the seduction of his early paintings, he worked on a series of very large paintings—serene and weightless—of limitless space, using the simplest possible means. He explained, "It took me a great deal of time to do them. Not to paint them, but to meditate them. It took an immense effort, a great interior tension, to arrive at the necessary simplicity. The preliminary stage was an intellectual one. Like before the celebration of a religious rite, yes, like taking religious orders. Do you know how Japanese archers prepare themselves for a competition? They begin by putting themselves into a certain state: expiration, inhalation, expiration—it is the same thing for me. I knew that I risked everything, one weakness, one error, and the whole thing would collapse.

"I began by drawing in charcoal, with great precision. I always start very early in the morning. In the afternoon, I look at what I have done already. All the rest of the day, I prepare myself. Finally, I start to paint: first the background, all blue, but it is not a question of simply putting on the paint, like a housepainter. All the movements of the brush, the wrist, the elbow, the respiration of a hand, also come into play. To work on the background puts me in the necessary state of mind to continue with the rest. This combat has exhausted me. I have not painted anything since. Those canvases are the fulfillment of everything I have tried to do."

Not everyone shared his enthusiasm. In the visitors' book for his exhibition at the Grand Palais, a disgruntled visitor had written, "This man should have his hands cut off." Miró was delighted, not offended. "That proves that it got through to him! It encouraged me to go on working."

In the summer of 1979 there was an exhibition of Miró's work from the last decade at the Maeght Foundation near Saint-Paul-de-Vence. I went to join him there and found him sitting in the shade of a large olive tree in the courtyard. A French television crew was filming him with some of the actors of a Catalan folk group called the Claca. He had designed costumes for them, sometimes painting directly on the white costumes they were wearing, sometimes delicately adding a star, sometimes sloshing whole bucketfuls of paint at them. The costumes transformed the actors into animated Miró sculptures.

Contrasting with these pneumatic multicolored apparitions was the artist himself: small, impeccable in his white suit, face as shiny and rosy as a ripe nectarine. We went into Maeght's house to talk. Miró sat down next to me, instead of opposite me, explaining that his left ear had gone partly deaf. This and a slowed-down gait were the only reminders he was eighty-six.

I told him I was thinking that it was twenty-five years ago that we first worked together. "Worked together"—his term, not mine.

He has the skilled artisan's respect for work seriously done. After the kind of conversation-interview we have had together over the years, he has invariably said, with satisfaction, "*Nous avons bien travaillé*"— "We have worked well."

I said how much I liked the background of the many drawings in the exhibition: the crumpled paper, the odd notations not from his hand, the strange surfaces. "I pick up anything," he said. "If I see a paper left on the ground that says something to me, I pick it up. Now, when I go back to Spain, there will be packages to open. Often I will keep the wrapping to use for drawings. Sometimes my wife, Pilar, comes back from the market with food wrapped in paper with stains—I take it for drawing. She is upset by this, but I can find a use for it."

I asked him if an object interested him in itself or simply served to make him think of something else.

"It can happen that a real object can prompt an idea, for a sculpture, for instance. It may start me off."

But for your drawings or paintings, unlike when you began, it's not the real world that interests you?

"No, not real objects. But if I see this"—he pointed to a space between the boards of the table in front of us—"or I see a shadow, or a crack in the wall, it can give me an idea. For example, this black spot here, or that little mark there." He touched them lovingly as he talked. "Spots excite me. Maybe I can get an idea for a large sculpture, or a drawing. The grain of the wood, that little eye, I am drawn to it—*pam*—it's like an electric current running through me."

I asked if he generally used a drawing as a point of departure for a painting.

"Sometimes I start with a drawing. I used to more often than now, now, more often an accident of the canvas or paper starts me off. An idea can be guided by the material. Sometimes I start with paintbrushes that are dirty. I wipe them across a new canvas [gestures of brushing them back and forth vigorously].

"I always have a great quantity of canvases in my atelier. I work many canvases at the same time. Maybe a hundred. Some I leave resting, partly worked, for years. Little by little they mature, and one day I am called by one of them. I've gone into the studio without a preconceived idea, and I am called to take it up again. A magnetic call, like an electric shock. I am forced to do it.

"After that comes a second stage. I attack [he makes the noise of someone charging]. Intellectual work establishes the equilibrium. The equilibrium of forms, colors, and volumes. One line calls another, one color demands another. After that, I rest. The next day, refreshed, I judge what I have done."

I told him I saw a documentary film about him in which he dips his fingers into the paint and paints directly on the canvas with them.

"Yes, I've worked with my fingers like this for years. Sometimes I use my whole hand [he slaps his open hand onto the tabletop, to demonstrate]. I used to work with brushes, often very fine brushes, but now I need to get my hands into the paint directly. I put my paws right into the paint, or ink when I am making lithographs. Sometimes I dip all ten fingers into the paint and play on the canvas, like a pianist!

"Sometimes I use an old rag [he makes the gesture of rubbing paint onto a canvas with bunched fingers holding an imaginary rag]. Or I begin with a piece of paper that I crumple up—*aaaaaaahhhhh*—like this [an imaginary ball of paper is rubbed into an imaginary canvas].

"And I like old brushes, uneven and flattened out, that produce 'accidents.' For example, when housepainters come to my place, I say to them, 'Keep the oldest brushes you have. Don't throw them in the garbage can, keep them for me.' An old brush has vitality [he clacks his tongue appreciatively]! It's a brush that has lived, that has already had a life of its own.

"I prefer objects that have already lived. For example, if I want to make a new painting. I buy a canvas at the paint store—but what is clean won't do. I begin to dirty it a bit; I splash it with turpentine, rub it with my paint-stained hands. I even walk on it. The naked canvas is cold, it doesn't excite me."

We talked about the past and his iconic painting *The Farm*, which is now in the National Gallery in Washington.

"Long ago, at the beginning, when you painted landscapes at Montroig, you worked directly from nature?"

"Oh yes [laughs], like Cézanne! I started *The Farm* at Montroig, and then I went to Paris, which is where I finished it. I took with me to Paris, in an envelope, some grasses from my home. As the grasses dried, I had to go to the Bois de Boulogne and pick some more."

Did anyone understand the picture in Paris?

"Certainly not! It was a very big picture, very hard to sell. I had no money, but I had to take a taxi to Paul Guillaume, Rosenberg. Then another to bring it back. Rosenberg said to me, 'It's such a big picture and people live in small apartments. Why don't you cut it into several pieces?'"

Then Hemingway bought it?

"For pennies. But he liked it a lot."

We talked about his interest in making large-scale sculpture.

"Besides monumental sculpture for its own sake, what interests me most of all is that it allows me to have direct contact with people. For instance, we are working on a ceramic mural—sixty meters by ten—for a German museum. It will be outside the museum, I don't remember the name of the town, but it is an industrial city, very depressing, I am told. What interests me is if I can bring a shock of humanity to those people who are sad in that industrialized city."

He was hoping to come to the United States in the autumn.

"I would like to go to Vee-she-ta [it took me a moment to translate this to Wichita]. I made a big mural for the university there, it is on the outside of the university. Every day, thousands of students go that way. So, evidently, it will fill the minds of these boys, the men of tomorrow. One of those might be president of the United States. Seeing that mosaic might have an impact.

"That's what interests me. It is the young people who count. Old dodoes don't interest me at all. I work for the future. I work for the men of tomorrow. I have always worked for liberty and openness of mind. Liberty of plastic expression corresponds to liberty of expression of ideas. If my personages have become grotesque, it is because we live in a monstrous era. I am more and more revolted by the world as it is.

"But the older I grow, I feel younger and more keen, more and more violent and more and more free."

There was a knock at the door. A car had arrived for us; Pierre Matisse and his wife were expecting us for lunch. By now it was one o'clock. There had been a business meeting for Miró, the television filming, my interview, yet Miró seemed genuinely disappointed to break off.

Before leaving, I asked him to sign the poster of the Maeght exhibition. I pulled off its protective wrapping; he uncurled the poster, looked at it intently, selecting a spot for his signature with great care. His pen hovered over it, then came down like a dragonfly alighting.

We walked together to the car. I realized I still had the crumpled wrapping in my hand and looked around for a place to throw it away. Suddenly Miró asked, "You permit?" and took the paper from me. He smoothed it out with eager anticipation, beamed, and with an apology went back into the house with it.

He came out still smiling. "It is superb! I will take it back to Barcelona with me for a drawing. We have not only *bien travaillé ensemble*, we have collaborated!"

For many years Miró never had much room for a studio. When, in 1933, he was making the large collages of minute machine parts that were shown at the Museum of Modern Art, he had no money and had to come back to live with his parents. He holed up in a small attic, so small that he strung strings across it and attached the collages to them, not having wall space.

"I used to dream of a large studio," he would say. Some time after he came back to Spain after the war, he finally had it. He had left Barcelona for Majorca, home ground for his wife's family. He was getting too much unwanted attention from the authorities in Spain; it was still the Franco days. His friend and fellow Catalan the architect José Luis Sert designed him a large studio outside Palma facing the water.

I went to visit him there several times; it was a short hop by plane from Paris to Palma. The last visit was in January 1980. He was waiting for me in the hall of the house, some way from the studio—arms outstretched in welcome, a small beaming figure with what I can only describe as goodness radiating from him. We sat down in the comfortable but conventional living room. "That is Pilar's domain, I have nothing to do with the house," he had said on a previous occasion. "The women sit here and talk about the price of onions."

We sat at a table near the window, overlooking the neatly planted garden and the big modern studio. I had brought a box of the traditional New Year delicacy marrons glacés. There was a bottle of Miró's favorite wine from Tarragona, Priorat. Pilar kept an eye out to see that Miró had only one glass of wine and a nibble of the marrons. "He is on a diet," she said.

He talked about an exhibition he had just seen at the Pompidou Center in Paris. "I came away bowled over all over again by Matisse. I had not seen the Matisses from Russia before. *The Dance* particularly—fabulous. What a great artist! I admired him so, I wish I had seen him more often, but I was shy, I hesitated to disturb him."

There were some souvenirs of his old Paris days—two canvases by Fernand Léger ("I liked him very much, a genuine human being"), a still life by Braque, Miró's own cartoon for a tapestry, incorporating evocative words: "*étoile . . . escargot . . . fleur . . . femme.*"

He had heard that through a personal upheaval I had lost many of my possessions, including my books. "Did you even lose the Dupin?" he asked me (Jacques Dupin had written a first-rate critical account of Miró's work). I had. Miró excused himself and left the room. He was gone almost half an hour. He came back with his own copy of the Dupin, and on a blank page he had made a full-page vibrant color drawing, with a touching inscription.

We went to the studio. On an earlier visit I had seen it almost empty, with cases ready to be unpacked. Miró had not seen the contents since before the war, when it was in storage. "When I took out works dating back over years, I began to make my autocriticism," he told me. "I corrected myself coldly, objectively, the way a teacher at the Grande Chaumière corrects a pupil. I was quite pitiless with myself. I destroyed a number of canvases, and especially drawings and gouaches. I would look at a whole series, then put them aside to be destroyed, then—*zac, zac, zac*—I tore them up. There were several big purges like that over several years. Some of the old canvases I wanted to rework; others I wanted to leave as they were. The work I did after that resulted from what I learned during the period."

Now, as Miró said, his studio "was like a forest." There were scores of canvases in all stages of progress. One canvas had a small pencil sketch pinned onto it—an idea for the future. Notes in black and red on bits of paper with penciled notations were filed under stones on a flat table. Miró was almost fanatically neat. Painting material was laid out in orderly fashion. Pots with brushes sticking out of them were lined up with military precision. He always kept a few Catalan souvenirs around him: a sunburst out of straw, painted Majorca whistles on which he enjoyed giving a vigorous toot.

He told me that when he is working, nobody, but nobody, could come into the studio. "I'm always alone there, no assistant. Never any music. Silence." He told me more than once that when he gets into the studio and closes the door, "I go completely wild. The older I get, the meaner and the more aggressive I get." I must say that if this was so, outside the studio there never was any trace of this ferocity.

I didn't want to tire him; Pilar had told me that he was exhausted, that during the last visit to Paris he had caught cold and had to sign too many engravings. Her brother, who is a doctor, had insisted that if things were entertaining, then it's all right, but he must not be bothered by unpleasant things. "He sees very few people now. But he wanted to see you," she said.

I went into the house to say goodbye to Pilar. Miró accompanied me to the door. A car was waiting. We embraced; both of us knew that this was probably the last time. I waited until I got into the car to shed a few tears.

Miró died on Christmas Day in 1983. He was ninety years old.

Henry Moore

When I started visiting Henry Moore in 1948 at his farm-house at Much Hadham, we often sat in what he called his ideas bank and what I thought of as his hermit's cell. It was a tiny space, more hut than studio, extremely uncomfortable. There was a small, hard wooden chair, an electric stove as big as a postcard, and the sort of table that wouldn't even make it to the thrift shop. For more than forty years, he sat there and waited to see what would come of it.

In that room there was an encyclopedia of natural forms. There might be anything from an elephant's skull to a vegetable form, no bigger than his thumb, that had caught his fancy.

He said, "Sometimes I come in the morning without a single idea, and just seeing a stone with an odd shape will set me off."

He demonstrated his favorite contrasts of forms, holding up a shell—a hollow form, hard outside, with a soft, vulnerable inside—a recurring sculptural theme: an external shape sheltering an interior one.

He rummaged around and came up with a large bone—the opposite, internal strength on which a soft outside depends. He looked at it with real awe. He turned it slowly, showing how it looked completely different from each angle. "That's what I want my sculpture to be like," he said. "You keep discovering entirely new shapes as you look around it."

But all his sculpture, he insisted, stemmed from the human body. "We only understand other forms from our own body. Our sense of scale is based on our person and the space we occupy. If we were the size of dinosaurs, or ants, we would see things very differently."

Drawing was all-important to Henry. "I'd make it part of everyone's education. It's the only way to make people look intensely. If you look out of your window at a view hundreds of times, you won't know it as well as if you drew it once."

But I also remember him saying that if husbands had to draw their wives, there'd be more divorces.

Henry was plain, direct, straightforward, and steadfast. He loved a good joke, and plenty of them, and he never prevaricated.

As a world-famous sculptor, he had to sit patiently through many long laudatory speeches. He would shift just a little when he saw there were still six or seven pages to go.

What he really liked was to shake the sawdust out of the stuffed shirts of officials and get them to play paper games in which he kept the score. By the end of the evening they were having as good a time as he was.

The Moores bought their modest house in the country in 1940. It dates in part from the fifteenth century, and in the early days you had no trouble believing that. No one was ever less nouveau riche than Henry. The house had begun plain, and in essentials it stayed plain.

And the house stayed small except for one light and airy sitting room that was built onto it—always called the New Room. I often sat there drinking scotch with Henry, chatting and looking with him at things he had lovingly collected. There were works of art that he never ceased exploring: a Seurat drawing, a big Degas painting of a woman brushing her hair, a small Rembrandt etching, a head of a woman by Courbet, a Vuillard panel. There was a fragment of a Romanesque pulpit and many pieces of the kind that had fired Henry's imagination long ago at the British Museum—examples of Cycladic, pre-Columbian, and African art.

And there were always things to pick up and feel: smooth stones, crystals, gourds, fruits.

Little by little Henry was able to buy more pieces of land. Gradually, more and larger studios were added. The garden was designed by his Russian wife, Irina. Henry was very proud of it, and the fields became a private anthology of his favorite sculptures.

When I first used to go and see the Moores, Henry was so impatient to get to work that he rode his bicycle standing up.

He loved his sculptures and took great trouble about where they were placed. He said, "There is no background to sculpture better than the sky, because you are contrasting solid form with its opposite—space."

One of his favorites was the *Sheep Piece*. He had installed it on high ground not far from the house. The great treat for every visitor in later years was to go and see this big piece. Not only was it meant for sheep to rub against, but Henry saw to it that when visitors came round the corner, sheep were there doing just that. Those sheep got to carry on like charter members of the National Theatre company.

Henry got to know these sheep intimately when his big studio became unusable because it was filled all day by over a dozen men hauling and carting his sculptures to ship off to Italy, where he was having a huge exhibition in Florence at the Belvedere.

He retreated to the small studio that had a window giving onto the field where his neighbor's sheep were grazing. When he tapped on the window, the sheep would look up and come closer—they couldn't see him in the dark interior. So he was able to study them at close range. "They were as good as life models. There is something ancient, biblical about sheep. And you know those sheep just love the piece."

For much of his long life Henry was one of the most famous men around. At one time, you could have written to him from almost anywhere in the world and known it would get there if you just wrote "Henry Moore, England" on the envelope.

Yet never, ever did he come on as someone "important." Our mutual friend the poet Stephen Spender said about Henry Moore at the memorial service in Westminster Abbey, "The son of a miner, Henry told me that in his whole life he had never had any sense of anyone being socially superior or, for that matter, socially inferior to him. People to him were equals, simply in being human."

Henry told us with amusement about being invited to luncheon at Buckingham Palace to meet the queen. The guests—there were a number of them—were instructed to file by the queen after the meal, and each in turn would have a few brief moments to address her. His place in the line inched forward smartly. But when a little man in front of Henry reached Her Majesty, the line stopped, and the queen talked to him with considerable animation. When it came to be Henry's turn, there were only a few seconds left for him. Who was the favored guest? The queen's jockey.

In 1974, I did two programs about Henry for CBS television. We were hooked up with microphones and left free to roam. Henry was completely unself-conscious, and we went on chatting as we had for years. We spoke of Alberto Giacometti, whom we both admired. Giacometti as a modeler started with nothing and worked outward, Henry explained. The carver, like himself, starts with a block and moves inward.

When we went by one of his big bronzes, Henry tapped it affectionately, smartly enough to make it reverberate. "I was just proving that it was hollow," he said. "A good cast should ring like a bell. One likes the sound and the feel.

"When the cast is well done, bronze would be good for twenty thousand years and be able to resist the elements rather better than any type of stone."

He spoke of the importance of placing sculpture correctly. "Of course, one can't go on worrying about every piece one's done, and whether it's well or badly shown. One's life would be just misery. But sculpture needs more care in its placing than paintings do.

"With a picture, the frame keeps you at a distance, and the picture goes on living in its own world. But if a sculpture is placed against the light; if you come into a room and see it against a window, you just see a silhouette with a glare around it. It can't mean anything."

Incidentally, if he didn't think that people had had the right idea, he was very good at getting his way. When his friend I. M. Pei built the East Wing of the National Gallery in Washington, there never was any doubt that Henry would be asked to contribute a sculpture to it. But what? And where?

He went to Washington to see what the National Gallery had in mind. He was taken to the museum in a very big car.

People of consequence in hard hats were waiting for him along the side of the new building where there was really quite a nice niche, in its way, for sculpture. It faced the traffic and would be seen by everyone who drove past on the way to the Capitol.

Henry got out of the car. He was already getting stiff by then, but he wasn't going to say yes or no in a hurry. He looked. He saw how

Walking down the aisle
with Aaron Copland at the
Philharmonic Gala, 1967

With John Russell, 1982
(Jill Krementz)

Lecturing about Henry Moore at the
Metropolitan Museum, 1972

With John leaving the Metropolitan
Museum of Art after a reception given
for me (Bill Cunningham)

Philip Johnson greets us at our wedding, 1974

Stephen Spender came from London for the wedding

Virgil Thomson and Leonard Bernstein

Andy Warhol feeds his dachshund a small sausage

Aaron Copland, who gave me away

Leonard Bernstein showing me that he was on time for my French decoration
(John Russell)

John, Philip Johnson, and Jackie Kennedy at John's sixtieth birthday
(Arthur Gold)

With Max Ernst in his Seillans studio, 1970

With Miró in the Park Güell, Barcelona, 1954 (© Brassaï)

A page from the first copy of *L'ŒIL*, January 15, 1955, signed for me by Braque and Picasso

The cover of the first *L'ŒIL*, a detail of Léger's *La Grande Parade*

Picasso reading *L'ŒIL* with his wife, Jacqueline, looking over his shoulder (Roland Penrose)

Picasso allowed me to reproduce his copies after Albrecht Altdorfer for the first and last time for *L'ŒIL* in 1957. The drawings disappeared after being returned to him and have never been seen since.

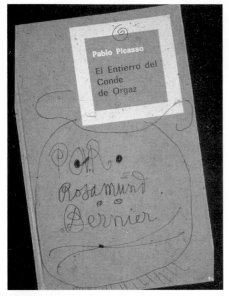

John and me with our hands in plaster (*top*) for a sculpture (*above*) for Louise Bourgeois

Picasso inscribed this copy of his book *El Entierro del Conde de Orgaz* on the cover and inside for me, 1971

Eric's sketch of me in a Paulette coif, Paris, 1947

Dresses worn over many years for my lectures at the Metropolitan Museum of Art. Most of these photographs were snapped backstage by John so that I would have a record of what I wore.

Alex Katz's double portrait of John and me, presented to the Metropolitan Museum
of Art in 2010

wide, or rather how narrow, the sidewalk was. He saw how the traffic raced by. He got back into the car, and he said nothing at all.

"Would you like to tour the building?" they asked. "Oh yes," said Henry. "That would be very nice. Let's see everything."

They pulled up to the front door. Henry got out. He saw how I. M. Pei had designed a main entrance that drew people right into the gallery and made them feel like empress and emperor.

He looked at the far corner on the left. He looked up, and he looked down. And then he pointed to that far left corner. "That's the place for my sculpture." And that's where it is today.

Among the treasures in what Henry still called the New Room was a torso by Auguste Rodin. He would point out the parts representing hard and soft parts, the bumps and the hollows. "I look at it every day. I keep finding new things in it," he would marvel.

"I couldn't remember a time when I had not admired Rodin more than any other sculptor since Michelangelo. So I was particularly moved to have an exhibition in the park of the Rodin Museum [in Paris]."

Henry would have me come over at the time—I lived just down the street—to circle around the sculptures, and to squat down to get the effect of the Eiffel Tower looming up in the distance as a backdrop for his bronzes.

In his late sixties Henry owned a cast of the headless and armless *Walking Man* that Rodin made as a preliminary to his *Saint John the Baptist Preaching*. Henry didn't miss, and in fact didn't want, the head and arms that made Saint John the Baptist look more "complete" in Rodin's day.

He said that the head and arms were in the late-nineteenth-century idiom, whereas the forms of the headless figure were timeless. "Because of owning the cast in the original scale—it's only half-life-size—and loving it, I know it very well. One of the parts in it which continuously astonishes me is the breast, the chest, the part on top of the chest, because you can feel that immediately, under a sixteenth of an inch, under the skin, there is hard bone.

"And this is something which Rodin had, this feeling for the interior bone structure, and yet the stomach part . . . you can feel that in the stomach there is no bone; for at least two or three inches, you could push through. So this feeling for hardness and softness, for roughness and smoothness, for the pushed-in and the pulled-out, for the hole and the bump, this is what Rodin brought back into sculpture, a reality of form."

One time in London, Henry took me to an exhibition of Degas bronzes. He pointed out the differences, as he saw them, between Rodin and Degas as sculptors of dancing figures.

Rodin's dancers are full of movement, as if caught at a fleeting moment that would not recur. He reminded me of how Rodin would have his models move around the studio any way they liked, until he got the split second's movement that he had never seen before and would never see again.

"On the other hand, the Degas seems to speak for attitudes that he had seen a hundred times over in the classroom and had had time to perfect at leisure. His dancers could have held those poses for five minutes, if they were told to. Rodin's, never."

In 1967, every publication in France was marking the fifty years since Rodin's death. As editor of the art review I had founded (*L'ŒIL*), I had to think of what I could do that would be completely different from anyone else's. Of course, Henry Moore was the answer. What could be better than to have one distinguished sculptor talk about another?

The only trouble was that Henry was at his summer studio at Forte dei Marmi in Italy, and I had a professional appointment in Athens, and the deadline loomed. Henry, amiability itself, readily agreed for me to come and see him.

So it was a question of flying to Milan, taking a train to Viareggio, then a bus to Forte dei Marmi. Then repeat the journey backward on the same day to catch the plane to Athens.

I had hoped that once I was at Henry's summer cottage, we could sit down and talk about Rodin. Not at all. Henry insisted on taking me to see the Henraux stone quarry. "It's a marvelous place," he said. "They have stone from all over the world." I was dismayed.

We got into Henry's Land Rover, and a perilous drive began: up the precipitous hillside, with a drop to the Mediterranean on the other side. (It made me think of landing my small plane at Acapulco.) Henry being English drove firmly on the left side of the narrow road. The Italians being Italian stuck to the right. To compound the excitement, Henry, not having seen me for some time, kept looking toward me to fill me in with his news. Somehow we made it.

I could understand why Henry loved those quarries. They're halfway to the sky, and when you walk into them, it's like being in an antechamber of the gods. John Russell, in his definitive biography of Henry (1968), wrote, "From his garden Henry could look up to the Carrara Mountains. These lie in the stretch of mountains in which Michelangelo is said to have gone in search of stone. Not only are the mountains themselves irresistibly grand, with their shifting cloudscapes and suddenly daunting fits of ill-humor, but the enormous concealed caverns of marble form a scene to silence even the most talkative among us."

A large sculpture was wheeled out that still had a long way to go, and clearly Henry was rejuvenated by the very sight of all that stone just asking to be used. He couldn't wait to manhandle it, with the energy of a man half his age. "When I take up a hammer and chisel, I begin to whistle and hum," he told me.

He described an earlier visit to the quarry. "There was one huge block as big as a room—turned on end and twice as high—and a ladder with a man perched on top of it, and in one corner, a man's bowler hat, a hat of about 1900 . . . and this hat and the ladder and the man on top of it combined to give one a sense of almost unbelievable scale and reminded me of things that I could try to get out of the block."

I had taken for granted that after the visit to the quarry we would go back to Henry's cottage and settle down for my interview. But not at all.

"We must have our bathe," Henry said (British for "swim"). That was the last thing I wanted to do with the clock ticking away. But there was no getting out of it.

Next thing I knew, I had taken my bathing suit out of my suitcase and we were bobbing up and down in the surf. "There's no time like the present," I thought. As Henry emerged from a wave, I asked him, "Do you really like those late marbles?" And the whole interview was conducted like that.

I just had time in Milan to type out my notes on the little Olivetti portable we all used in those days, and I actually got to Athens on time.

Max Ernst

I met Max Ernst in the early 1940s in New York. He had managed to get out of German-occupied France and had arrived in the United States thanks to the support of Peggy Guggenheim. She prized him as a catch on several levels: he was a leading figure of the Surrealist movement, and he was outstandingly handsome. He looked like a cross between a noble bird of prey and a fallen archangel. He was known for his beauty of person, his laserlike intelligence, his idiosyncratic command of at least three languages, and his gift for the lapidary phrase that stops the stuffed shirt dead in his tracks.

Although he had lived in France since 1922, German born, he had never bothered to take out French nationality. As he described it, he arrived in the United States by plane: "Splendid view of the Statue of Liberty. I was met by immigrations authorities, who sent me straight to Ellis Island. Splendid view of the Statue of Liberty."

The only way out of this impasse was to give in to Peggy Guggenheim's insistence that he marry her, giving him American citizenship. I don't think either of them expected a smooth crossing. As Peggy put it to me, "When Max paints a picture, I like him. When Max sells a picture, I love him."

We happened to be fellow houseguests for a weekend in the Hamptons. A group of us had been swimming. The beach was a short walk to the house, and there were bicycles. Max and I rode back to the house on bicycles, and so we arrived a few minutes before the others. When Peggy arrived, she made a terrible scene, accusing Max of dalliance with me. Max commented drily, "Not even I can make love on a bicycle." Later, Peggy told me about this herself and said, "Wasn't I foolish?" which was endearing.

Not much later, Max was sent by Peggy Guggenheim's organization in New York (the gallery she established there was called Art of This Century) to select work by women artists for an exhibition. A singularly unwise move. One of the artists on his rounds was Dorothea Tanning. He went to her studio. She was pretty, a good painter, and she could play chess. They played chess and fell irrevocably in love.

After the inevitable skirmishes and recriminations, the painter Matta lent them some money; they bought a broken-down Ford and headed west, to Sedona, Arizona. I lost touch with them for a while because I went back to Europe. A few photographs arrived, showing a very sunburnt Max, shirtless, and Dorothea (with shirt), literally building their own house.

We met again in the early 1950s in France. The Ernsts had a house in Touraine in a village called Huisme. We had a weekend house not far from them at Suèvres. An evening with them usually turned into a hilarious romp. Max kept a hamper with ridiculous disguises and joke elements—it was not for nothing that he used to say, "To take the banal and make the marvelous." Max and Dorothea always outshone us in creating new and often farcical identities. For a fancy-dress ball given by Marie-Laure de Noailles, a famous Parisian hostess, the guests were meant to appear as figures from paintings. Dorothea was a personage from the Netherlandish Master of the Female Half-Lengths: she had half a table cut out and somehow attached to her person, laid out with a complete meal.

The Ernsts moved to Paris. I was living there too. There were many outings together—going to see the movie *Jules et Jim*, a rerun of a favorite, *King Kong*, sampling restaurants, going to the Natural History Museum to look at rows of exotic beetles.

I soaked up stories of his peripatetic life. He was born in Germany in 1891 but left it for good in 1922. He left on a passport borrowed from the poet Paul Eluard, who had come to see him with his wife, Gala, who later married Dalí. Max moved in with the Eluards and became Gala's lover, all this routine according to Surrealist tenets that ruled out conventional rules.

He was an émigré and occasional enemy alien in France and the United States. For his first sixty years and in practical terms, he was over and over again a paperless near pauper, a man on the run who belonged nowhere. While he may have had uncertain nationality, he never lost his hold on the ultranatural.

He never lost his faith in chance. He told me that when he was still interned in southern France as an enemy alien, he agonized about how to get his great premonitory painting *Europe After the Rain* safely out of France. (It is now in the Wadsworth Atheneum in Hartford.) In this painting he had set down once and for all the worst that could happen to a Europe that was overrun, broken-down, and returned to the jungle. How could the painting be kept safe? He decided there was only one way. He would roll it up, wrap it up, and mail it to the Museum of Modern Art in New York. He did, and when he got to New York in 1941, there it was waiting for him.

It took the world a very long time to recognize Max Ernst as one of the major artists of his century. But when it finally happened, nothing was too good for him. He won first prize at the Venice Biennale of 1954, but not even official honors seemed to follow their ordinary course where Max was concerned.

He had gone to the award ceremony with his old friend Jean Arp, who had won the sculpture prize. The president of Italy, who was to make the presentations, got so carried away by the list of foreign dignitaries attending that he forgot to give the prizewinners' names.

Then Max was stopped in the park grounds, where the Biennale is held, by the carabinieri—the Italian national police—who asked for his pass. He fished ineffectually in his pocket, he had left it behind at his hotel, but he told the guards that he had won the "*primo premio*" (first prize). The men stepped aside and talked, gesturing to each other, clearly indicating that they were saying, "This guy is nuts." Whereupon they marched him smartly to the exit.

"That," said Max, "was my triumph at the Biennale."

In 1970, I was involved in a divorce—mine. I was living on the rue du Bac, and the Ernsts lived nearby on the rue de Lille. At one point the situation grew unpleasant, and I wanted to move out. Max declared that as long as he was alive, I would never go to a hotel in Paris; in fact, he said, you must come here. The Ernsts had leased an apartment above theirs so that there would be no noise. This became my temporary headquarters. I arrived to find the Ernsts had improvised a welcome party, and Max had written my name in white icing over a chocolate cake.

I was actually working at that time on lectures I was to give, in French, at the Grand Palais. One of them was on Max. He had to go to Cologne to collect an honorary bachelor of arts degree, so I had the place to myself. His studies had been interrupted by World War I. As he said, "To get a degree, all you have to do is wait."

It was curious, and moving, to sit at Max's desk with its miniature red devil on a bicycle (which I now own) and work on my Ernst notes. The lecture went well, but it gave him the wrong idea.

One morning he called me to come down. Usually, I only joined them at drinks time. There was a group of men waiting there, looking expectantly. They were from French television. They had been trying to persuade Ernst to let them do a feature film about him. He always refused. This time, to my dismay and the dismay of the television people, he announced, "This is Rosamond Bernier, she will make your film." He gave us all a glass of champagne and left.

So French television and I were locked into a shotgun marriage. Max apparently was under the illusion that since I had lectured about him without bothering him, I would do the same thing here. Naturally, I wanted to record him on camera and keep out of the picture myself.

I thought Max might be more relaxed in the sunny atmosphere of Seillans, in the south of France, where Dorothea had designed a large house for them, with a studio at either end.

I had visited the Ernsts there a number of times. Roland Penrose, the English collector and champion of Surrealism, and I had stopped by when the Ernsts were just moving in. Max was eighty, but he was already planting the vegetable garden, some fruit trees, and two kinds of American corn—unknown in these parts—a taste acquired during his stay in Arizona.

So off to Seillans, with a director, a soundman, a lighting man, and a few hangers-on.

It was not easy. My subject was skittish. He might tell me fascinating stories at lunch, but when I asked him to repeat them on camera, he would say, "You know all that. I just told you." And there was the inescapable impression that Dorothea thought the film should be about her.

I doubled as director and occasional guest chef. In the morning, on request, I would make the menu, naming each dish after one of Max's paintings. He liked my cooking, so I would stir up one of his favorites. A photograph records me on the job in the pretty tiled kitchen, a towel around my waist, having just emerged from the pool.

I finally managed to capture Max on film and kept myself out of not only the picture but also the sound track. Unfortunately, French television had a heavy hand in the editing room and added a most inappropriate, grandiloquent sound background.

Some time later, there was a Max Ernst retrospective at the Guggenheim Museum in New York, and I was asked to give a lecture about him. I did, with the artist sitting in the front row— somewhat disconcerting. When I came off the stage, he had tears streaming down his cheeks. "No one has ever spoken like that about me before," he said.

The German chancellor, Willy Brandt, was in town and wanted to see the exhibition. Normally, the Guggenheim curator who organized the show would have been asked to show him around. But Max insisted that I do the honors, so I did.

I went with Max and Dorothea to Cologne, where Max's eightieth birthday was celebrated. This prodigal son who had been ignored by his compatriots for half a century naturally enjoyed all the attention. Now the Ernsts were guests of the town in the presidential suite, and he was amused by the flowery tributes, special boat trips down the Rhine, tea with the president of the republic, and the inevitable bottles of eau de cologne. With his usual irony, however, he enjoyed reminding his hosts that his rare exhibitions in Germany, until very recently, had been "total flops."

He was born in a modest little house in Brühl, near Cologne, which now has a plaque identifying the rare bird that was hatched under these eaves. Just down the road is the great baroque Augustus Palace, once the residence of the prince bishops of Cologne, now used for special state occasions. It has a spectacular staircase by Balthasar Neumann. That is where the state dinner in his honor, hosted by the chancellor of West Germany, was held. It took Max Ernst about eighty years to make the few steps from cottage to castle.

The setting was an exuberant south German rococo fantasy of multicolored marbles, putti sailing through space, angels blowing trumpets, caryatids projecting from a foam bath of stucco ornaments. After numerous courses and speeches, the composer Karlheinz Stockhausen, his long blond hair held by a barrette, appeared. He announced, "This is for *lieber* Max," whereupon a few acolytes twisted some dials and a blast of electronic music thundered out loud enough to project the putti right through the painted dome.

During one of our many conversations, Max told me that the Impressionists lived in a happy period when people could believe that the retina played the essential role in the creation of art. "One could take one's easel, canvases, and paints and brushes and go off for the day to paint in front of the subject—the landscape or whatever—and come back in the evening more or less pleased with what one had done. But this concept of painting was finished by my time. I had decided to become an artist. I had to devise my own answers to the problems.

"I said to myself, when I'm forty, I will stop painting. At the time, that seemed so old to me. I told myself that most painters, once they have achieved a certain result, content themselves with the result. This is not what I wanted to do.

"An artist who finds himself is lost. I had the good luck not to find myself. So I didn't stick to my promise. I went on painting."

I did not know it at the time, but my future husband, John Russell, was working on a major biography of Max Ernst. When, a few years later, our stories combined, Max wanted to join us formally at Seillans. Only a heart attack thwarted this master of the marvelous from his generous plan.

Chanel Comeback

In the autumn of 1953, I was in Paris, busy preparing to launch *L'ŒIL*, when I received a telephone call from Alexander Liberman, *Vogue*'s art director, in New York. He asked me to interview Chanel, who was about to relaunch her couture house, which had been closed since before World War II.

I had not been connected to *Vogue* for some years, but had remained on friendly terms with the Condé Nast people. So I accepted.

There had been a good deal of talk swirling around this event. Chanel's couture house had been enormously successful in the 1920s and 1930s.

Britain and France had declared a state of war with Germany in 1939. Three weeks later, Chanel closed her place of business without warning and laid off her entire staff. Only the boutique selling her perfume, the famous Chanel No. 5, remained open.

France was occupied by the Nazis. Gabrielle Chanel continued to live in her quarters at the Paris Ritz. She took up with a handsome, tall blond German who had been an attaché at the German embassy, Hans Günther von Dincklage, known as Spatz. Their liaison was public knowledge.

At the liberation, Spatz was already back in Germany. Chanel's position as a collaborator with the enemy could not have been more perilous.

Two weeks after de Gaulle's triumphant return to Paris, in 1944, Chanel was arrested. Two young men with the armbands of the FFI (a French resistance movement), revolvers at the ready, called at the Ritz to escort her to police headquarters.

Exactly what happened, under what circumstances, has never been revealed. The fact is that after only three hours, Chanel was released.

Her lawyers advised her to get out of the country immediately. She left for neutral Switzerland. Eventually, Spatz joined her there.

Rumors began circulating in 1950 that Chanel wanted to reopen her house. It seemed preposterous. But aside from her restlessness after years of inactivity, there was a practical reason why her business associates, who owned the perfume business, needed a jolt to spur sales of No. 5. It is the perfume business that supports the couture houses.

And she was piqued to hear of the triumphs of new people in the couture, especially of her bête noire, Christian Dior.

She decided, at seventy, to make a comeback. The date was set for February 5, 1954.

My interview with Chanel ran in the February 1954 issues of American and British *Vogue.*

LISTENING TO CHANEL

Eric [*Vogue*'s star fashion illustrator] and I went to see Chanel on the rue Cambon, where she lives over her salon and ateliers: vast premises, until recently empty, dormant. We went through the boutique with perfumes, soaps, sweaters, and scarves, into the mirrored hall of a mirrored staircase, strips of mirror breaking space, into a cloudless Cubist maze beyond time and space, hushed with carpets. Past massive dull gold Spanish arabesques, past the darkened showroom sliced with lacquered screens, up the famous staircase where Chanel's openings had crowded her high-titled employees and the most brilliant personalities of the day. "It's like a dream," said Eric, "nothing has changed."

Now an entrance hall dark with paneled Oriental screens; pushing through the looking glass (more mirrored doors) into a small, dim study to find—not Sleeping Beauty—but a small, brown idol hung with jewels, perched on the edge of an outsized brown sofa. A spare, taut, compressed figure; widely spaced large dark eyes, so alive that they deny the lines around them; a broad, shrewd face; wide mouth pulled straight across the face, turning down at the corners; determinedly penciled eyebrows. Black wisps of hair break from the navy blue felt hat spreading a little protective shade. A knot of diamonds and a great unblinking emerald pendant at the throat of a white crepe collarless blouse, the cuffs turned back with art, caught with jewels; brief navy sweater; a plaque of jewels at the waist; earrings, pearls caught in a swarm of diamonds; short gray jersey skirt—the legendary unchanged Chanel elegance. Her extraordinary hands, monumental on a small scale: powerful, broad knuckled, the hands of a sculptor, strong long fingers, short unpolished nails, massive emerald ring.

She leans forward as she talks, the angular jaw thrust forward like a Toulouse-Lautrec lithograph of Yvette Guilbert. Without prelude the talk flows endlessly in rapid-fire, dry, intense monotone. No full stops, no rhetorical effects, an uninterrupted long-playing record, no change of tempo or volume. A first-person-singular whirlpool, flinging off interpolations or questions, following its own course . . .

"What is Fashion? *La mode est un métier* and not an art—it is a *don* and not *du génie*. We keep hearing this word *génie*—everything has genius—a handbag, a pair of shoes. I tell you there is no *génie* to this business but *don* and taste—I happen to have both. I make my dresses like a watch—if one tiny little wheel doesn't work, I remake the dress. A dress isn't right if it is uncomfortable, if it doesn't 'walk' properly. A dress must function or *on n'y tient pas*. Elegance in clothes means being able to move freely, to do anything with ease.

"I shall show a collection on the fifth of February—maybe it will not be what is expected of me. Sometimes, *j'ai le trac*. I make everything in my collection, from bathing suits to evening dresses, one personality all the way through. Not like those houses where *modelistes* do some things, the designer another, there is no unity—with me I do everything down to the last button. And on the subject of buttons: no button without a buttonhole.

"Look at today's dresses: strapless evening dresses cutting across a woman's front like this [she cut an angry finger across her own]. Nothing is uglier for a woman: boned horrors, that's what they are. As soon as a woman is over twenty, she can't show all her upper arm that way; she needs the grace of a little something over the shoulders, or over the top of the arms. Nothing shows age more than the upper arms, the arms in general, and the hands, then the neck, then the face. I wouldn't want to sit in a sleeveless dress next to a girl of twenty. I introduced the strapless dress, it's true; but gracefully done, with 1830 feminine charm. And these heavy dresses that won't pack into airplane luggage, ridiculous. All those boned and corseted bodices—out with them. What's the good of going back to the rigidity of the corset? A woman in an evening dress like that has to hold herself like this [and she ramrodded, chin thrust forward].

"Now women go in for simpler lives—the big receptions are gone, the way of living has changed—small apartments, no servants. No good having dresses that must be ironed by a maid each time you put them on. No good *des robes a grand tralala.*

"My collection won't be a punch on the nose, it is not to disconcert. It will not be too simple—women don't want to dress like their concierges. Changes must not be brutal, be made all of a sudden—the eye must be given time to adapt itself to a new thought. It will be a collection made by a woman, with love. I want to make women look pretty and young.

"I once made a sudden change in fashion. Working on the collection, in 1929, I believe, I first lengthened evening skirts to below the knee, then I gradually brought them down to the ankles. My vendeuses wept when they saw what was happening; my people were in despair on the day of the presentation. I had been seeing it for two months, so it no longer looked strange to me. Afterward everyone had to follow me. As Monsieur Bendel used to say to me, I made the wholesale dress trade—because, before Chanel, dresses were too complicated to be copied *en gros.*

"I am no longer interested in dressing a few hundred women, private clients; I shall dress thousands of women. But [and this seemed the core of her fashion philosophy] a widely repeated fashion, seen everywhere, cheaply produced, must start from luxury. At the top of the pinnacle—*le point de départ* must be luxe.

"I have always been copied by others. Half the women

one sees today are wearing Chanel (inspired) dresses. If a
fashion isn't taken up and worn by everybody, it's not a fashion but an eccentricity, a fancy dress. An eccentric dress
doesn't make an eccentric—a woman is just as dull in an eccentric dress if she is dull without it.

"I want mannequins with bosoms and hips, with a real
shape. I don't care about their faces, they must have elegance.
Today's look [she struck a pose characterizing hollow-cheeked
fashion models], *c'est l'élégance des cimetières.* They aren't
women, *ce sont des ombres.* [Here she confirmed that her mannequins at one time wore hideous white cotton stockings:
plain faces and those stockings kept attention riveted on the
dresses.]

"The most important things are health and joie de vivre.
To diet and be underfed in order to lose weight—then one
looks sad! What difference do a few kilos make? To be good-
tempered and young in spirit is what counts. I tell these women
who only gossip and say unpleasant things, 'Nothing makes
you uglier than being malicious.' And if one wears ridiculous
clothes or a silly-looking hat, it makes one bad humored.

"Women's clothes must be more glamorous, even Romanesque. Dresses are never gracious and flattering enough.
My dresses make women look young. Women must do anything not to age, in their appearance and outlook. Aging is a
state of mind, one must keep enthusiasm and curiosity. I said
to a twenty-five-year-old friend of mine, 'My poor girl, how
very old you are!' She wasn't interested in anything. Americans are wrong to overestimate very young girls—these are
not the only beautiful women; for me, women become interesting after forty.

"Real elegance means elegance in manners, too. Look at
women at table—how they take out boxes and things between courses, put them on the table—they are not even
pretty most of the time, these objects [and she screwed up
her face, dabbing at it with an imaginary powder puff, then
scrubbed her lips with a nonexistent lipstick]. How can one
be elegant doing that? And all those women who leave lip-

stick all over table napkins and on glasses. I tell them, when you come to my house, I will provide you with paper napkins, my table linen is too fine to be spoiled by you. Yes, elegance in living is very important.

"You ask what I feel to be my most important contribution to fashion history? Perhaps the suppression of many things . . . no, the ensemble of what I did, not one thing. I began by making sweaters because I didn't know how to make other things; I began my career not knowing how even to sew on a button. Then I discovered I could do everything. I worked with enthusiasm, with love. Nothing distracted me from my work, or does now. I am implacable. I do everything myself. I won't fit a client, but I'll spend hours on my knees in front of a mannequin perfecting a dress. I give sketches to my ateliers, showing exactly how I want a dress to be put together; then I work on the figure, it is really sculpture. I always respect the body, and let it move freely under my clothes. No false bosoms, making breasts like bombs [she plucked her blue sweater into two points]. My men friends say it is no pleasure to dance with a woman wearing armor, they want to feel a living body.

"It is deplorable that women all dress alike—to please each other rather than to please men. Look at them, playing canasta, all dressed in the identical 'little black,' screwing up their faces over their cards. Why waste all that time over massage, pedicures, depilations, hairdressers, to reach this uniform result? Anyhow, I find that men have better taste and judgment about clothes than women. When I want an opinion about what I have done, I ask some men friends to come in and tell me what they think: not professionals in the couture, just friends. I value their reactions much more than women's. Women should always bring a man with them when choosing dresses. A woman friend will probably give them an insincere opinion; the man can be trusted.

"About this collection: I am starting with the most difficult, *des petites robes de sport*. They are the basis of a collection, but they are not what is suitable for photographs, or drawings, or descriptions. I am making many cocktail dresses—this category didn't exist before, I never made any before. And, of course, dresses for *les belles soirées de printemps*, many of these. A woman can never be overdressed in my clothes; nothing is worse than being overdressed, and that goes for the mind too. A woman showing off intellectually is as bad as a woman wearing satin for breakfast. Now women have started showing naked shoulders at five o'clock, even at the races; that never existed before. It must come from all the nakedness on beaches; people lose their sense of the appropriate."

The telephone rang; someone suggesting a mannequin for Chanel. *"Elle n'a plus ses vingt-cinq ans?"* Coco echoed her interlocutor. *"Alors, moi je les lui donnerai!"*

This break, the only one since we arrived, made it possible for the first time to look fleetingly at the surroundings. (Not a pause ever, she didn't even light a cigarette.) For she projects the tentacles of her talk with such intensity, riveting one with her black tragic gaze, that for over an hour I saw nothing but herself. Only now did I take in a fabulous Louis XIV clock—a wonderful baroque pile of bronze—a sober, imposing mirror, Louis XIV too, in a gold frame with double coat of arms on top, flanked with exuberant Italian baroque gilded wood scrolls and cherubs, in an entirely different tempo. On a low table in front of the sofa, the clear cool surfaces of Chinese rock crystal, rose quartz, jade animals: "I always arrange them in couples, somehow it seems *plus gentil.*"

In her four-room apartment, Chanel lives, has meals, and receives friends, but she actually sleeps at the Ritz. "If I didn't have to go out to sleep, I would never get out at all, and I don't like to sleep in a room where I've been during the day, filled with objects—just white walls, empty space, and quiet for real rest."

The apartment is dimly lit and filled with treasures of the most diversified periods—all of superb quality. Throughout her famous collection of Coromandel screens. She likes moving her objects around and buying new ones. She is impatient with the idea of decorating in one style. ("How ridiculous to say 'this Louis XV chair won't go in my Empire room.' If the elements are beautiful, that's all that matters.") She enjoys ruling out architectural demands in a room by a lavish use of mirrors ("I've made small rooms large and large rooms small by my mirrors"). She loves large pieces of furniture in a small room—note the outsized sofa in her living room.

Chanel was back again (the small boy's figure, furrowed face, flat shoes). The web of words began again, this time to be interrupted by knocks on the door. Chanel sprang to her feet. "*Je viens, je viens,*" and to us, "Now you must go—but you must come back. Yes. I'll show you my dresses, and look, I'm arranging a new room." She opened a door, a glimpse of dark Coromandel screens with fan designs. "Come back and I'll show you everything, and we'll talk!"

At first, the new Chanel collection seemed dead on arrival. The neat little suits, the easy-to-wear black dresses, looked déjà vu. Where was the explosion of the new that was expected?

Karl Lagerfeld, that canny seismograph who was to take over the Chanel house in 1983, summed up, many years later, his reactions: "You had a feeling you were seeing something prehistoric, but I loved this look that harked back to a prewar world I hadn't known but found more intoxicating than any current fashion.

"Chanel was so alive and intuitive, and she found the right compromise between her style and the 1950s look."

The press was damning. "A fiasco" was the verdict of London's *Daily Express.* But her American fans, including Carmel Snow at *Harper's Bazaar,* beat the drums for her. And it worked. She had done it again. By January 1971, when she died, sales were zooming. She had made a positive of retro designs that evoked what people had loved decades earlier—but always with a witty twist. She had tapped into the zeitgeist and given the look they wanted.

Visiting Karl Lagerfeld

Almost forty years after my visit to Chanel, Anna Wintour, the editor of *Vogue*, sent me to Paris to interview Karl Lagerfeld, Chanel's present mastermind.

Unlike some of us who might wish to change our physical appearance and take on a new persona, Karl Lagerfeld has actually done it. The original model, whom I met in 1991, was a thick-set, solid man in a dark suit (made in Japan), a white shirt, black tie, a discreet cameo for a tiepin, gray hair pulled back in a ponytail, black glasses de rigueur.

The dark glasses are still there, but the image has dwindled: an unforgiving diet and an iron will—no alcohol, a low, low no-cal drink—have honed Lagerfeld to a Giacometti look-alike, ninety-two pounds gone, and they stay gone.

The hair is bleached snow-white. There is a stiff white collar as wide as a hand, the skinniest of jeans, various metallic hand embellishments, fingerless gloves.

If there had been a Shakespearean stage direction for our first meeting, it would have been "Enter, talking."

What has not changed is the rapid-fire, flat staccato voice. It greeted me on my arrival and continued with nary a largo. French and English moved seamlessly in and out of the talk. Had I been proficient in German and Danish, no doubt those languages would have come into play. Karl is of German and Danish extraction.

He told me, "If I had not been in fashion, I would have studied languages. My big regret is that I don't speak more languages. I have French, English, German, and vaguely Italian. I'd like to know Russian, Spanish, Swedish (which I can understand), and Danish because I come from that area."

He told me, "I love your English." I learned that before meeting me, he had acquired some of my tapes and played them. It shows how thoroughly he watches his publicity. He commented on my name: "Rosamond. That's the English spelling. Not like Schubert's Rosamunde. It's like Rosamond Lehmann." And it is, of course. But I wondered how many people in Paris still remembered the author of a once ubiquitous novel, *Dusty Answer*.

He said, "I can never have enough dictionaries. I want to know everything. Life is a continuing lesson. There is not a stupid subject."

And "I want to *have* everything" might be added to the mantra. That includes houses, clothes, works of art, books, people.

He has owned a number of houses in a number of places and disposed of them all. When I first met him, he occupied, and had restored at vast expense, a splendid eighteenth-century Paris mansion, of the kind referred to in French as an *hôtel particulier*. It was furnished in the grandest eighteenth-century style: all the furniture had pedigrees like racehorses. Of the stupendous Savonnerie carpet in magenta and clear yellow, he let drop, "Louis XV ordered it."

At the time of my visit, he referred to an apartment he had had in Monte Carlo: "All Memphis furniture—I only went to Monte Carlo for the annual Grand Prix automobile races, so I got rid of it." What he didn't say is that he is a frequent visitor to Monte Carlo because of his close friendship with Princess Caroline (the daughter of Grace Kelly and Prince Rainier). To his credit, he never name-drops.

He had had a mansion in Biarritz, which he described as completely refurbished and stocked with over two thousand books and a full contingent of servants. "I realized I hadn't visited the place in two years, so I sold it."

There were passing references, usually punctuated with "Hmm?" to his Art Deco collection that had furnished an apartment near Saint-Sulpice. "It looked too much of a set." All gone now. And there was a Wiener Werkstätte ensemble, a high-tech apartment, and a group of Pop Art artists. "I bought David Hockney and Tom Wesselmann and the others, but when it got to be such a trend, I gave them away as Christmas presents."

Now the whole grand eighteenth-century package of the Paris *hôtel particulier* and its furnishing has left the radar. Karl has acquired several floors of a handsome house on the Quai Voltaire and no doubt will surprise us when he has finished with its transformation.

He claimed he was in a minimalist mood, and he spoke about wanting one day a really modern house—like one designed by Tadao Ando. Where to live has always been a presiding passion. It is an inherited trait. His very entry into the world hung on the choice of a house. His father was a Swedish widower in Hamburg, his mother a divorced German.

"But she knew what she wanted. When my father took her to see the house he had built for himself, she said, 'I'm very sorry, but this is a horrible house. Anyone can see that a widower built it. I'll never marry you in this house.'

"So they walked around the city until they saw a very pretty neoclassical Biedermeier house in a big park, and then she said to my father, 'I'll marry you if you buy this house. Otherwise, forget it.'

"So they got married. I was born ten years later."

Like Catherine the Great, Lagerfeld obviously believes in excess. According to a recent documentary about his living quarters, there are reams of shelves with what looked like hundreds of those collars and white shirts, hundreds of fingerless gloves, dozens of pairs of jeans, belts laid out in the hundreds, a treasure trove of necklaces, rings, brooches, buckles, clasps, pins.

In a separate room, there are some dozen clothes racks on wheels with some five hundred suits, all in shades of gray or black.

Clearly, Lagerfeld does not subscribe to the "less is more" school. According to a profile in *The New Yorker* by John Colapinto, these days Lagerfeld is apt to appear with a large belt buckle "encrusted with diamonds" and wearing a tie "looped with silver chains" that is "fixed with a jade Cartier clasp" from the 1920s. He wears "fingerless black biker gloves" that bear "silver grommets" on each knuckle. A "chunky Chrome Hearts ring" worn over the glove completes the look.

Like the eighteenth-century French encyclopedists Diderot and d'Alembert, who believed everything worth knowing could be listed and classified, Lagerfeld wants to know everything, especially about what is happening right now.

For this he has an immense collection of books, and magazines and publications of all kinds, spilling out from a succession of rooms. He has read a surprising number of them. How he can find the time is utterly mysterious—and in four languages. The fact is that he really loves books, and even has his own bookstore at 7, rue de Lille. It specializes in his particular interests—fashion, photography, poetry, architecture, history, and design—and he has his own imprint.

Incidentally, he is a highly proficient photographer who has been exhibited abroad and does many of the publicity shoots for Chanel.

I am perhaps one of the few people who remembers that the well-publicized Freudian analyst Jacques Lacan practiced and lived at the same address where Lagerfeld now has his bookstore.

After my interview with him appeared in 1992 in *Vogue*, for years, heavy packages of the latest books and art catalogs would arrive from La Hune, the best Paris bookstore, sent by Karl.

He had not met my husband, John Russell, but admired him. He told me, "Let me know when John is next in Paris." In due course he arranged a lunch with just the kinds of people John might enjoy. The director of the Versailles Library was one of them.

After lunch we did a tour of some of the book-filled rooms, books overflowing on a succession of tables, even on the floor. Karl noticed John had picked up a book by Paul Léautaud, a seldom-read author today. Next day, he sent around a copy to where we were staying.

Not so long ago, unexpectedly, I got a note from Karl, handwritten, as usual: "Tell your husband I enjoyed his translation of Roger Martin du Gard." Who else would even have heard of this author?

It may not be long lasting, but his generosity is princely. After our first encounter in 1991, he sent me right to the Chanel Boutique. I understood I was to choose something. I chose a suit in black. "But it comes in red too, don't you like red?" the chic salesperson asked me. I explained that I thought I was only to choose one thing. "But you don't understand, madame, Monsieur Lagerfeld wanted you to have everything!" And I got everything: not just the outfit, but the blouse, the shoes, the gloves, the costume jewelry. And that went on for a decade, every time I stopped by the boutique when I came to Paris.

And at each arrival in Paris, there would be such an opulent arrangement of flowers from Karl that it practically took an Olympian weight lifter to deliver them.

What do you give the man who has everything? I owned two complete sets of the years I edited *L'ŒIL*, my magazine, handsomely bound, each year in a different color (1955 to 1970). They were my most precious possessions. I got a hefty messenger—they were extremely heavy—to deliver one set to Karl's residence, with my note (in French): "I have given you the best of myself."

Some years ago, John and I came to Paris to go to the eightieth birthday ball of the very erudite Baroness Elie de Rothschild (she and John had just celebrated fifty years of friendship). I was wearing a pink ruffled dress by Carolina Herrera. Karl, a fellow guest, complimented me extravagantly on my appearance. Next day, a sketch from memory of me in that dress arrived. I can't imagine any other designer making such a gesture. I sent the sketch on to Carolina.

It is inevitable that a certain ruthlessness is involved in Karl's determination to keep renewal at the forefront of his preoccupations. People are not exempt. This remarkable man is an immensely disciplined perpetual-motion machine, in quest of—if not eternal youth—the eternal new.

He hates nostalgia. It's new trends, new ideas, new people, new favorites. This entails sloughing off old baggage, human or material, but renewal is the name of the game.

Once Upon a Time:
Life at Mouton Rothschild

I first started going to Mouton—as it was called *tout
court*—in the mid-1950s. My friend Pauline Potter, an American
educated in Paris, had married Baron Philippe de Rothschild, owner
of the famous wine château Mouton Rothschild, in 1954. Then began the union of money with taste and determination.

Pauline had decided that life *chez elle* would be exceptional, and
it was. The attention ranged from the sharpened pencils, magnifying glass, and pads by each guest telephone to the bottle of scotch
and its accompanying soda on the night table of every male guest,
following English country house tradition.

The visit began with the visitor's suitcase or suitcases being immediately unpacked and the contents stored away.

Each bathroom was an oasis of Guerlain soaps, Floris bath oil,
and scented potted plants. The bath was drawn by the *femme de
chambre*, of course. Denise, the *femme de chambre* who had been
allotted to me, whisked away any garment that might have touched
my skin so rapidly that once, having arrived with only one evening
bra, I took to hiding it.

The bed linen was of gossamer fabric. The turndown sheet was
starched and pleated, with an in-and-out wide strip of satin ribbon.
Every morning two maids in pink uniforms would arrive with a
small ironing board and an iron and meticulously re-pleat the top
sheet. In fact, anytime a body rested on a bed, however briefly, the
iron came into play. Incidentally, Philippe chose to have a maid, not
a butler, take care of his needs.

The breakfast trays were little masterpieces with every kind of
toast, croissant, jams, a pat of butter like the moon, and a minute

basket of pansies. The only sounds that could be heard at breakfast time were the cooing of the doves and the gravel of the driveway being raked into perfect shape by a small man in a black beret who was at it even on Sundays.

Although called a château, the original building was not a castle but an old Victorian house, with a warm crimson Napoleon III décor of tassels and poufs, a carpet celebrating the Anglo-French alliance with full-length figures of the English queen and the French emperor, and a full-length portrait of Philippe's wasp-waisted mother. Philippe told me that she kept her figure by picking delicately at unshelled baby shrimps throughout the gargantuan dinners of the period.

Soon Philippe and Pauline had taken over the spaces adjoining and over the original cellar, henceforth called Grand Mouton (as opposed to the old house, Petit Mouton), and added a long living room overlooking the vines, a series of handsome bedrooms, and a library. This long gallery was paved with faded pink tiles copied from a medieval manuscript. The grand décor combined Renaissance sculpture, Venetian chairs, some pieces of baroque sculpture. A rare foray from Philippe's bachelor days, when he was a famous racing-car driver: a gleaming Brancusi *Bird in Space*, with its suggestion of speed. In his racing days, Philippe was known at railroad crossings because he would toss out gold coins to the gatekeeper, who hurried to let him through ahead of other competitors. A contrast to the Brancusi was the immaterial, freestanding Giacometti.

"When you live in the country, you need variety," the Baronne Philippe said. The tables for those famous meals at Mouton were set in different rooms from both houses: the long gallery over the vines, a small intimate salon, the library, a corner of the house, and even . . . the dining room.

At lunch there were patterned Provençal tablecloths. They were inventoried, and a sample of each was pasted in a book so Pauline could point at what she wanted for that day. The same was true of an enormous set of Creil dishes, each with a different printed illustrated scene, collected all over France. Each model was photographed, numbered, and listed in an album. To choose the set for the next day's lunch, the hostess just had to indicate the desired number. Even for a long visit, guests never saw the same series twice.

This system was borrowed from Marie Antoinette, who had swatches of her dresses in albums. She would place a pin in the one she wanted to wear that day or evening.

For dinner, there were always white tablecloths and eighteenth-century porcelain. Table landscapes were created by a woman trained by Pauline who collected ferns, grasses, branches, berries, and whatever was at hand that season and built little still lifes in the middle of the table, directly on the tablecloth.

At dinner there were usually five wines, served in identically sized glasses, which made a crystal garland around the table. Each guest had a card listing the menu and the wines. Wine was served in tall-necked beakers, the neck tied around with a kerchief dyed wine red, a custom from the austerity period postwar, when laundry was difficult with little soap available.

On occasions when really great vintages were to be served, the *maître de chais*, not a butler, came himself to pour the wines, wearing a wine-colored jacket.

Philippe often seated me next to him, not because of any particular charm on my part, but because he knew me so well that I was no effort. He would place his foot firmly over mine under the table, and I thought, if it gives him any pleasure, why not?

The inventive, really historic, meals were presided over by the chef, Maisemain. Pauline had poached him from Princess Marthe Bibesco, from whom she had rented an apartment each year when she was on furlough from her job as designer at Hattie Carnegie, New York. Maisemain was only a modest *homme à tout faire* at the time, but Pauline sensed his potential and whisked him away, to the fury of the princess. When Pauline took over the Bibesco apartment for her Parisian stay, she used to bring her own luxurious curtains that trailed to the floor.

When I left France for New York, I found a cache of Mouton menu cards dating from the 1950s to 1969. Some samples:

Le 30 Octobre 1960

FILETS DE SOLES AU CAVIAR
BAS ROND DE PRE-SALE ROTI
RIZ AUX RAISINS

PETITS NAVETS AU BEURRE
ARTICHAUTS FARCIS
SALADE
FROMAGES
GLACE AU CITRON

Margaux 1934
Haut-Brion 1908
Mouton Rothschild 1881
Yquem 1937
Moulin 1909

Le 4 Janvier 1964

CREME DE MOULES
POULET A LA RUSSE
SOUFFLE STAUNTON HILL
SALADE
FROMAGES
GLACE AU RHUM
POMMES GLACEES

Riesling 1949
Lafite 1949
Mouton Rothschild 1929
Mouton Rothschild 1879
Climens 1929

It was of course black tie every night, and for women practically ball gowns were encouraged. Balenciaga made a series of billowing creations for Pauline to wear for Mouton evenings. She called them "*mes Moutons.*"

Guests were expected to hold up their end, preferably in at least two languages. There were often English guests, literary types such as Stephen Spender and Raymond Mortimer. No excuses of headaches or any other ailment were allowed; you were expected to perform regardless of the fact that you might have just heard some very bad news.

There was a steely, relentless quality to Pauline. If someone who had been an intimate friend for all her New York years was introduced to Philippe and Philippe found her boring, that person was dropped irrevocably and never heard from again. On the other hand, a future biographer of the Rothschild family was courted assiduously, his wife given luxurious presents from Dior. The Philippe de Rothschilds received extra favorable coverage in the family biography.

Pauline, a great reader, kept stacks of books in baskets under her bed. She went to bed later and later, and emerged for meals later and later. At night, she was always the last to appear for dinner. Cecil Beaton said her appearance was a work of art. She created the aura of a beautiful woman through sheer will, although in fact she was not a beauty.

Philippe had thought for some time of creating a museum that would marry works of art with the making and drinking of wine. In 1962, with the impetus of Pauline's flair and energy, the pair began assembling the contents of a Museum of Wine in Art. They had a spectacular head start with the collection of seventeenth-century vermeil ceremonial pitchers and goblets inherited by Philippe from his great-grandfather Carl von Rothschild—very much in what was called "*le goût Rothschild.*"

The pair traveled from America to Anatolia on their treasure hunt. Soon cases began rolling into the vast hangars of the domain: exotic objects, elaborately mounted, so-called unicorn horns, nautilus shells, ostrich eggs, coconut shells . . .

A suite of fifteenth-century tapestries shows some stylishly dressed young men in miniskirts harvesting grapes. There is a jade cup from Agra, English monteith bowls, seventeenth-century Venetian glass, blue-and-white Chinese porcelain, still lifes by Willem Heda and Georg Flegel. The twentieth century is represented by a Picasso sketch, a Rouault, a Juan Gris, and a wire sculpture by the American Richard Lippold.

These were displayed in rooms adjacent to the vast, always cool, musty-smelling cellar, where there were barrels of Mouton Rothschild as far as the eye could see. Pauline had lined the museum cases in raw silk, in various shades of eggshell.

I had been in on the project since the beginning, and before the museum opened, I worked with my photographer to prepare a feature for *L'ŒIL*. I chose the objects, but instead of shooting them in their cases, I placed them in unexpected backgrounds: like chess pieces on the tiled floor, or emerging from forests of cobwebs in Philippe's own private cellar, where he kept his most precious bottles.

I got to know the museum so well that I was pressed into service as guide to the various notables, including André Malraux, who arrived. I had everything except a guide's uniform.

There were two particularly grand dinners on consecutive nights to mark the opening. Philippe insisted that the menu be identical for each so he would not be tempted to overeat.

Mouton continues today under the skillful guidance of Philippe's daughter, Philippine. Obviously, Mouton has changed as the world has changed—no more pleated sheets—but the high standards for excellence nevertheless remain. Philippine, whose background as an accomplished actress might not be expected to form an accomplished businesswoman, has multiplied the Mouton activities worldwide and maintained Mouton itself as a continuing delight for her friends.

Louise Bourgeois,
a Loving Memory

I had the privilege of seeing Louise Bourgeois very often starting in 1995, when I was preparing to lecture about her at the Metropolitan Museum. Naturally, I knew her work, which I very much admired, but I hadn't met her before.

I was warned that she was extremely difficult; she was very small but very fierce and apt to show the interviewer the door after five minutes. It was with some trepidation that I telephoned to ask for an appointment. "But of course come over, in fact come tomorrow, to the Brooklyn studio," I heard to my surprise. We were speaking in French (the best possible introduction), and we almost always spoke in French from then on, with free swings into her highly idiomatic but charmingly French-inflected English.

The Brooklyn studio was an immense former industrial space that had become a forest of disciplined clutter. Later, she talked about the role of clutter in the family life. Meanwhile, rounded-off spaces were filled with rusty implements whose function had long been forgotten, found objects, made objects, reflecting surfaces everywhere—mirrors, glass, shiny bronze, marble—textiles, dilapidated chairs.

All this was about to be moved out for a major exhibition where these disparate objects would take their places as sheer magic.

The sculptor herself was a diminutive figure in her always personal assemblage of mysterious overgarments, trousers, baseball cap, chains, and boots. Shrewd, mischievous, appraising blue eyes.

By her side, towering above her, was her indispensable assistant and friend, Jerry Gorovoy. It would be more accurate to qualify him as her guardian angel. He warded off angst, intruders, the corrosion of daily living, not to mention that he was the globe-trotting installer par excellence of her exhibitions all over the world.

After this, Louise allowed me to visit her often at her narrow lair on West Twentieth Street, where she had lived since 1960.

This is where she used to meticulously iron *The New York Times* every morning and flame a spoon and slide it directly into the jam pot for her breakfast. "No toast," she explained, "but no germs."

She told me that all her subjects for at least the last sixty years found their inspiration in her childhood. It has never lost its magic, its mystery for her. "I need my memories, they are my documentation," she said.

As we all know from the movies and the great French novelists, French family life is often full of secrets not quite covered up and hatreds that leave their mark for a lifetime.

Louise grew up in a large house at Choisy-le-Roi outside of Paris. It was very large because some thirty people lived and worked there, besides the family. The family business was repairing tapestries. Living with tapestries was a form of education for her, she said. "Through tapestries I learned what I did not learn in school: stories from the Old Testament, and the New Testament, antiquity, history, mythology.

"The characters from the Old Testament were crafty and bloodthirsty. People just loved that. The New Testament was full of pieties. As subject for tapestries they had no appeal. Scandalous subjects were successful. Pious ones bored people."

There were elements in the Choisy house that made her feel unwanted, betrayed. One was the fact that her father already had two daughters and had no wish for another. Louise's tactful mother tried to mollify him: "Can't you see she looks exactly like you, *comme deux gouttes d'eau* [like two drops of water]?"

The betrayal that was to haunt her for many years was the fact that in 1922 a young Englishwoman called Sadie came to live in the house. Ostensibly, she was there to teach Louise English, but very soon it was clear that she was sleeping with her father and had been engaged for that purpose.

Sadie lived in the house ten years. Louise said, "The motivation for my work is a negative reaction against her. It is the anger that makes me work. I thought she was going to like me; instead, she betrayed me. I was betrayed not only by my father but by her too."

I had a lively example of this simmering resentment. One time when I was visiting Louise, she was showing me a video that had been made from a montage of family photographs. She told me she has some 650 family snaps and has always kept diaries faithfully. As she put it, "The story of the past is very present. Everything is documented."

We each had a mug of tea and a plate of cookies. As she watched the faded images—so vivid to her—she suddenly let out a cry: "Jerry, stop the film there, right there!" And he had to back up to get the right picture on the screen. It showed a debonair figure, her father, in front of the mantelpiece. You could dimly make out a bust behind him.

It was a Houdon bust of the Princesse de Lamballe that made the most of her generous endowments.

"I just hated that bust," Louise almost hissed. It evoked the father's numerous dalliances. "Every night I dreamed of smashing it."

"Did you ever do it?" I asked.

"Of course not, but I destroyed it in my heart. And to this day I hate terra-cotta, I hate ceramics, I hate porcelain."

Then, to my amazement, she grabbed the plate of cookies and flung it onto the floor, breaking it with a dramatic crash. Then she crunched the pieces into the floor, stamping on them with her boots.

Then she burst out laughing, and our conversation continued as before.

Louise's memories were not only embedded in photographs and diaries. Once I was allowed into her attic, and there hanging in rows were all her old clothes from girlhood on and all those of her late husband—the primitive-art historian Robert Goldwater.

With French frugality and ingenuity, she used snippets of material from them to clothe the stuffed figures she made in 1996.

Because Louise never stopped working, when the physical labor involved in sculpture became too much for her, she made large-scale engravings, drawings, gouaches. She was an insomniac, and at night—besides listening to rock bands on the radio—she drew, endlessly, on music paper. A few years ago, the Hermitage Museum of

St. Petersburg presented a large exhibition of these Insomniac Draw-ings, some 220 sheets, giving them a noble imprimatur.

We talked about the Left Bank quarter in Paris, where we both had lived. "That neighborhood is very dear to me," she said. "I was born above the Café de Flore. My brother and I amused ourselves by throwing our mother's scissors out of the window and over the balcony. We aimed them at passersby on the street.

"*C'était méchant*. But what happened was that the scissors always got stuck in the awning outside the Flore, so we never hit anybody.

"My mother never got her scissors back. But she wasn't fussy. She just said, 'Well, my scissors seem to have gone again.' She never ac-cused us.

"This was quite another age. Montparnasse was all the rage at that time, and Saint-Germain-des-Prés was completely provincial. The Flore was just a little café for the locals. We are talking now of 1922–23."

An important element in Louise's formation was her school, the Lycée Fénelon. She still remembered the names of all the girls in her class and had written their names on the back of the class photograph.

"It is not so much what I learned there. It was the discipline that it gave me. When you come out of Fénelon you know that you are a disciplined person. And it is a help in everything. If you can over-come it, push it away, manipulate it; that is a help too.

"It's like manners. You don't have to have good manners, but if you have them, they can be of help to you.

"My French intellectual background is very important to me.

"But it was not a social education. The lycée taught us every-thing except how to deal with other people. Being logical, being very severe and pure, does not make you a diplomat."

I asked if she saw that as a shortcoming.

"Absolutely, I missed being a diplomat. That is why my work means so much to me. It is a compensation for my difficulty in deal-ing smoothly and evenly with people."

On one of my visits Louise talked about her father—he came up very often in these conversations. "It took me a long time to make peace with him," she said, "but now I feel—well, the guy was not very good—he was awful. But, first of all, I owe him life. My parents told us that all the time. 'If you are in this world, it is because we gave you life.'"

"Many people would say, 'I did not ask to be here.' But I am not like that."

She said that it was because of her father that she was always surrounded by sculptures. "He was really crazy about sculpture; he collected lead sculptures. Our garden at Saint-Cloud was full of them.

"He had his big Panhard, all his other cars. He was always on the road, looking for sculptures. He would put them on the rumble seat.

"He never knew that I made sculptures; he would never have tolerated it. He detested artists. They were always out to steal other people's wives, he said. He was projecting of course. As he saw it, every artist was out to swipe his daughter.

"So he put his sculptures all over the garden. Apollo was a favorite subject. My mother would not have allowed them in the house. We had great respect for my mother's wishes—no cluttering allowed.

"No cluttering became the number one characteristic of the house. We had no animals indoors, no dogs, no cats, for that reason. Tapestry doesn't clutter. You fold it up, and it doesn't take any room.

"My father collected chair frames, but they did not clutter the house, because they were hanging from the ceiling, in the attic.

"Hanging is safe, and it allows for a lot of movement. So the floor belonged to my mother and her tapestries."

Louise said she still had this very much in her mind's eye. Suspended ladders and suspended plants turn up in her work of the 1940s. Many years later she used rubber in the ambiguous image of two elongated legs, which hang from the ceiling.

In the 1960s Louise started working with marble and going to the Henraux quarry at Forte dei Marmi, just below Carrara in Italy. She said it was not a great change for her to work in marble.

She told me that if you are making an outdoor sculpture, it is important to have the right kind of marble and to know what not to do with it. If you leave a small chink, and if rain falls into it and it freezes, the marble will crack.

"That is why there is so much marble in Italy, where there is supposedly no freezing point. In the North you have to use granite or bronze. That is why there is Rodin in France and archaic sculpture in Greece."

By a fortunate coincidence, Louise met Henry Moore at Forte dei Marmi, where he had a studio. Henry didn't stay there during the hottest months, so he lent the space to Louise.

As Louise tells it, "One day Henry Moore came into the studio to find a chisel, or something, and there I was. He was very friendly, and he didn't waste his time.

"He didn't talk about himself. He talked exclusively about sculpture. There was nothing that he didn't know about marble.

"I was very impressed by his simplicity, his direct style, and his professionalism. I was very impressed by his wife too. She was a no-nonsense Russian woman.

"We were lucky because we met in the studio, with lots of plaster around. He felt at ease and I felt at ease. It was not personal. It was really a matter of talking shop."

The architecture of the human body—its elements and appendages—is a recurring theme in Louise Bourgeois's work. Hands in particular are as revealing to her as faces. "I consider the hands a signature," she told me.

During the summer when I was visiting Louise every week, my husband, John Russell, was grounded by a torn Achilles tendon. His leg was in a cast, and he was in a wheelchair. Very solicitously, she always asked, "How is John?"

Then she announced that she was making me a present—a cast of my hands. After a pause, she added, "And of John's hands too." Another pause, then she said, "And of his foot too, as soon as he is out of his wheelchair."

So eventually we were summoned to the Brooklyn studio, where a plaster technician was in attendance. A board was put on my lap. John gamely put his large foot across it. Louise posed our four hands and the foot in question, and we became an instant Bourgeois composition.

We were coated with Vaseline, and the technician whipped up a great soufflé of plaster.

Our appendages were plunged deep into the plaster. It took two full hours to harden.

"It's an act of faith," Louise commented. "You can say that

again," I muttered. This was especially true when the plaster specialist hacked at the hardened mound with an enormous knife.

The plaster shattered into a hundred fragments as he prized us out. I would have thought them irretrievable, but somehow, unlike Humpty Dumpty, they all got put together again and turned into a mold.

We thought it indiscreet to inquire about our plaster alter-members. Then one night in November, when I was about to give a lecture on Louise at the Metropolitan Museum, we suddenly saw ourselves—or rather, selected parts of ourselves—right there on the stage. Louise had managed as a surprise to have it installed next to the podium.

Subsequently, she had it sent to our apartment. And her generosity went beyond the initial gift. Two brawny men delivered a massive wooden cube that she had retrieved out of a magnificently weathered old pier. It was a perfect base for the sculpture.

I complimented her on her jocular colloquialisms in English. She referred to herself as a fussbud-GET. She referred to an unreliable person who made things up out of ALL CLOTH. She said she owes her easygoing English to her family: her husband and her two boys. "When I married my husband, Robert Goldwater, in 1938, we made a pact. I would never criticize his French if he would never criticize my English. We kept to it. I make mistakes with the greatest assurance."

In spite of her deep resentment of Sadie, Louise had learned a passable amount of English during those painful years. This came to be very useful when, as a young person, she wanted to study art in Paris. Her father would not give her enough money to take courses. "Let her starve, and she'll get married" was his attitude, straight out of one of Balzac's novels.

But Paris was full of Americans who wanted to study art, and she was the only applicant who could translate for them; she got to take the studio courses for nothing.

Fernand Léger was one of her teachers. She said she learned a lot from him—much of it at a silent, unspoken, visual level.

"He was satisfied with the third dimension on canvas, but I needed to move around the object," Louise said.

Louise would not travel. For years she had not left the house. She had no interest in attending affairs in her honor or receiving awards in public. For years she asked me to go to represent her. I went to one recently, at the Municipal Art Society. Often some young person has come up to me at such an event and, looking at me admiringly, enthused, "Madame Bourgeois, I so admire your work." Sometimes I just smile modestly, accepting the praise.

Another time Louise was having a large exhibition in Finland. Hoping to tempt her, the organizers sent along a travelogue film with many a photogenic lake. Also, it seemed that the Finns have a passion for the tango. There are large halls where they come from all over Finland to dance it. There were sequences of this on the promotional film, showing impassive dancers, the men built like *des armoires à glace*, solemnly dancing the tango.

Louise ran the film for me. Then she hummed an air that she thought was a tango. "No, Louise," I said, "you are thinking of a *java*, the tango goes like this," whereupon I hummed and danced a few tango steps.

"*Voilà!*" Louise exclaimed. "Just the thing. You will go to Helsinki and dance the tango at my opening."

I said, "Louise, I would do practically anything for you, *but* no tango in Helsinki."

Sitting for David Hockney

My husband, John Russell, picked out David Hockney as a winner when David was still in the Royal College of Art, more than fifty years ago. His paintings were not like anyone else's. He himself was not like anyone, either.

He had black hair then—soon, and for most of his life, it was bleached blond—and very large glasses, which were to remain a fixture. In 1961 he made an etching called *Myself and My Heroes* in which he appears with Mahatma Gandhi and Walt Whitman; it bore a written message: "I am twenty three years old and I wear glasses."

His humor was infectious. Once he saw a picture in a Berlin museum of a leopard in full pursuit of its prey. It impressed him so much that back at his hotel, he made a drawing of it from memory and added two men standing talking in the open. Immediately above them was the leopard, coming down at top speed to make its breakfast of the two of them.

Underneath the two men he wrote, "They are perfectly safe. This is a still."

John wrote about him, "Over the next forty years it turned out that he could do just about anything that he wanted. He could paint, he could draw, he could make prints, and he could give the word 'photograph' a whole new meaning. He could give technology a fair shake.

"Along the way, he has become regarded as someone who is a joy to have around, both for what he has achieved and for his golden good nature."

We had heard on one of those frequent long-distance calls (David in London to us in New York) that David had just had his portrait painted by his old, though highly dissimilar, friend Lucian Freud.

We were naturally curious to know how it went.

He told us about it when we got back to London: "I walked from my studio to his studio. It's the prettiest walk, through Holland Park, and I was there by 8:30 every morning. I sat for him eight hours a day, for days.

"It's up six flights of stairs. He always runs up them. I would sit for several hours. But he let me smoke and talk, and I had lots and lots of marvelous conversations. His energy was fantastic.

"He works very slowly, because he scrutinizes every tone. I could tell what he was doing. He uses quite a small palette, for seven colors perhaps. He has piles of tubes, but knows at once which one he wants. Just once, he looked a little longer. I realized that he had to look longer for the blue because he hardly ever uses it."

We didn't see the portrait of David, but Lucian showed us a photograph: a solid, middle-aged Yorkshire man who knows exactly who he is.

In return, David Hockney asked Lucian to pose for him. "He agreed," David told us, "but he was not going to sit for six hours. The first time he came, he fell asleep in five minutes."

The next time he came to pose, Lucian arrived with his assistant, and the two of them sat for one of the series of double portraits that David was working on.

"They're in watercolor," we were told, "and very large—four feet by three. I may show them in London next year."

We had no idea that we might be involved in this project. But suddenly we got a message (2002) in New York from David in London, asking us if we could be at his studio in London at 8:30 a.m. on Friday, November 8. As I was lecturing at the Metropolitan Museum on the sixth, and again at the Met on the thirteenth, it was a tight schedule, but we weren't going to pass up the invitation. So we flew to London.

When he is working, David gets up early, checks the light and the weather, and prepares himself in good time. Sitters are expected to be prompt, and we were on the nose, like a Swiss express.

We had our backs to a long row of double portraits in watercolor.

As portraits in watercolor go, they were uncommonly, and quite possibly uniquely, big. Each was four feet high and three feet wide.

The sitters included some of David's painter friends—Lucian and Howard Hodgkin among them. Others, like ourselves, were invited for the ride.

Those portraits could never have been painted on one sheet of paper or on a conventional easel. The paint would have run, and the paper would have wrinkled.

So David decided to work with sheets of paper that would be of manageable size and could be laid flat on a board. Each one was twenty-four inches by eighteen inches.

Each double portrait consisted of four of those boards. Once they were fitted tightly together, they could stand tall and be hung on the wall like any other painted portrait.

Sitters were expected to pose, motionless, for six hours the first day and to be on call for a second day if needed.

Anyone who shifts by as much as an inch gets reprimanded. He works in complete silence, no talk, and no music.

Behind him, to our left, were white circular dishes, already filled with differing flesh tones and reds.

To our right were brushes, bottles of water, small glass cups to be used for mixing the pigments with water.

David in daily life is the easiest of men. But when on the job, he can look like a man on the rack. He doesn't exactly groan, but he shivers and shudders. His face darkens. He peers down at the painting as if daring it to disagree with him.

Then he looks at the sitter with one eye screwed up and his face contorted as if he had just seen an appalling sight.

His concentration was almost painful to witness. We had front-row seats, since David did most of his work standing directly in front of us, just a few feet away.

We were thoroughly looked over, in that our feet were not just auxiliaries. Feet and shoes got star billing.

The sitters sit in identical poses, side by side, but an inch or two apart. They sit on identical office chairs.

To begin with, he takes a smaller pad and roughly blocks in the two figures. Then he takes a quick look, with brush poised. If it's a small brush, he makes brief pecking motions toward the paper, or broad flat marks with a larger brush.

At the initial stage, the paper is laid flat on the board, and he paints a neutral pale gray across the upper part of the paper. It will remain unchanged as the background.

When he started on my face, he first laid a pen and then a cigarette on the paper to indicate where the top of the head should come.

Every so often he reached for his pack of cigarettes, pulled one out, lit it, took a few puffs, and then threw it on the floor and stamped it out. After a while I counted seven discarded cigarettes on the floor. "I don't smoke them much," he said, "but I can't work without them."

The sitter sees the paper at an angle that is almost but never quite horizontal. David began by taking two big panels of paper on a board and laying them flat in front of him.

The initial deposits of paint on the paper are difficult to read. They are pure color and of a purity that is rarely met, with such intensity and with so little that identifies the future subject matter.

Progress is slow but methodical. We see blobs of red and pink whose purpose we cannot identify. But there will come a moment at which, without warning, everything suddenly snaps into place. But there are none of the broad sweeps of the loaded brush that we find in what the English call swagger portraits in oils. The brushes are often tiny, as are the amounts of paint that they can carry.

Half an hour may pass before we get our bearings. Those tiny but vivacious deposits are not going to help us out. They have no volume as yet, but then we suddenly identify them as our fingers, our knees, and a flash of the light from our carefully polished shoes.

Hockney gives a gala finale to the group portrait. The shoes and feet cut a dash—if I may so put it—that the heads and shoulders don't always equal. David features John's signature red socks. It is below the ankle that some of the sitters live life to the full.

This is a high-wire act, without a net, and occasionally Hockney checks his watch. His double portraits have the tone of friendly conversation. His hand lets his eyes get on with their work. Nothing can be corrected, rubbed out, or redone. And if the result does not seem to the sitter to be "lifelike," he simply isn't interested. "That's the way I see you," he will say, if pressed.

That seemed to us a fair deal. To have sat for David Hockney was an experience, and a proof of long friendship, on a scale that does not come every day.

Jerome Robbins

In 1985, John and I were in Leningrad in one of those once-grand hotels. Our salon was peopled with large pieces of somewhat worn furniture, with the unexpected addition of a bulky Frigidaire—empty and unconnected.

There was also a small, fancy telephone, left over from some other era. We presumed its function was purely decorative. One time, to our astonishment, it rang. It was Channel 13 calling from New York to ask me to interview Jerome Robbins for their *Great Performances—Dance in America* series.

I thanked them for thinking of me but said I was not a dance critic, they must be thinking of someone else. "We didn't think of you" came the answer. "It was Jerry's idea. In fact he said that if you won't do it, he won't do it at all."

Jerry and I had been friends for many years. He had often given us tickets for his ballet performances. He had come to my lectures at the Metropolitan Museum. But our conversations were more apt to roam on such general subjects as movies, or trading recipes for exotic sherbets—he was an excellent cook.

I was touched that he had singled me out to be his interviewer. So in spite of misgivings, I finally accepted.

Some time later, we were together in a studio in New York, and Jerry proved to be as eloquent with words as he was with gesture.

Asked about his early days with Ballet Theatre—as a member of the corps de ballet—under Bronislava Nijinska, he said:

> She took an instant dislike to me. She singled me out of everyone and said, "Please do a double air turn." I don't think she

said "please," just "Do a double air turn." I did my best and landed in a fifth, slightly off balance, and had to put my foot down. She said, "Ha!" and from then on nothing I could do ever pleased her.

However, I thought *Les Noces*, a remarkable piece, one of the great works of the ballet repertory.

I also like *Les Biches* very much.

We were very fortunate because at that time—there were Fokine, Massine, Lichine . . . It was a great school for me to be able to go from rehearsal to rehearsal in the same day and work with different choreographers and see how they approached their various ballets.

It was very, very Russified. There was one year when I never got out of boots and Russian bloomers.

It was somewhat against all that that my feeling came to do something American. I thought, why must we only dance Russian subjects? We have American subjects we can dance about. Those feelings turned into *Fancy Free*—about sailors in wartime in New York.

The material for research was all there in front of us. We were at the old Met, a block away from Forty-second Street, where every sailor who came to New York gravitated. One could see them walking down the street, eyes and mouth wide open to all the sights that were New York. They usually went in threes, which struck me.

Another approach to *Fancy Free* was that I had been submitting scenarios to the company for quite a while—little things like five-act ballets [laughs]. Casts of thousands. Finally, someone wisely said to me, "Why don't you compose a scenario with just a few people which won't be difficult to put on." So I did just that, and wrote a scenario which is the basis of *Fancy Free*. They said, "Now, find yourself a composer and you can put it on this spring." So I searched and searched and found Lenny Bernstein, who was unknown then.

He had been suggested to me by a number of other composers who didn't want to bother with *Fancy Free*. They didn't know who I was, why should they spend the time.

They all said, there's this guy named Lenny Bernstein, if you can find him.

Oliver Smith, who was to design the set, said, "Oh, I know him." So I called him up and went over. I walked in and said, "I'll give you my scenario and you play me some of your music and let's see how we get on."

We both liked each other's ideas and that was that. We were off and running.

He was writing the ballet score while I was touring. We were all so young we didn't think of the complications. He would send me records, of him and sometimes even Aaron Copland, playing the music so that I would hear what the music was like.

Then I'd either write or call him and say, "I'm sorry, Variation Three is much too long, or this is too fast, or this is wonderful." This correspondence went on right until we came back off tour.

I was inventing the ballet as we toured . . . in cellars, lobbies, gyms, any place I could find room. On top of normal rehearsals and performances.

I was told I never had my nose out of the score during the whole trip. On the train, everywhere, I was fascinated by it.

The dancers that I wanted were all pals of mine, we were all in the corps de ballet, we had been bumming around together on four continents.

When the ballet was finally put on, it was a surprise, to all of us. A Hurok press agent had come and watched a rehearsal and said, "I think you're in for something here." The ballet opened, we did our best, and then came this reaction which was the wildest reaction I've ever had.

We had an unprecedented amount of curtain calls—twenty-two, which is really extraordinary. It was such an abrupt change from what the ballet audiences were used to.

The second night, we were so nervous we almost fell down, and did all the wrong things.

It was difficult being both choreographer and dancer. I had choreographed a role for myself in *Fancy Free*, the Third

Sailor. I hadn't quite finished choreographing my own variation by opening night; I think I improvised a bit.

After the success of *Fancy Free*, unfortunately, for a while,
I became known as a jazz choreographer who did New York
subjects, contemporary work. It took me a long time to dispel
that classification.

"You're very physically aware of the way people move."

Not only the way they move, the way they move in space,
because that's what ballets are about. That volume, that space,
is the stage. The drama is how people move in and around it,
or separate from each other, or more come in, or move to one
side of the stage, move forward or backward.

That is the fascination of choreography. It's an empty studio when you start a ballet and the first dancer begins. It's
rather an awesome moment because it is like putting the first
mark of ink on a piece of blank paper. From then on, your
whole structure is going to be connected to that.

I always feel that choreography is a little like building a
bridge. You start on one side, you build a step, then you build
another step, and another. The structure has to contain itself
so that it meets at the ends of the ballet and makes an architectural structure that is satisfying.

It was Oliver Smith who suggested making a musical out
of *Fancy Free*. We made the adventures of three sailors in
New York into the musical *On the Town*. We had fun doing
it. It was our first time out with the genre, there was a lot we
didn't know, we were very brash, but we got away with it.
Then that became a movie.

There was a period when I alternated doing commercial
shows and working on ballets. I sandwiched in *West Side
Story*, *Fiddler on the Roof*, and *Gypsy*, and I became a director
of those, as well as the choreographer.

How do I start a ballet? Mostly I feel that working on a
ballet is like knowing there's an island out there, which you've
heard about, and you have to find your way to it. Once you

get on it, you have to explore. By the time you finish the ballet, you've explored the island.

I don't always know how my ballets are going to end. I have to find that as I go along. I do have a conception, somewhere in the back of my head, of the total arch of the music.

I know none of the steps before I begin. I have to work that out in the studio, with the dancers. What comes out of that leads me to the next move, always guided by the perimeters . . . the perimeter is the score.

Choosing the composer, the music, is a very subjective thing. At one moment you can hear something that appeals to you because of what's going on in your life, it really hits you. Another time, you might not have reacted to it.

I know this was true of Alban Berg. When I heard a recording, I was intensely moved by it. A friend of mine pointed out that I'd heard it with him several years before. At that time, it didn't stay with me enough to want to work with it. But then I was ready for it.

I followed the actual structure of the score. That score is a marvelous cryptogram on many, many levels. The story behind it is that Alban Berg was very fond of a daughter of a friend of his, Alma Mahler. She contracted polio and died after a lot of suffering. Berg was so upset that he stopped working on *Lulu*, or the last act, and wrote this piece in memory of her. My ballet is *In Memory Of . . .* The structure of the music is a portrait of the girl, and her society, and her struggle with death, and then her transfiguration.

So much of his own biography was incorporated into that score. It was written in 1935. The Nazis were rising up. He was also very ill himself. In it are his notes about his love affairs, an illegitimate child he had when he was very young, his relationship with another woman.

All this within the structure of twelve-tone serial music. At the same time he was a wonderfully dramatic, lyric writer. Finally, the ballet should not be connected to one person, but to the sense of losing people, and the struggles they go through when they're ill and die. And hopefully, arrive at a peace for themselves.

I had a difficult time with that ballet. I got quite despairing halfway through it, up to the point where Death enters. I didn't know how to use the rest of the music. I got very depressed because the music is very depressing.

But by chance, Adam Luders was at that rehearsal. I dismissed everyone else, thinking I am going to stop the ballet here. I still had half an hour, so I said, "Come on, Adam, stand here," and I started working on a pas de deux.

I didn't know that I was going to use that music for a pas de deux until that moment. Everything opened up. I couldn't go wrong.

You have to remember I had studied the score very closely so that I knew musically what was going to happen even though I didn't yet know physically. It was almost like automatic writing. I felt I couldn't make a mistake.

The same thing happened in rehearsal with Adam and Suzanne Farrell, we all fused in an extraordinary way. I've never had a rehearsal like that, it was almost as if it had already been done. No matter what I asked them to do, it led immediately to the next thing, and then we moved on to the next.

I don't know what I will be doing next. I have a list of ballets I want to get to sooner or later, but you have to be ready for them.

Sometimes you can force yourself, and that isn't bad, the discipline can turn into something interesting.

Whenever we did our festivals that Mr. Balanchine organized, suddenly we were all doing Stravinsky ballets, or Tchaikovsky ballets, or Ravel ballets, whether we wanted to or not. And that wasn't bad discipline.

Sometimes it is good to work not where you feel the most comfortable or the most ready.

What I find about rehearsals is that on the days that I do not want to go to the theater, and do not want to choreograph, because I don't know what I am doing, and I'm the most upset about it, is the day when something happens.

As choreographers, we're stuck working not when we feel like it but when the company can arrange a rehearsal. Terp-

sichore has to come down between three and six on Friday
afternoon, even though you may feel like working between
ten and twelve.

So we have to work when we can get the dancers and when
the schedule permits it. That too is a wonderful discipline.

I did one ballet without music, called *Moves*. I had commissioned a score from Aaron Copland , this was for my own
company. He was late writing it, I was already in rehearsal.
So I'd go over to Aaron and he'd play me a fragment, and I'd
go to the rehearsal with some of the tunes and certainly the
rhythms in my head. I started to choreograph it, even though
there was no score. I was doing it to counts. Suddenly I looked
at it and thought this is very interesting without any music.

So I went ahead and choreographed the whole ballet in
silence. The dancers got used to it very fast.

It was really about what happens to roles when they're not
being danced. When *Petrushka, Giselle, Hamlet,* or *Traviata*
are not being performed, they're sort of hanging around
somewhere, waiting for an actor or a dancer or a singer to
bring them to life.

I had started a ballet called *Antique Epigraphs*, and it was
only when I got near the end that I realized that what was
haunting me were some statues in Naples at the National
Museum. Many years ago I had walked into a room, and
there were four or five bronze life-sized statues with enamel
eyes. It was like walking into the middle of a silent ritual. It
was almost alarming.

Near the end of my ballet, I turned my dancers, more or
less, into those statues. It was the idea of stillness, which we
find in Greek sculpture and vases, that comes into the ballet.

When I started the ballet, I didn't have those sculptures in
mind. It wasn't until later on that I thought, "There's something in my head that's trying to get out." Then I remembered the statues, and felt yes, this is where I was going.

For choreographers, our work is composed of our experiences, which are conscious or unconscious. Dance is so abstract, nonverbal, nonanalytical that you can't put your finger
on it, which I think is why it is so exciting.

A reason that dance is so popular now is that it is one of the few experiences that a person coming to the theater can have which they cannot have from television. It is a magical ritual of an abstract kind, a fantasy. It puts you in a place that no other theatrical experience can match.

I see dance as an experience, the way music is. When you listen to Mozart, you don't look for a story. There's this glorious sound coming at you. But some ballets can be stories, some can be more abstract. I don't think there should be any rules.

Fancy Free was as much a story ballet as you can get. I did it in 1944. The Berg, *In Memory Of*..., I did in 1985, fifty-eight ballets later. You change and see your art somewhat differently. I don't think I could ever do a ballet now like *Fancy Free*, just as in that day I never could have done *In Memory Of*...

I first met Mr. Balanchine on Broadway, when I was a chorus boy in a show he was involved with, called *Great Lady*. Then he picked me to understudy José Limón in another show he had choreographed, *Keep Off the Grass*. Then I met him on a boat coming back from Nantucket, and we had a long conversation about dance. Then I finally saw what is now the New York City Ballet. I immediately wrote him a letter and asked, "Can you use me, any way you want. Dancer, choreographer, anything." And he wrote me and said come along.

One year later I was assistant artistic director to him. It was such a privilege, such a remarkable time that any moment with him, at work or socializing or at a rehearsal, was a gift.

We shared a dressing room for many years, it was nice having those relaxing moments with him. Once he told me how much he admired my ballet *Watermill*. He said, "We choreographers get our fingertips on that world everyone else is afraid of, where there are no words for things. I think that is what dancing is about. For ballets—there are no words. But we aren't afraid to go into that world.

"You take time away, there is no such thing as time in that ballet, *Watermill*." He was fascinated by it.

I actually worked with him, choreographed certain things with him. He'd quite often call on me to ask me to help him do, for instance, a big hunk of *Nutcracker* or *Pulcinella*. Quite often they were things he wasn't too interested in doing. I didn't mind that. It was fun to ask him what he had in mind.

I remember in *Firebird*, particularly, getting all the instructions about how he wanted me to proceed. But most of all, it was fantastic to be in that milieu, where this enormous creativity was always pouring out of him. He was so prolific. He could do four ballets where any of the rest of us could do one.

It is different without him; it has to be. He is not there guiding his own ballets the way he sees them; he's not creating new works. I think that what he has left us, which is very much alive, is a certain kind of dedication to dance, and to those ballets which act as inspiration for us all.

The Editor as Talker

My next life took me back to the United States and an unknown future. My friend of many years Michael Mahoney, who had been a curator at the National Gallery of Art in Washington, was the newly appointed head of the art department of Trinity College in Hartford, Connecticut. Before taking over, he was traveling in Italy with his friend Dr. Raymond Bahor. I joined them in Venice.

While I was lying in the sun (I know better now) on the Lido, Raymond asked me to explain Cubism. I talked away. Later we were in Paris. "Will you explain Surrealism?" Raymond asked, and I did my best. Michael said, "If you can talk like that off the top of your head, you should be lecturing." I ignored this.

Some time later, I was back in New York, Michael telephoned. "We are all looking forward to your lectures." "What? What lectures?" I asked in alarm. He claimed he had written to me all about this. To this day I don't believe him. "What about?" I asked. "The background of Twentieth Century Art," came the answer. "How many?" "Fourteen" came the answer.

Well, I did it. With death in my heart I would take the train to Hartford every week, muttering my opening lines to myself—I had no text—and twice a week spoke to the students, all male at that point. I firmly decided never to do that again.

Somehow another old friend, Dominique de Menil, whom I knew in Paris, but was now living in Houston, Texas, tracked me down at my father's house in Philadelphia. "Come to Houston and speak to my students at Rice," she said. I thought I had an out: "I can't. I have no slides."

Dominique was very persuasive. I would live at their house, could use their library, her art department would make my slides.

Dominique and her husband, Jean, had come to Houston to escape the occupation. Dominique's father, Conrad Schlumberger, had invented a system needed for the exploration of oil fields. Jean was appointed head of the Schlumberger operations in North America. Later, Jean anglicized his name to John.

I finally agreed, curious about Texas, territory unfamiliar to me. Dominique asked for my telephone number. I gave it to her. "What is the area code?" she asked. I had no idea. That didn't exist when I left the United States.

So off to Texas. Dominique received me in the famous Philip Johnson house with—to Houston—the controversial flat roof. The walls and even inside the cupboards were painted in striking colors by the until-then dress designer Charlie James. There was a Cubist Braque near the entrance and a big Max Ernst sculpture in the garden. I was given the guesthouse a few steps away, with its treasure of a library.

I was geographically in Texas, but it was a French enclave. Only French was spoken in the house, and the gentle-voiced black domestics were from Louisiana, their French colored with a charming eighteenth-century vocabulary.

The other imported element was a jolly French Dominican monk, Père Duployé, who was there to teach French literature at Rice. He spoke no English, and the students knew no French, so I imagine I benefited more than anyone else. But I enjoyed him very much, and we had lively discussions walking along the Rice campus. "Do you think Apollinaire really understood Cubism?" he might ask me.

He had been lent a house. "Come to supper and I will make you a boeuf bourguignon that you will never forget," he told me. He was right. It was delicious.

Jean and Dominique went off to distant parts. They were very active in ecumenical matters and civil rights. The next houseguest was Roberto Rossellini, who was involved with several Menil projects to do with cinema.

Roberto spoke no English and my Italian was shaky, so French was the lingua franca. We would meet at breakfast, and Roberto would announce as an opener, *"Pascal n'avait pas raison"*—"Pascal wasn't right"—and he was off.

He told me that although he was divorced from Ingrid Bergman, she still relied on him and kept telephoning him with complaints. She was in a play in Washington and complained about the other actors; she complained about the director. "She was always like that," he said resignedly. The next subject was the twins. He was very worried about them, he said. They had fallen into bad company in Rome. "I slapped them," he said. "Both of them?" I asked. "Both of them," and he demonstrated. So Ingrid shipped them to Hollywood to stay with Loretta Young. "Why Loretta Young?" I asked. "Ingrid said she would teach them good manners."

Roberto was still worried about them. "Why don't you have them come here?" I asked. "You wouldn't want them." "It's not my house, and I am sure Dominique would want you to have them."

So the twins arrived, with a young Indian boy who was the son of Roberto's current wife. The twins spoke no French, only Italian, the Indian boy spoke English. There was no one common language. We would gather around the dining room table in the evening and play an animated game that they taught me called *Battaglia*.

Meanwhile, I was working feverishly to prepare a series of lectures. The slides were indeed made for me by the Rice art department under the direction of a bonny long-haired student, Susan Barnes. Since then, she has become the leading expert on Van Dyck and an ordained minister.

When the Menils were in residence, there would be a knock on my door promptly at six o'clock, and Jean—wearing his signature orange tie—would hand me a scotch and soda.

The dread day of the first lecture arrived, and I got through it. To my surprise—since he didn't understand a word of English— there was Roberto coming up to congratulate me. He said the equivalent of "You've got it. You haven't a worry in the world. When we get back to Paris, I will film all your lectures." I was immensely moved to have such appreciation from a professional. Naturally, he never did film the lectures; he never had the money. But it was the intention that counted.

Roberto gave me the most romantic present I ever had. He drove me to Rice. We got out and walked along endless corridors. We went into a room. He said, "Sit down, close your eyes, and put out your hand." I felt something being put into my hand. "I have given you the moon," said Roberto. It was in fact a fragment of the moon—Rice was one of the universities that were given samples of moon rock to analyze. I had to give the moon back, but I had had it for a moment.

I had only seen cowboys in the movies, so I rushed out in my best Cartier-Bresson manner with my camera, when Fat Stock week brought the cowboys and cowgirls riding into town. They had camped outside the town for the night, then rode into Houston in a brave procession.

I had never heard country-and-western music before, but I became addicted to the immortal Hank Williams and Loretta Lynn. The Menils did not have a television then, but I heard them on the radio and loved it.

I had wanted a proper cowboy hat and was advised to go to Stelzig's, which had the real thing. To my disappointment, they had already stocked up with their spring line of straw hats. I wanted the proper hard-hat item. I spied a cowboy high up on a ladder getting something, wearing a fine dark brown cowboy hat with the proper swagger. I called out to him, "Want to sell your hat?" "Sure," he answered. "How much?" "Twenty bucks." "Sold!" So I got the real thing. It had a reinforced crown for rodeo riding and it said "Rick" inside.

When I left Houston, I was wearing my new hat and holding a sheath of yellow roses—a symbol, I was told, that I was wanted back. I stepped into the Menils' private plane that was to take me back to New York. It had a Max Ernst on the wall. Where else?

Lecturing Notes

It was a great way to get to know this country. Although born here, I had seldom lived in America for long. Now, through the lecture circuit, I got to know not only the major museums but also the rural ones tucked away in this vast continent.

I had no agent. Agents only wanted television stars, I learned. But one way or another, it got around that I was a possible number, and soon I was crisscrossing the country. You name it, I've been there.

I was amused to be greeted at the Yakima, Washington, airport with a large electric sign: "Welcome to Yakima, Rosamond Bernier." It was a letdown on leaving to see that the electric sign was still there but just said "Welcome to Yakima" and any name of an arrival was added.

In Portland, Oregon, I was teamed on the local theater marquee with Comedy Hour and Mother's Day.

An agreeable woman named Wilma Lewis had a series in California, the A.M. Talks. I stayed at her house, and at six every morning I got into her station wagon, along with her sister Fran and the coffee machine, and we drove to Walnut Creek or Sacramento, or to one of several other places. The routine was that the assembled ladies got coffee and a chance to chat, and then they got me. The program was always the same, but in six different California suburbs.

At first I rather dreaded the Ladies' Luncheons that were invariably hosted by the head of the women's committee. It was part of the package. What on earth could I talk to them about that might interest them? Cubism was hardly an opener.

I hit on two surefire subjects: gardening and cooking, both of which interested me. I would ask my neighbor on the right, after a suitable lead-in, "Do you have an acid or a lime soil?" And to my neighbor on the left, "Exactly at what temperature do you bake your ham?" I would return from these forays with illegible scribbled notes made on my knee during these meals.

During the first years of my lecturing, there were still dry states. John was appalled to think I couldn't get a drink after performing, so he gave me a little silver flask and filled it with whiskey so that I could retire to my hotel room after speaking and take a nip.

The change in this country was rapid. Now, in the smallest coffee shop, you get a choice of white, red, or rosé—the quality may not be high, but it is cheering to the traveler.

It was not always smooth going. I arrived in Chicago to speak at the Art Institute the next evening. I felt a bit odd, then a raging fever took over. Luckily for me, my husband was with me. He telephoned James Wood, the director of the museum (unfortunately, he died recently), who very kindly dug up a doctor, even though it was after hours. I was pumped that evening and the next morning with powerful potions.

It turned out that I had been bitten by a spider when I was lunching in Houston in the open air the day before. I had survived scorpions all those years in Mexico; I hadn't thought of urban Houston as dangerous territory.

I managed nevertheless to stagger onstage that night.

I was booked to speak at the University of Utah at Salt Lake City, a Mormon redoubt. They sent me a stern warning, the gist of it being that these artists I was going to speak about led highly irregular lives and they counted on my censoring my remarks. I wrote back equally sternly that these artists led magnificent lives and enriched ours and I was in no way going to misrepresent them.

I spoke in the gigantic gymnasium; several thousand attended. It apparently was a custom that if one of the pupils was moved with a message, he or she could stand up and deliver it.

When I finished, to my astonishment, a young girl came forward, grabbed the mike, and thanked God for bringing them Rosamond Bernier. That was the first and only time I have been linked to the Almighty.

Still Talking

In my new persona as professional talker I roamed far, if not wide. This phase started in Paris in 1970, when I was invited to give four lectures at the Grand Palais—on Matisse, Picasso, Miró, Max Ernst—in French.

I was still mired in the legal tangles of my divorce, so I was living at the Max Ernsts', rue de Lille. There was only one key to their apartment, always left with the concierge. The day of the first lecture, which was to be at 6:00 p.m., both Ernsts were in Cologne, where Max was being given an honorary degree. I had prepared an elegant but subdued outfit for the evening: a strawberry-pink cashmere skirt that Halston made me, and a Zandra Rhodes blouse. Meanwhile, I was out on my rounds in wool dress and boots. It was pouring rain.

When I came back in time to change, catastrophe! The concierge was nowhere in sight. No way to get into the apartment. So the lecturer had to appear onstage in dripping boots and soggy wool dress. I rallied and told the audience that they must imagine this was Shakespearean theater and that I was splendidly arrayed to perform, complete with twinkling jewelry. I got a warm round of applause and sailed into my story.

Nothing as dramatic happened when I next spoke in Paris, at the Pompidou, and this time I had my husband, John, with me to steady my nerves. The high point came a few years later, when I was invited to speak, twice, at the Louvre. To see my name posted in that august institution, where I had worked so often, made my heart beat faster.

John came with me when I was invited by the Indian government to lecture in Mumbai (it's still Bombay to me) and New Delhi.

I arrived in India completely jet-lagged from the long flight, and had just slumped into heavy sleep, when the telephone rang. A perky Indian voice speaking from the lobby said, "I would like to come up for a little chitchat." He was from the *New Delhi Times*. I managed to get myself dressed and somehow got through the interview without falling asleep like Alice's Dormouse.

In Jerusalem the government provided us with a comfortable guesthouse complete with kitchen and a magnificent view of the Old City. I spoke at the art museum and then, as a thank-you, at another cultural institution. This was before the heartbreaking strife of today.

After Jerusalem we went for a dip in the Red Sea, then onward by car through the Sinai desert. Thanks to an introduction from the Metropolitan Museum, we were received at the Saint Catherine monastery, perched high up on the rocks. We were shown some of its spectacular icons, but the dim light was frustrating. We were introduced to the newest arrival: a young English monk. I think he was thrilled to hear his native language.

He invited us to sit outside his cell under the roof and offered us tea. There was a slight delay while he prepared this, and he came out a bit shamefaced, with a kettle—he had no teapot.

We chatted, and he told us his family ran a nursery in Sussex. As one gardener to another, we discussed the difficulty of growing anything in the arid desert climate. Then he told me that only a very small plot of earth was available, where the monks were buried—one at a time. After a while, the defunct was dug up to make room for the next occupant, and the remains put in the ossuary. My gardening experience having been mostly in the tropics, I could not contribute much help, but I think we both enjoyed this unlikely conversation in this unlikely setting.

Later, I was able to send him a teapot via a Hong Kong connection.

A year later the Metropolitan Museum put on a large Byzantium exhibition with magnificent examples from great monasteries. A large contingent of black-robed and black-coiffed visiting ecclesiastics were on hand, each one standing by the vitrine displaying his monastery's treasures, just as collectors hover by their own displays.

We found ourselves by the Saint Catherine exhibits and greeted the head abbot. He made an almost imperceptible gesture toward John and whispered to his attendant, "*New York Times.*" Then he handed me a card with his e-mail address.

Back on this continent, a new experience was speaking for television. John and I did some programs together; he wrote, I spoke. We did programs for the National Gallery of Art on Luminism; we went to France to film a program on the spot on France and French painting for the San Francisco Legion of Honor Museum. For CBS, I was on my own interviewing Henry Moore, Paul Mellon, Joseph Hirshhorn, Philip Johnson, and a number of others. A friend looked it up on the Internet and found that I had done sixteen television programs for CBS and Channel 13, one of which won a Peabody.

Along the way I was awarded two French decorations: Officier de l'Ordre des Arts et des Lettres and the Légion d'Honneur. And the king of Spain, Juan Carlos, bestowed the Cross of Isabel la Católica on me, with a lovely yellow-and-white ribbon to go with it.

John and I were both named "National Treasures" by the Municipal Art Society of New York in 2004, and the New York Landmarks Conservancy named us "Living Landmarks."

Aside from this, Alexander Liberman lured me back to Condé Nast, and for years I wrote first for *House & Garden*, then for *Vogue*—some hundred articles. I never got around to counting them.

Hilde Limondjian, who had directed the Concerts and Lectures series at the Met since the late 1960s with brio, took a chance on me—completely unknown here at the time. I started in 1971 and was still at it over two hundred lectures later, when, as I said to John, my motto was "Stop at the top," and I did.

They were happy years, and backstage at the Met became my second home, with Mikel Frank, Steve Rotker, and Felix Cotto as a convivial support team, and John always keeping me company until I had to go out onstage.

P.S.

In an interview in *The New York Observer* on July 13, 2010, about her retirement from the Met, Hilde Limondjian answered, when asked who were some of the influential speakers in the lecture series:

> In the early '70s, a very gifted speaker, Rosamond Bernier, revolutionized what I like to call the "art of the art lecture." She spoke from the 1970s until just recently and gave more than 200 lectures. Her glittering speaking style, the immediacy of her delivery and the fact that she had known many of the famous artists in Paris in the '40s turned her lectures into the hottest ticket in New York.

Philip Johnson and Our Wedding

I met Philip Johnson in the early days of the Museum of Modern Art. He took an almost avuncular interest in me and, when I moved to Paris to work, made sure that I checked in when I passed through New York.

That often meant meeting him for lunch at the same corner table of the Four Seasons restaurant on the ground floor of the Seagram Building. It is not surprising that he felt at home there, since he designed both the bar and the dining room itself. He may well have told the chef how to make the excellent crabmeat dish that he often recommended to his guests, and he certainly explained just how he wanted the vermouth that turned up automatically in front of him when he arrived.

I was privileged in that most of the people who lunched with him were in some way concerned with architecture. They might be young or old, American or from overseas, but no matter who they were, they would find him formidably well-informed—and not least about the latest gossip.

He followed my adventures in creating an art review in Paris. He offered introductions to architects I should know about: Frank Gehry and Paul Rudolph were among them. He supplied moral support during certain upheavals in my private life.

Whenever I had the time, he invited me out to the Glass House and provided a car and driver to bring me. The first time I went, however, was with Alfred Barr (the first director of the Museum of Modern Art) and his wife, Marga. Philip was fanatically neat. His décor was as sparse as his person. When Marga noticed I was about to put down my coat, instead of hanging it up immediately, she whispered a warning, and added, *"Admirez! Admirez!"* I did.

Although the Glass House is accepted today as one of the classic buildings of the twentieth century, Philip told me that it didn't always get too easy a ride from some of the architects he most admired.

Frank Lloyd Wright, for instance, walked in and kept his hat on. "Should I keep my hat on or should I take it off? Am I indoors or out?" Apparently, the Glass House made him very uneasy. It didn't give him the sense of shelter that he got from his own houses, with their wide overhanging eaves and their rows of little windows.

The great French architect Auguste Perret didn't like it either. He came in, he sat down, and he said, "Too much glass," and that was that. Later he made a great effort and said, "Well, I suppose it's a little more comfortable than a railway station," but he really missed the concrete that he had worked with all his life.

As for Mies van der Rohe, whom Philip revered, he almost took the house as a personal offense. He just hated it. Philip said that at first this made him very unhappy, but then he realized that the Glass House was both too close to Mies's own style and yet not close enough. What seemed to Mies the "mistakes" drove him quite crazy. In fact he disliked it so much that he refused to spend the night there, and Philip had to telephone all over to find him a room in a decent hotel.

Some years later—we are in the early 1970s—the brilliant English art critic John Russell had come to New York to join *The New York Times* and me. I had left my magazine and my former matrimonial attachment and moved to New York. Although completely committed to John, I hesitated at the word "marriage." Philip was enthusiastic about John from the start and thought I should act. "You kids ought to get married," he said. "Kids? We're a couple of middle-aged birds," I objected (we were both in our fifties).

But by 1975, Philip had taken over as father and mother of the bride and planned the whole wedding with the attention to detail given to designing a new skyscraper. He corrected my guest list (I had been away so long that I didn't know the abbreviation for "Connecticut" was no longer "Conn." but "CT") and sent out the invitations. He arranged a musical program to be given in his new Sculpture Gallery. He somehow got a small organ flown in and engaged the organist John Weaver to play Bach chorales. He hired young trumpeters from Juilliard to provide flourishes at appropriate moments. For all I know, he figured how many hors d'oeuvres would fit on each one of the many buffets that were circulated.

Our only contribution was to provide ourselves, and we had asked our great friend Irene Worth to recite some Shakespeare sonnets and Millamant's speech from Congreve's *Way of the World*.

We had negotiated with our host: no crowds at the actual wedding, just a few close friends. The guests poured in after the actual ceremony was over. Pierre Matisse was John's best man, excruciatingly nervous because he thought he had to make a speech (he didn't). My old loved friend Aaron Copland gave me away. Lenny Bernstein was John's witness; his wife, Felicia, and daughter Nina—holding a bouquet of wildflowers—were my attendants. Stephen Spender flew in from London, bringing me a notebook in which he had handwritten my favorite poems.

Incidentally, it was the hottest day of the century. Stephen heroically ignored suggestions that he take off his jacket. "She hasn't seen it yet," he explained. He had bought a new suit for the wedding.

Photographs record the festive scene, with some two hundred guests wandering over the immaculate lawn and spilling into the new Sculpture Gallery—such shots as Lenny walking arm in arm with Virgil Thomson, Andy Warhol feeding his little dog a cocktail sausage, Louise Nevelson with her usual triple layer of eyelashes, Leo Castelli chatting with John Ashbery, Helen Frankenthaler sitting on the grass with her shoes off, Philip giving the first toast, the bride and groom looking blissfully happy.

In fact, May 24, 1975, was the happiest day of my life.

I lost John on August 23, 2008.

They were wonderful years. I am grateful for every one of them.

Some of John's Musical Friends

Although officially an art critic, my late husband, John Russell, had been deeply involved with music and musicians all his adult life. He had written a biography in 1957 of the German conductor Erich Kleiber, one of the major conductors of the period between the two wars, and in the course of this had become familiar with the whole Kleiber family.

Carlos Kleiber, the charismatic son, also became a conductor. Although he was well into middle age when I met him, John still referred to him as "young Kleiber." John told me Carlos got absolutely no encouragement from his stern father. When, as a teenager, Carlos came home to report excitedly, "Papa, I have been accepted in the chorus of the Stuttgart opera," the elder Kleiber answered, "What? They have room for *you*?"

He became one of the most-sought-after conductors alive. He combined profound musicality with irresistible personal seductiveness. To watch him conduct was almost to hear the music. But it was not easy to hear Carlos Kleiber; he must have had the Guinness world record for canceling performances.

We went especially to Munich to hear his *Rosenkavalier*, and at the last moment he canceled. He came to have lunch with us the next day at the Hotel Vier Jahreszeiten. We complained about our disappointment. "Oh," he said offhandedly, "I had a spat with the soprano." She happened to have been a former mistress of his—one of many.

Did he like being in such demand all over the world? Not at all. "Eating well and making love is what life is for," he once said.

After his son had realized that his father was being offered unbelievably high fees and turning most of them down, he said, "Papa, I think I'd like to conduct too."

"And why is that?" asked Carlos.

"Well," his son said, "I've noticed that the less you work, the more money you make."

One of the great Russian artists who was finally allowed to go abroad was the pianist Sviatoslav Richter.

John described his debut in London in July 1961. "He made an unforgettable and distinctly curious impression. He had a mighty head, mighty shoulders, mighty legs and mighty coattails. He had compact but very large hands with which he dug deeply into the keyboard when the music asked for what he called 'a singing sonority.'"

I got to know Richter, Slava, as we called him by then, in the 1970s and 1980s, when he came every summer to a little festival he had founded not far from Tours in the Loire valley.

As the guest of a music publisher friend of John's, Francis Van de Velde, he had come across a noble thirteenth-century tithe barn the size of a small cathedral. Richter saw at once it had enormous possibilities, and he guessed the acoustics would be perfect. They were: what came to be called the Fêtes Musicales en Touraine opened there in June 1964 and continued to draw a full house (or a full barn) of music lovers, not only from the region, but from all over France. Richter chose all the other performers, and the programs, himself.

During the Fêtes, Richter and his wife lived in a secluded house on the estate of the Van de Veldes. We were also fortunate guests there.

For a few weeks each year, as John described it, "life was a Franco-Russian paradise. There were no regular hours. Conversations drifted this way and that in Chekhovian style. Hugely gifted people drew upon their sense of play, as when the great violist Yuri Bashmet rode round and round the house on a tiny child's bicycle.

"Dinner was at no particular time and for no foreseeable number of people. It usually ran late. With good food and good wine, collegial good humor drew near to wildness."

One evening it leaked out that we had to move on the next morning. Richter pulled one of his more terrifying faces. "But you can't

go," he said, "we're going to play the Stravinsky Concerto for Two
Solo Pianos tomorrow evening!" Then he paused. "Well . . . if you
really must leave, we'll play it for you now."

The dining room seated eight or ten and was an extension of the
small living room that had two pianos, side by side. Richter and
Vassily Lobanov came over and sat with their backs to us, just an
inch or two away.

Whether in public or in private, Richter gave all he had. The Stravinsky concerto in question is strenuous, from beginning to end. In
high-summer short sleeves, Richter played as if he were laying his
life on the line. That massive head, that rocklike back, and those
formidable arms and hands radiated an implacable power. "That's
not the whole program!" Richter said at the end, and added two
sizable encores before the evening was over.

My husband and I had known Yehudi Menuhin for quite some time,
though he was someone who had to be caught on the wing, so constantly was he on the move.

I had seen him in Detroit, where he was conducting and I was
lecturing. We were staying at the same hotel and leaving the same
day. The concierge warned me to check out early because there was
a convention going on and hundreds of people would be checking
out at the same time. "But there is only one Madame Bernier," Yehudi said gallantly.

Some years later John and I were waiting in the Frankfurt airport for a connecting flight to St. Petersburg. We spied an unmistakable small figure in the lounge—it was Yehudi, accompanied by his
wife, Diana, who towered over him. We embraced, and we found
out we were all going to the same hotel in St. Petersburg and that
Yehudi would be conducting two concerts at the conservatoire, just
across the road. "Of course we will be there," we said. "Then do
come and see me during the intermission."

Wouldn't he need a rest? "Not at all," he answered. He was conducting the Hungarian Symphony Orchestra, which dated from the
year the Russians marched into Hungary. It was not a great orchestra, but Yehudi remained loyal to it. "Besides," he said, "the Hun-

garians are the only people in Europe who really have rhythm." He had programmed Bartók, by the way.

Yehudi was well into his seventies, but from the back, on the podium, his svelte silhouette and vigorous movements suggested a far younger man. He kept himself in top physical shape by a regimen of yoga and a complicated program of vitamins he invented for himself.

After the concert we were to meet for supper. He told us he had to go to an official reception for him. "But I won't stay more than two minutes. Do go and get us a table for four at the restaurant."

We didn't hurry after the concert, because we didn't believe about the two minutes. We were strolling along when a stocky figure in a big high-necked fisherman's sweater came bounding down the stairs to the restaurant, leaving us way behind. It was Yehudi.

Yehudi not only talked but listened, as if one's story was of high interest to him. His incorruptible goodness and sweetness drew people to him everywhere.

John remembered that Diana sometimes thought that he carried this too far. She never hesitated to give her opinions.

"That violinist who played with you last week was just awful," she said. "Admit it, now, she played like a pig."

"But she brings something of her own," Yehudi answered mildly, and changed the subject.

Another conductor who is in demand everywhere—every major symphony orchestra did a dance of seduction to try to lure him—but who doesn't cancel is Simon Rattle: *Sir Simon* since we spent a week with him a few years ago in Birmingham.

John was commissioned by *The New York Times Magazine* to write a major article on the conductor who was causing an international buzz, from a city not previously associated with star performers. So we went to Birmingham to watch him in action.

As a very young man, Simon took over a minor orchestra—the Birmingham Symphony—and stuck with it year after year in spite of all inducements to move elsewhere.

This dynamo with an abundant halo of graying curls is not swept away by adulation. He was, and is, totally unpretentious.

We attended rehearsals, and concerts, and saw how he worked with the orchestra, with a chorus, with soloists. He was preparing Verdi's *Requiem* and, for another program, a cello concerto with Lynn Harrell as soloist.

In his usual rehearsal gear—a baggy multicolored sweater (perhaps knit by an admirer) over slacks—he worked with demanding but endless good nature. Orchestra sections were rehearsed separately, their members spoken to like colleagues. The tutti finally blossomed seamlessly.

When we went out to lunch together, he pulled a pile of scores behind him on a little platform on wheels, "my little dog," he called it.

As a music student, he had been a percussionist. He had played in jazz concerts. Still an avid jazz fan, he would go after what should have been exhausting concerts that week to Ronnie Scott's, a popular jazz hangout, and stay until the late hours.

Later in London we heard Simon conduct a remarkable performance of Stockhausen's Symphony for Three Orchestras. It was in the vast Royal Festival Hall with the three orchestras so widely spaced apart that three conductors were needed.

At the end of the symphony Simon turned to the audience: "Now I would ask you all to move to another part of the hall, and I will play the Stockhausen all over again, and you will see if it sounds different." Everyone was happy to comply.

He resigned from the Birmingham Symphony Orchestra after his long tenure there. There was much speculation as to where he would go next. He could write his own ticket. He finally decided on the prestigious Berlin Philharmonic, making guest appearances elsewhere.

An accurate picture of John's musical friends must include the German lieder singer Dietrich Fischer-Dieskau. John was devoted to him, and I inherited him when Dieter, as he was known, came for recitals to New York.

John had met the young baritone in London in the 1950s. John had always cared for German music and was deeply moved by the exceptional artistry and the magnificent voice of this large blond Berliner.

Besides their musical interests, Dieter was knowledgeable about painting; in fact he painted himself. The two toured the galleries together, and John helped him make some, at first, modest acquisitions.

Fischer-Dieskau became world famous. Besides giving recitals all over Europe and in concert halls here in the United States, he sang leading roles in the major opera houses. John was still living in England in 1962 and went to Coventry Cathedral to hear his friend Fischer-Dieskau sing his friend Benjamin Britten's *War Requiem*.

I never saw him in an operatic role, but a DVD of *The Marriage of Figaro*, with Fischer-Dieskau singing the role of the Count, showed him to be a gifted actor with an unexpected flair for comedy.

Later, when both Fischer-Dieskau and John were in New York, there were always reunions. Naturally, we were right there when Dieter sang Schubert's *Die Schöne Müllerin*, with that superb accompanist Gerald Moore at the piano. I was struck by the fact that even for a daytime recital, Fischer-Dieskau wore Pan-Cake makeup. Apparently, it was routine in Europe for performers at that time.

In the 1970s Dieter arrived with a new wife: the Hungarian soprano Julia Varady. She was gifted, dark haired, lively, considerably younger. I took her to Ken Lane's to buy some stage jewelry. John did the galleries with Dieter and helped him buy a Monet.

John always kept a framed photograph of young Fischer-Dieskau and his two, then, small children, part of his personal pantheon: along with photographs of André Gide, Albert Schweitzer, Arnold Schoenberg, Cyril Connolly, and Henry James (he did not know the latter). Next to them was a childhood drawing by Lucian Freud for his mother.

After a long and glorious career, in 1992 Fischer-Dieskau retired from the concert stage as a singer but took up conducting, with great success.

Fortunately for us, recordings bring that ringing voice right into our living room.

I can't end this prestissimo gallop down a gallery of musician friends without including two remarkable but totally dissimilar artists: the conductor and harpsichordist William Christie and the composer Elliott Carter.

We have heard Christie, Bill to us, on numerous occasions conducting in New York, where he draws a standing-room-only audience for concert performances of such operas as Lully's *Atys* and
Purcell's *King Arthur*, sometimes conducting from the harpsichord.
He pays meticulous attention to every detail of the staging, including the outfits worn by his young singers.

One time, we went with him to Caen, some four hours' drive
from Paris, where he has built a devoted audience and was welcomed
from the stage by the mayor. One might not think that a whole evening of Purcell would be a crowd-pleaser in a French provincial
town, but it was.

That nonstop day started in Paris, at eight in the morning. There
was a long rehearsal at Caen, the concert, a reception afterward, then
the drive back, with Bill lying fast asleep on the luggage. We arrived
after one in the morning. We were completely exhausted, but Bill
awoke refreshed and talked excitedly about forthcoming concerts—
he performs all over Europe—and of his new plans for his country
house in the Vendée. His garden has been classified as a national
treasure.

In January 2010 he had the prestigious honor of being made a
member of the Académie Française. I went over to Paris to watch
Bill, a former American, being welcomed *sous la Coupole* (under the
Cupola) of this august institution. The building itself is magnificent—Louis Le Vau, late seventeenth century.

The Academicians (there are by tradition forty; a new one can
only be admitted to replace one who has died) filed in one by one,
in their traditional uniform. Designed in the early nineteenth century, the black cutaway's lapels and collars and the sides of the trousers are lavishly embroidered in green; a cocked hat sets it off (this
was originally trimmed with black feathers, but they must have given
up on this, I didn't spot any); and a multiple display of ribbons and
medals on many Academicians' chests added what Diana Vreeland
used to call "pizzazz." A sonorous rolling of drums accompanies
each entrance.

Another tradition: the new Academician must deliver a eulogy of
the departed member whose place he is taking. Bill's task was to
speak about the famous mime Marcel Marceau. For a musician who

deals in sounds to speak about an artist whose specialty was silence would have daunted many, but not Bill. He spoke eloquently, and in perfect French, about gesture and movement. He even evoked Michael Jackson's moonwalk—I doubt that any of the Academicians had ever heard of him. Christie illustrated his points about the French tradition of singing and playing baroque music by living examples: some of his young singers and instrumentalists were grouped in the audience and performed elegantly.

In 2010, Christie made his debut at the Metropolitan Opera conducting *Cosi Fan Tutte*.

No one is younger than Elliott Carter, who turned 102 in 2010. He didn't hesitate to hop to Berlin or Paris or London or Milan to hear one of his works performed; until recently, he was far more widely played in Europe than in America, and incidentally speaks the languages of these cities fluently.

Now it would seem hardly a week goes by without another new work by Elliott Carter being featured on a concert program.

James Levine had been a particularly eloquent champion. We have had the good fortune of having Levine sometimes leave his post in Boston long enough to conduct his Met Orchestra group in New York, often with compositions by Carter on the program.

Carter is a cherubic man with endless intellectual curiosity and a keen appreciation of good food and wine. I sent him the last bottle of my former French cellar for his birthday and received a handwritten letter of thanks, promptly, the next day.

We ran into him at an opening in 2008 and discovered that he keeps all his curiosity about current events. He told us with a chuckle that Carnegie Hall had booked him for his hundredth. He made it! He climbed up onto the stage with only minimum help and, beaming, waved his stick at the cheering audience.

Now a salute to our friend Ned Rorem, who lived in Paris during the decades I was there—the 1950s and 1960s.

He was the prized composer in residence at Marie-Laure de

Noailles's handsome town house, a gathering place for the most interesting people of Paris: painters, poets, composers, assorted eccentrics.

Over the years, Ned has composed some of the most ravishing songs of our times. And he has published diaries that are acute and poignant testimonies of a rich and civilized life.

And I must include two beloved friends who, alas, are no longer with us, that superb two-piano team, Arthur Gold and Robert Fizdale.

We first met in Paris in 1948, when Virgil Thomson sent me "the kiddies," as he called them, about to make their European debut. I helped launch them with a large party—very important in Paris. (Alice B. Toklas came, almost disappearing under an exuberantly flowered hat—she bought one a year, she told us. Truman Capote sat on Janet Flanner's knees.)

But soon their artistry and personal charm had won over everyone who counted in the musical and intelligent social worlds. Francis Poulenc so admired the way they played his Piano Concerto that he composed a sonata for them.

The leading French composers all wrote for them.

Once when they were staying at the Hôtel Pont Royal in Paris, they were desperately waiting for a taxi to take them to their recital. Poulenc happened to come by. Seeing them in distress, he sank to his knees in the middle of the hotel lobby, spread out his arms, and implored aloud, "Saint Francis, please send a taxi so that the boys can get to their concert, and send another so I can get to my dinner."

Whereupon, two taxis pulled up in front of the hotel.

Back in the 1950s in Paris, Pierre Boulez was the prestigious—but not yet well-known—conductor of the Jean-Louis Barrault–Madeleine Renaud company, which occupied the Théâtre Marigny.

Perched upstairs was a small hall, with excruciatingly uncomfortable seats. Here Boulez directed a series of concerts, called the Domaine Musical, of what was then extremely far-out music: Xenakis, Ligeti, Berio, Berg. The small public was made up of the cream of

Paris intellectuals, with a few artists like André Masson thrown in (his son was a professional percussion player).

I never missed a concert.

I had never met Boulez until many years later, when we were both in Edinburgh for some celebrations of Leonard Bernstein's birthday put on by Columbia Records.

I introduced myself and thanked him for having made my contemporary music education with his Domaine Musical concerts.

He kindly thanked me for having made *his* education with all those years of *L'ŒIL*.

After that, John and I often heard Boulez not only conduct his own music but brilliantly elucidate such scores as *Le Sacre du Printemps*; both as a conductor and as a narrator, Boulez speaks excellent English.

Recently, a double bill at Carnegie Hall had both Boulez and Barenboim presenting their view of Schoenberg: one coolly analytical, one surprisingly romantic.

In 2010, Boulez celebrated his eighty-fifth birthday. Now he sells out the house wherever he appears. What a contrast to those years when he was conducting the New York Philharmonic and the critics could not write a good word about him.

About John

John Russell, that most elegant and civilized writer, came, as he would say, from nowhere. He was born at the end of World War I, in January 1919. He never knew the identity of his father. He wrote in an unfinished memoir: "For a long time I fantasized that my never-known and never-named father had died a gallant death in action in France. But I knew nothing about him then and have learned nothing about him since."

The baby was placed in an orphanage. That would have been the end of the story except for his grandfather Isaac James Russell, who came to have a look at the baby. "That boy is never going to stay here," he said, and took the baby home and gave him the family name. He and his wife were well into middle age, with no child at home. John grew up believing that his grandparents were his father and mother. They raised him with all possible kindness but in isolation, to hide the "shame" of the family.

John's grandfather owned a string of prosperous pubs. The family was comfortably off, but no one ever read a book, or went to a concert, or listened to music on what was then the wireless.

"We lived first in Strawberry Hill, a London suburb that was dignified at that time by the presence of the former King of Romania," John wrote. "Although I saw the top of the ex-king's head every morning as he passed by our house on his solitary walks, I was not yet alert enough to reflect on the ups and downs of fortune but merely wondered why he always left his crown at home."

John always knew he would be a writer. He had a severe speech problem and wrote:

For one thing, there was nothing else I could do. At a time that I could hardly talk and did not want to be a burden to others, I found I could put down whatever was in my head; I had always thought it through. To my surprise and my relief it turned out that there were people who would pay for it.

I was eleven or twelve when one of my more convivial aunts urged me to enlarge my experience of life. "If you can't have amusing people at home, you simply have to read," she said. "Go to the public library, sign up, and get yourself another life."

And "another life" is exactly what I got. Not only did I enjoy it hugely, but it made it possible for me to get a fix on a cultural wonderland that none of my schoolrooms had signaled to me. It was often way above my head, but at least I looked into James Joyce, Marcel Proust and T. S. Eliot. I was often baffled, but I knew at once that these were the giants of the day.

By the time I reached adolescence I was already precocious in my expectations of life. When I was thirteen and at prep school we were asked to write about the summer holiday that we would most enjoy. I wrote that ideally I would like to go to Paris and tour the town in the company of one or two of Mr. Cochran's "Young Ladies" (more or less the equivalent of a later day Ziegfeld Follies).

My essay was passed at once to the headmistress of the school. Never in her long career had anything of the sort been presented to her. If I was not forthwith expelled, it was for two reasons. One was that there was no sign that I would ever be able to put my ideas into practice; the other was that the school was broke and needed the money.

To their great credit, John's grandparents, after his prep school, sent him to the best day school in the country, St. Paul's, in London. There he had brilliant, eccentric masters, as they are called in England. There was Mr. Cotter, as John always thought of him (E.P.C. Cotter), who came on like a man of leisure who was doing the school a favor for turning up. After setting the day's tasks, he would sit back and continue the correspondence in Latin verse that he kept up with a fellow staff member.

Then there was G. E. Bean, who later became known for his studies of Turkey in classical times. He was immensely tall and a very good tennis player; in fact, in the 1930s he competed in the men's doubles at Wimbledon. At that time at Wimbledon, all men played in long white flannel trousers. When Mr. Bean and his partner were scheduled to play, their match was always put on last on the day's program. This made it possible for Mr. Bean to complete his work in the classroom, change into his almost unbelievably long white trousers, and arrive at Wimbledon in time.

And there was a magnetic form master, A.N.G. Richards, a classical scholar who was a gifted musician and sang the tenor role in Handel's *Semele*. He showed young John how Toscanini had conducted the scherzo from Mendelssohn's music for *A Midsummer Night's Dream*, so that, John wrote, "I could almost hear those fast-fluttering strains."

In 1936 the talk of the town and that filled the press was the large international Surrealism exhibition. Major Surrealists were there, including Salvador Dalí, who gave his speech from a diving bell. John had studied the catalog and the press clippings with great excitement. One day in class, the high master of St. Paul's, John Bell, said something like: "Everyone seems to be talking about Surrealism. I can't make any sense out of it. Can any boy in this room tell me what Surrealism is?"

John found his hand raised of its own accord. And he heard, for the first time ever, his voice raised in class. "Sir," he said, "I can." He was asked to go into the next room and write it all down.

Two hours later, he sought out the high master in his sanctum and gave him a sheaf of papers. It was not a work of genius, but the right facts were in the right place, and the current controversies were summarized.

The high master read it through line by line. Then he looked at John with a new curiosity and said, "Russell, you could make a living out of this." Within twenty-four hours John's situation in the school, and his entire future, had changed.

John wrote in the sketch for his memoirs:

My general education was further enriched by the fact that I had been given a small sum for my lunch. This was meant to be eaten in a down-market tea shop no more than a minute's walk from the school.

I soon realized that I could find a better use for my money. Every day I took the tube to Leicester Square and fanned out among the second-hand bookshops and print shops.

Up the road was Covent Garden, where during the annual season of Colonel de Basil's Ballets Russes de Monte Carlo, the topmost seats at either side cost little more than a shilling. Or if I got out at Green Park, the art galleries of the West End were no more than two minutes' walk away. I could not always afford to go to concerts at Queen's Hall, but if I timed it right I could slip into the back at the end of the concert, and watch Richard Strauss or Toscanini or Artur Schnabel, as they came back for one more tumultuous bow.

In this way, and with the help of substantial teas at home, I was able to get a supplementary education on which I built for a lifetime.

With his speech problem and a shaky hold on the required classics (Latin and Greek), John had little hope of a scholarship for Oxford or Cambridge. But unexpectedly, his history master, Philip Whiting, took him aside and said, "I think you'd better try this June for a scholarship in the history department."

John sat in a big upper room at St. Paul's and wrote and wrote and did his best. His pen seemed to move effortlessly.

When a letter arrived from Oxford asking him to present himself for an interview, he wrote:

I said to myself: "I am not nervous, I shall not be nervous. I shall be buoyant, self-assured and above all talkative." I still believed, until I reached the front door of the Master's lodgings, that I would do well in the interview. But I could not get out a single word. After several minutes, the Master said, "Why don't we continue in the garden? People often feel more comfortable there." I still could not say a word. It was the all-time low point of my life. I had given up all hope for Oxford.

I went back to London and I never mentioned it to anyone.

Then one day I bought the *Times* on my way to school. I turned the pages at random. Suddenly I saw the results of the examination I had taken. I had come out at the top of the list.

I can only quote the *Shorter Oxford Dictionary*: "Bliss: perfect joy or happiness."

He had three very happy years at Oxford, at Magdalen College. He was so ecstatic at being in Oxford that he did very little work. He never went to a faculty lecture and skipped seminars. Nevertheless, he was finally awarded what was deemed "a perfectly reasonable second." Brian Urquhart, his contemporary at Oxford, described him as "tall, handsome, golden-haired, and always surrounded by the prettiest girls."

Those times were shadowed by the state of hostilities between Britain and Germany. Hardly any of his contemporaries had been able to finish their three years at Oxford. One after another, they had been called up for war service, from which many of them did not return.

Rejected for military service because of his speech difficulties, he accepted an offer from Sir John Rothenstein, then the director of the Tate Gallery, as an unpaid honorary assistant.

As the Tate was then closed, and its collections were by then in safety either in country houses or in suitable caves far from London, there was nothing for him to do but to type, month by month, sixteen separate copies of the minutes of the trustees' meeting (no carbon paper). He then joined the Tate's emergency outpost in Upton-on-Severn, Worcester.

This was a town that had been briefly in the news when it was named as the location of a pioneering novel about two lesbians. However, John commented, "At no time in my two years in residence was there any sign of sexual activity, whether regular or irregular."

With time on his hands, John roamed the countryside with a publisher of successful guidebooks of Britain, Harry Batsford, who had a petrol allowance. The result was John's first book, *Shakespeare's*

Country. "It had to do with whatever could be reached within an hour or two by car from Upton-on-Severn. None of the places in question were related in any way to Shakespeare, but nobody pointed that out and I had a very easy ride with reviewers," the young author wrote. It was the first of twenty-three books to be written by John Russell. He was twenty-three years old at the time.

Later in the war John had a job in Naval Intelligence on the editorial side of the weekly review of intelligence. Detailed accounts of individual actions at sea were spelled out. These often involved the movements of U-boats, which were decisive as to whether the war would be won or lost.

With other figures from the literary world, he spent nights on fire duty at Westminster Abbey.

The war over, he began writing for publications such as Peter Quennell's *Cornhill* and Cyril Connolly's *Horizon*. Through his friend Ian Fleming, not yet creator of James Bond, he began reviewing books for *The Sunday Times*.

What he described as "a disgraceful episode" occurred in 1951. At the annual dinner of the Royal Academy, the owner of *The Sunday Times*, Lord Kemsley, sat next to the president of the Royal Academy. At a late stage of the proceedings, during which wine had flowed freely, the president said to Lord Kemsley, "There's something terribly wrong with *The Times*. It's your art critic, he's a disgrace, and he's dragging the paper down."

"Do you really think so?" said Lord Kemsley.

Deeply troubled, Lord Kemsley reported the conversation next morning to his staff. The editors protested, "Eric Newton is widely admired and he is a pleasure to work with."

"That can't be helped," said Lord Kemsley. "We can't ignore what the president said." Someone asked if he had a successor in mind. "I don't know about art critics," Kemsley retorted, irritated. "Just get one."

Someone then said, "We have Russell on the staff, sir. He knows about art."

"Who's Russell?" asked Lord Kemsley. "A book reviewer, sir." "A book reviewer?" said Lord Kemsley, none too pleased. Then he said, "Oh, well, get Russell."

In this way John became the art critic of *The Sunday Times* and remained there for twenty-five years, until he left for the United States.

He had married Alexandrine Apponyi, from a distinguished Austro-Hungarian family. They had a daughter, Lavinia (now Lady Grimshaw), of whom he was immensely proud.

As for the years at *The Sunday Times*, he never had trouble finding something to say. "Nor did I ever use fancy language. It was precisely the life I had always dreamed of."

In the immediate postwar years in Europe and elsewhere, as a new generation of artists emerged, John traveled widely, chronicling developments in France (he wrote and spoke perfect French), Germany, Greece, Italy, Austria, Denmark, Australia, and the former Soviet Union. Speaking of the growing international popularity of modern art, he wrote, "The critic . . . could go to a new country every month of the year if his editor would stand for it."

Those postwar decades saw a transformation in the art world. New money and new publicity primed the newly expanded auction market, and enterprising dealers challenged the comfortably established auction houses with their country house connections. Two Viennese Jewish refugees, Frank Lloyd and Harry Fischer (with a future duke on their board), made the Marlborough Gallery the hot place to see and be seen.

Contemporary art had a new role in national self-awareness. Modern Britain had for the first time a living artist of unquestioned international eminence, Henry Moore. John, who traveled abroad with Henry for several exhibitions, said that Henry was well aware of his reputation but was never the slightest bit pretentious. He was scrupulously attentive to the local artists when he was feted in foreign countries. If he thought someone would never make it as a colorist, he would say, "Black-and-white's your thing, you know. Black-and-white!"

John wrote, "Fifty years ago, the life of an established art critic in London was unhurried and hugely enjoyable. There were not too many shows, but we got in first to see them, and the dealers made us welcome, no matter what they privately thought of us, as did museum directors both at home and abroad. We had congenial colleagues. World-wide publishers sent us their new books. We travelled throughout Europe at our employers' expense. I always felt I was being paid to educate myself."

John discovered and wrote about Lucian Freud, Francis Bacon (the subject of a book), Gilbert & George, David Hockney, Anthony Caro, R. B. Kitaj, Bridget Riley, Howard Hodgkin—all of whom made us welcome when John brought me to meet them years later.

While still a British citizen, he was awarded the CBE (commander of the Order of the British Empire), the French Arts et Lettres, the Légion d'Honneur, and heavy crosses from Germany and Austria. We had quite a struggle adorning him with all of these to go to a white-tie dinner at the Royal Academy. I resorted to pins and Scotch tape.

I wrote earlier about John's appearance in the pages of *L'ŒIL*, and then in my life. Eventually, our previous attachments unraveled. I was about to move to New York, when John announced he had resigned from *The Sunday Times*. "I am a writer. I can earn my living anywhere," he said, and he followed me, jobless, to New York.

Within a week he was invited to lunch by Hilton Kramer and offered a job on *The New York Times*. John accepted immediately. "Don't you want to know more about it?" asked Hilton. "No," answered John.

Whereupon he went right to the *Times* office and wrote his first article.

His colleague Michael Kimmelman described John arriving at the office just before lunchtime one day, as usual in a finely striped British shirt, highly visible tie, and red socks (he loved color). While his colleagues were struggling to finish their articles, John sat down at his computer, dashed off his piece in his usual elegant prose, just the right length, and left for his lunch. His speed, facility, and wide-ranging frame of reference never ceased to astonish. He had the rare ability to write a finished draft on the first go-round.

Over here, his subjects in those first years included Willem de Kooning, James Turrell, Gilbert & George, Joseph Beuys, and Anselm Kiefer.

John flourished in his new country. He became a U.S. citizen and was amused to be asked if he could read and write.

He combined impeccable scholarship with a generous curiosity about young artists and women artists, who had been somewhat neglected in the press until John came along. He was good nature itself, with a somewhat antic sense of humor.

There was still a telephone switchboard at the *Times* in those days. It was manned (an inappropriate word!) by an intelligent young black woman named Lucy. She wanted to continue her education with night courses, but there was a conflict with her schedule. Permission was not granted for a change of hours, whereupon John wrote to the managing editor that if Lucy was not allowed the time off for her studies, he would take her place at the switchboard, in drag.

Lucy got the change of schedule.

Having a huge reading public in a very large country after what John felt in the end to be the narrow confines and jealousies of writing in Britain was immensely stimulating. The *Times* editors gave him free rein and even sent him, as an onlooker from Mars, to cover the Republican convention in Texas in 1984.

Over his thirty years writing for the *Times* (1974–2004), he cast his net wide. Besides covering exhibitions, he tossed off articles on such subjects as the color green and the fact that "wisteria" rhymes with "hysteria."

After settling in New York, in proper British clubman manner, John joined the Century Association. He drank its signature Silver Bullets and enjoyed the stimulating assortment of its members, so much so that he undertook to write the club's monthly bulletin. He went on writing it for twenty-five years, from 1981 to 2006.

Incidentally, I was one of the Century's first woman members.

Just as he had written that "the history of art, if properly set out, is the history of everything," he managed to harbor the most varied and unexpected bedfellows in these pithy, witty dispatches.

Seurat found his place with Moselle wine, reflections on existentialism, macaroons, and the experience of driving on the Merritt Parkway. Incidentally, in spite of taking some driving lessons from the Smith Driving School in Connecticut, John never really mastered the intricacies of life at the wheel. He acknowledged this himself. When someone asked him who was the most courageous person he ever knew, he answered without hesitation, "My driving instructor."

John was remarkably prolific. Besides reams written first for the weekly London *Sunday Times,* then the daily *New York Times,* he published monographs on Seurat, Georges Braque, Max Ernst, Henry Moore, Francis Bacon, and the conductor Erich Kleiber and travel books on Switzerland, London, the palaces of Leningrad, and Paris. He edited the correspondence between Henri Matisse and his son Pierre and translated several texts from the French.

As he wrote of himself, "He published a slew of books that he cannot for the moment remember, much as he loves them all."

As a critic, John never saw the point of going through life "snarling and spewing," as he put it. If he didn't like someone's work, he simply avoided writing about it. But he could speak his mind. When his fellow Centurion Nick Weber was planning to write about the painter Balthus, John, who knew both the man and the work well, having curated a Balthus exhibition at the Tate Gallery, warned him, "As a liar, he is without equal."

And as Philippe de Montebello pointed out at John's memorial at the Century Association, on November 14, 2008, John could sling it out:

> When the art historian Albert Elsen wrote a quarrelsome letter to the *Times* about what I thought was a tempered review by John of Rodin's *The Gates of Hell,* when it was shown at the Met, John let him have it. Here is what John wrote: "I am well aware that *The Gates of Hell* draws a crowd. So would a public hanging, if it were allowed. There is room today for more than one estimate of the old rascal and his overblown activities. For the rest, I see less reason than ever to budge from my point of view, which is that *The Gates of Hell* is to serious art what a disaster movie is to *King Lear.*"

The Century has hung John's portrait, by the painter Marc Klionsky, over the stairway as one gets out of the elevator. It is heartening for me to see what looks like dear John's welcome: "Come on in and lift a glass."

To the Met with Alex Katz

One day in 2007, our friend Alex Katz told us he would like to do a double portrait of John and me.

Of course we were delighted, but wondered if we were up to joining Alex's gallery of insouciant, unlined young people.

We showed up and posed, one after the other, in profile. Alex worked away swiftly, in silence. We were sorry that our moment of glory was over so soon.

Out of discretion, we asked no questions. Then, in June 2010, I learned that courtesy of Alex, we were entering the Metropolitan Museum.

The Met organized a little ceremony. Alas, I was the only one of the duo who could attend. There were hospitable drinks. Alex spoke. I spoke. And this is what I said:

A few years ago, John and I had the good fortune to be invited by Alex and Ada to visit them in Maine.

We went. It was blissful. We felt ourselves becoming Alex Katz personages, radiating well-being, not unlike the characters Alex immortalized in his cocktail parties series; as John described them: "No one has ever looked vicious, nasty, hungover, left out of the party or bored."

We had the best company. We had our own little house with a view of the lake. There was a rustic bench and table just outside where I could spread out my texts and work on my next Met lecture. John, as usual, was reading.

Alex would disappear for long-distance rambles. We would meet in the evening for congenial drinks and Ada's delicious meals. We had our first-ever lobster rolls.

Alex and Ada had been coming to Lincolnville, Maine, for many years, where Alex, as he put it, became aware of "the great Maine landscape to be devoured." They have lived in their present house for summers since 1954.

He became an intrinsic part of the Maine fabric when he extended his interest in Colby College with epic generosity. He gave a large body of his work to the college. The powers that be at Colby were delighted at this opportunity for the students to live with such quality. They built a new museum dedicated to the work of one artist, Alex Katz.

John esteemed Alex Katz, both the work and the man. For John, Alex was the archetypical American. He wrote: "If it turned out that in first youth he had been chosen for the United States pole vault team, we should not be at all surprised. Something of that is there in the work, if we know how to look for it—the concentrated spring of the run-up, the delicate but decisive way with pole, and the well-hidden effort that takes the vaulter over the bar."

John found Alex a champion verbalizer: "His abrupt and often astonishing phrases come at us one by one, fast and unexpected, the way the little black ball comes at us in the squash court. If we don't catch them on the bounce, they are gone."

John wrote, "Alex Katz had looked a great deal at European Old Masters, and has an idiosyncratic 'take' on each one of them. (Who but he would have said: 'Titian was a hired gun, and everything he did was cool. Whatever anyone wanted, he'd do it'?)"

Of Veronese, Alex said: "He's big and bland—no hot spots, he's just all over. He makes Rubens seem like he is kidding around."

As it happens, "bland" is a word sometimes used for Alex Katz's own paintings by people who do not notice the surgeon's sharp knife, the ferocious editing, and the ever-present feeling of risk that go into those simple-seeming images. In those images, Katz himself appears quite often as founder-member, along with his wife, Ada, of the repertory company of human beings who turn up year after year. Unfailingly tender with the others, he occasionally pushes his own full-length profile to the very edge of parody.

John once wrote in a review of an Alex Katz exhibition for *The New York Times*, "If we had to be reincarnated, one of the better ideas would be to come back to life in a painting by Alex Katz."

We did the next best thing: Alex painted a double portrait of us.

When Alex told us about the project, we were surprised, touched, and pleased, in that order.

And I am happy that Alex has brought John and me together forever, even if it is only on canvas.

Afterwords

Foreword to
John Russell's *Paris*

This is my foreword to the enlarged and updated version of my hus-
band John Russell's Paris. This new version was published by Abradale
Press, Harry N. Abrams, Inc., Publishers, New York, 1983. (It was orig-
inally published in 1960, in London.)

When I first read John Russell's *Paris*, I remembered particularly a very small room halfway to the sky in what was then my
favorite Left Bank hotel. The rooms on the top floor of the Pont
Royal are not as large as the ones lower down, but after trying some
of the others, I decided to perch above, where each room had a small
balcony and you could step out through the French windows and
there in front of you was a clear view across Paris.

You could look down to the right and follow the rue du Bac on
its straight reach for the Seine. Eighteenth-century town houses with
flat stone facades—not yet sluiced clean on André Malraux's orders—
and elegant doorways lined one side of the street, rising to steep,
humped roofs (gray tile, usually) bitten into by mansard windows
with projecting triangular hoods. Across the river was the cluttered
mount of Montmartre, topped by the ridiculous but endearing white
fantasy of the Sacré-Cœur. To the left was the Eiffel Tower and, still
farther, the gold-ribbed dome of the Invalides. Paris in my pocket.

This is where I came to live in the late 1940s, when an American
magazine sent me to Paris to report on the arts. The Pont Royal was
cheap in those days, and it was near to everything I wanted.

I was extraordinarily lucky to be starting a career at that time,
when Paris was still a great center of intellectual and artistic energy.
Art and life were beginning again after the long dark night of the

German occupation. As Cyril Connolly once wrote about French writers, "Intelligence flows through them like a fast river." The river was indeed flowing fast. The great figures of twentieth-century art were still in full activity. There were new magazines, new books, new art galleries, new plays, new hopes. Even new music was beginning to make its way.

Writers, publishers, and art dealers from all over stayed at the Pont Royal or met there. Fred, the Swiss concierge, knew them all and kept a fatherly eye out for me. When I came home from work, he might tell me, "Monsieur Skira left this morning to visit Monsieur Matisse in Vence. Monsieur Matisse didn't sound a bit pleased when he telephoned." (The Swiss publisher Albert Skira was chronically late and never answered letters, which infuriated the supermethodical Matisse.) Or he might say, "Monsieur and Madame Miró are arriving tomorrow from Barcelona for a week. Monsieur Curt Valentin is expected from New York Tuesday." (Curt Valentin was the most imaginative New York art dealer of the day.) "Monsieur Stephen Spender came in from London and was looking for you."

My room with its Turkey red carpet, brass bed, and nubbly white coverlet offered few amenities: one chair; an old-fashioned stand-up wardrobe; watery lights. The telephone was cradled uneasily on two metal prongs. Its function was mainly symbolic. Even the most exasperated jiggling rarely caught the attention of the *standardiste*. Often it was quicker to go out, buy *jetons*, and call from a café. Once, in a rage of frustration, I stormed down to confront the telephone operator face-to-face, only to find her standing in her cubicle, tape measure in hand, intently fitting a friend for a dress while her switchboard flashed futile appeals.

The bar, downstairs from the lobby, was conspiratorially dark and filled with deep and overstuffed brown leather armchairs and sofas. This was my club, a quintessentially Parisian listening post where you went to find out who's in, who's out, and who's gone away and will never come back. Publishers and authors negotiated over the new fashionable drink in France: *le scotch*. The painter Balthus, more Byronic than Byron himself, would drop by and give me news of Picasso. Jean-Paul Sartre and Simone de Beauvoir were regulars. At that time their fame and the provocative aura that surrounded the word "existentialist" (practically nobody knew what it meant) had made them objects of universal curiosity, and they had abandoned their previous headquarters at the Café de Flore for the less exposed Pont Royal.

Later, when I had an apartment, I continued to see Jean-Paul Sartre and Simone de Beauvoir, though neither of them cared much for Americans in general. Once, when Sartre came to lunch, he gave an offhand demonstration of mental agility: without stopping the general conversation, he deciphered, one after another, the formidably difficult word-and-picture puzzles on my Creil dessert plates.

Although I moved from the Pont Royal, I never left the quarter. It was, and is, a neighborhood of bookstores and publishing houses. The grandest, Gallimard, is a few steps from the Pont Royal. I used to go to its Thursday afternoon garden parties every June; they were long on petits fours and short on liquor. Alice B. Toklas lived around the corner from my office and was always ready to receive the favored visitor with enormous teas. She was exquisitely polite, and even when very old she would insist on serving the guest herself.

In Paris, you are on easy terms with the past. I would nod to Apollinaire, a favorite poet, as I went by 202, boulevard Saint-Germain, where he lived after coming back wounded from the front in World War I. I liked going by the Jesuit-style Eglise Saint-Thomas-d'Aquin, set back from the boulevard, where Apollinaire was married, with Picasso as witness. On my way to Nancy Mitford's, I would go by 120, rue du Bac, a handsome house from which Chateaubriand set off every afternoon to visit Madame Récamier. Ingres, Delacroix, Corot, George Sand, Madame de Staël, Voltaire, and Wagner (he finished *Die Meistersinger* in Paris) were among the friendly neighborhood ghosts.

It is often said, and with some reason, that Parisians are not hospitable to the foreigner. But what an abundance of generosity and hospitality came my way! I remember Picasso rummaging through the indescribable chaos of his vast studio on the rue des Grands-Augustins to try to dig up some drawings I wanted to publish. Fernand Léger lined up his recent work for me and asked which canvases I liked best. Matisse received me with all the books he had illustrated, meticulously opened out so that he could explain in each case what problems he had solved and how. The admirable, austere Nadia Boulanger (who taught so many American composers, beginning with Aaron Copland) invited me to her icy apartment on the rue Ballu to hear her latest protégé. The composer Francis Poulenc, a bulky, pear-shaped figure, was droll beyond words and yet indescribably poignant as he accompanied himself on a small upright piano and sang the soprano solo of a woman desperately trying to hold on to her lover—from his *La Voix Humaine*. President Vincent Auriol took me on a tour of the Palais de l'Elysée after a press conference to point out the famous Gobelins tapestry. And I remember the ultimate Parisian accolade: a great French chef, the late René Viaux of the restaurant in the Gare de l'Est, named a dish after me. It is reproduced in color in the Larousse *Cuisine et Vins de France*. He later became the chef at Maxim's, where I always got special treatment.

A few years after my Pont Royal days I was starting my own art magazine, *L'ŒIL*, in a minute office at the back of a cobbled courtyard on the rue des Saints-Pères.

For the magazine, we needed good writers and got in touch with a young English art critic whose weekly column in the London *Sunday Times* was indispensable reading if you wanted to know what was going on not only in England but on the Continent as well. It was clear that unlike many critics, he loved art; he wrote about it with informed enthusiasm, and he wrote in crystalline prose. There was not a dull phrase to be weeded out in translation (French translation did wonders for some of our German, Dutch, Italian, and English-language contributors), and, what's more, he knew France and the French language very well.

We corresponded. He sent in his articles—on time. We met. Our conversations centered on ideas for features and deadlines. I had the intense seriousness of the young and the harassed, and I was producing a monthly publication on a shoestring as thin as the one Man Ray wore in lieu of a tie. In private life both of us were programmed, to use computer language, in other directions. Unlikely as it seems, I had no idea that while I was discovering Paris and the Parisians, he was working on a book about Paris.

Some eighteen years later, reader, I married him. Only then did

I discover John Russell's book *Paris* (originally published in 1960). Here was sustained delight. No one else could combine the feel and the look, the heart and the mind, the stones and the trees, the past and the present, the wits, the eccentrics, and the geniuses of my favorite city with such easy grace.

Reading this book, for me, was like sauntering through the city where I had lived so long. By my side was a most civilized companion who casually brought all the strands together and made them gleam—not forgetting to stop for an aperitif and a delicious meal en route. The book was long out of print, and I felt it unfair to keep this to myself. I showed it to a publisher friend. He immediately agreed that others would enjoy John Russell's *Paris* as much as we did. He suggested it be brought up to date, in an illustrated edition.

The author and I went to Paris to gather the illustrations. There was some confusion about our hotel reservation, and the receptionist at the Pont Royal apologized for giving us a small room on the top floor. Here the circle closes in the most satisfactory of ways: it was the identical room, No. 125, in which I had lived when I first came to Paris. The Turkey red carpet was now royal blue, the furniture was spruced-up modern, there was—is this possible?—a minibar. And there was a push-button telephone that clicked all of Europe and America into the streamlined receiver.

We stepped out onto the little balcony. Deyrolle, the naturalist's, where I used to buy crystals and butterflies, was still across the street. There were some new chic boutiques, but the noble eighteenth-century facades still stood guard over the past. We looked around happily: there they were, our cherished landmarks—the Invalides, the Paroisse Sainte-Clotilde, and the Eiffel Tower on the left, and on the right the former Gare d'Orsay, soon to be a museum of late-nineteenth-century art, the Sacré-Cœur, and the Grand Palais.

The huge open sky overhead had drifted in from the Ile-de-France. The bottle green bus bumbled down the rue du Bac. The tricolor flew the way it flies in Delacroix's *Liberty Leading the People*. I was back again, this time in John Russell's Paris.

Janet Flanner (Genet)

In 1990, I wrote an introduction to the former New Yorker *writer Janet Flanner's book* Men and Monuments: Profiles of Picasso, Matisse, Braque, and Malraux, *which was originally published in 1957 and then republished by Natalia Danesi Murray for Da Capo Press in 1990.*

I can still see Janet Flanner as I first caught sight of her in the late 1940s, when I was a young woman in Paris on my first job and she had been for almost a quarter of a century the acclaimed author of the "Letter from Paris" in *The New Yorker*.

She had arrived in Paris from her native Indiana in 1922, at the age of thirty. Like hundreds, if not thousands, of other American would-be writers at that time, she couldn't wait to make the most of the freer air, the richer culture, and the smaller expenses that Paris had to offer.

Before long, her letters back home struck her friend Jane Grant as just what was needed for the new magazine of which her husband, Harold Ross, was editor. Its name was *The New Yorker*. And in October 1925 it carried the first "Letter from Paris," for which Janet was paid forty dollars. Like all the letters that were to follow, it was signed "Genet"—the nom de plume that Ross had chosen for Janet.

I did not of course know at the time of our first meeting that Janet was to go on writing for *The New Yorker* until she was in her eighties. Nor could I know of the lengthy profiles that she was to research with such exemplary care and yet manage to present, in print, as if they had given her no trouble at all.

The day-to-day detail of life in Paris was her prime and lifelong concern. Like the Parisians themselves, she loved a good murder and was fascinated by scandals of every kind. She was forever in touch with whatever was newest in art, in the theater, in literature, in music, and in the fashion industry. Nor did she neglect the sociabilities to which those interests gave rise.

She had a very good eye for an eccentric, and—again like the Parisians—she adored a good funeral and could sum up the deceased with an admirable and lively concision. She enjoyed state occasions, too, and brought them alive in a way that was the envy of every other foreign correspondent. On the American in Paris, from Gene Tunney to Edith Wharton, and from Alice B. Toklas to Isadora Duncan, Marian Anderson and Josephine Baker, she was at her most observant. But she was in Paris primarily for the Parisians, and in dealing with them—Georges Clemenceau, Paul Poiret, Suzanne Lenglen, the Duchesse d'Uzès, Maurice Chevalier, François Mauriac, Erik Satie, in no particular order—she was consummately and enviably at home.

Much of this came out in just a phrase or two. But she could also turn her hand to monumental reportage with a skill that caused William Shawn—the most perceptive of editors—to rank her with Rebecca West. What Rebecca West was to the Nuremberg trials, Janet Flanner was to the looting of art by the Nazis and its subsequent salvaging by the victorious American forces.

Characteristically, it was in a bar that I first saw her. After the end of World War II, foreign correspondents in Paris lived in the Hôtel Scribe and used its bar as their meeting place. Later they moved for drinks only—the rooms were too expensive—to the Hôtel Crillon. And that is where I saw her, talking, talking, talking. What she said was always incisive, well modulated, with the words so well chosen that they could have been wafted, unchanged, onto the printed page. She smoked the whole time, eyes crinkled above the smoke. And, from that small frame, there would emerge a surprisingly Falstaffian laugh.

For Janet, though not frail, was small—delicately chunky, one might say. With good reason, she was proud of her elegant little feet. (She wore size four and a half.) When custom-made shoes were a luxury but not a financial catastrophe, she had all her shoes made by a famous *bottier*. In her chosen mannish style, she was always very well dressed. Every year, she had one suit made by a top couture house—Chanel, it might be, or Molyneux. She loved bright silk scarves and usually had one—knotted with seemingly casual care—round her throat. In later years, the red ribbon of the Légion d'Honneur made a bright accent on her every lapel.

For decades, she lived in a mansard room in the Hôtel Continental on the rue de Castiglione. How she could live permanently in such tiny quarters was a mystery to me. She had a little balcony with a view over the Tuileries, but I doubt she ever took the time to step out and have a look round.

Some of the furniture was hers. Its main feature was a boulle *bureau plat*—heaped, of course, with books and papers. She had spied this luxurious table in the front window of a butcher's shop on the Left Bank. Maybe a client had left it there on consignment. Anyhow, Janet marched right in and bought it. There were papers of all kinds everywhere. Janet read all the newspapers, and there used to be a great many of them in France. She had a batch of fat red and blue pencils, and she would go through the newspapers imperiously marking any item—however small—that might nourish her fortnightly "Letter from Paris." "You have to look even at the smallest items at the bottom of the page," she used to say. "That's where you might find something." She clipped and clipped. There were mounds of clippings all over the place. Perhaps only Marcel Proust's bedroom had such a shifting sea of papers.

Underneath the boulle desk, she kept a wicker hamper stuffed with papers. And then, when Janet was going away for a few months—to America, to Italy—the papers got shunted elsewhere. Marie, the floor maid, and her husband, Emile, one of the hall porters, would transfer Janet's clothes into the hamper, which would then be taken down and stored in the bowels of the hotel.

The staff of the hotel adored Janet. They waited on her, took care of her, took pride in her. She was a particular favorite with the barman, who acted as informal host to the streams of people who came, in later years, to see Janet (or in hopes of seeing her). She gave appointment after appointment in the bar, and people took their turns, edging along the narrow banquettes until they were next to the large leather armchair that was her throne.

She was totally undomestic and quite proud of living, as the French say, like a bird on a branch—with no permanent anchor anywhere. She lived the life of a convivial *homme de lettres*—monocle and all—who just happened to be a woman.

She was generous—with her time, her person, her resources. I only discovered after her death that a number of people—Alice B. Toklas, among them—were getting small (and sometimes not so small) checks from Janet. It was in character that after a friend of hers had dropped dead when about to have dinner with her, she paid for the funeral expenses.

She loved to invite her friends for a splendid meal in a good restaurant. On festive occasions, or to celebrate when, for once, her "Letter from Paris" had gone off to *The New Yorker* on time, we used to go to a bistro called L'Ami Louis that she especially liked. I still remember the foie gras sautéed with grapes, followed by little roast birds. She was a good judge of food and wine, yet she didn't know the first thing about cooking.

Although her Paris letters and her profiles read with seamless clarity, she agonized over them. How many telephone calls did I get at the small office where I edited the art review that was my reason for being in Paris! "I can't get it finished!" she would moan. She could only write at the last minute, with the deadline hanging over her like a sentence of death. Only then would she attack her typewriter in a frenzy, working through the night until four or five in the morning. On some of the longer pieces, and after months of research, she would be closeted in her room like a desperate bear, working on her private marathon until driven out in search of food.

Though she knew her worth as a writer, she could be curiously shy and uncertain of herself. When she was preparing the profile of Georges Braque, she asked me if I would mind taking her to Braque's house on the rue du Douanier (now renamed the rue Georges Braque), up by the Parc Montsouris. Perhaps I could introduce her and generally hang around? Later, she sent me two pages of typewritten notes, along with an affectionate scrawled message, asking me to correct or add anything that I remembered from the interview.

Until age and infirmity slowed her down, Janet went everywhere—to concerts (she loved music), art exhibitions, political meetings, cabarets, parties. Deep down, she disliked the theater, perhaps because as a child she had been pushed onto the stage in amateur productions by her mother, who was a passionate and gifted amateur actress. But the fact is that she could have been an actress. When called upon to speak in public, or on television, she was immediately in command. She never used notes. Her wit, her unexpected and cogent turn of phrase, never failed her.

News was her business, but it was not in her nature to intrude in order to get it. For a long time, after the end of World War II, she would sit just a few feet away from Picasso night after night in the Café de Flore. She never presumed to speak to him, but some fifteen years later, when she was taken to his house in Cannes, he said, "But of course I know you! How often did I not see you at the Flore! Why did you never speak to me?" and threw his arms around her.

As a talker, she could be sharp, incisive, jaunty, and ribald, though never malicious. But she was also—unlike André Malraux—a natural listener. She had great reserves of compassion and was poignantly responsive to the tribulations of others. One morning, when she was sitting over a cup of coffee in the garden of the Ritz in Paris, she heard of a friend's bad news. On the instant, heavy tears began to course, uncontrollably, down her furrowed cheeks.

She often complained that she could never get down to the books that she ought to write and wanted to write. In private, she would admit that it was not only her demanding work for *The New Yorker* that was responsible. The long haul was not for her. As she wrote to her friend Kay Boyle, "I seem to live on in a steady conflagration of matches, easily burnt out, but always re-lighted." She did actually write two articles for my magazine, *L'ŒIL*—one on her old friend Mark Tobey, the other, less predictably, on Helena Rubinstein—but although we commissioned her to write the text for an illustrated book on Paris, she backed out.

Happily, she lived to know that her reports from Paris and elsewhere were being reprinted in book form. She enjoyed the belated personal recognition—her pseudonym, Genet, concealed her identity for many years—and toward the end of her life, when debilitating illness prevented her from writing, she took an enormous delight in reading herself in book form. She would laugh uproariously. "I must say," she told her friends, "that nobody ever amuses me as much as reading myself!"

That amusement is contagious. Janet Flanner was a person of very strong convictions, but she never preached. Delight was what she offered, from one decade to the next, and it has never staled. The profiles in this book are as fresh as they were on the day that she wrote them. As for "The Beautiful Spoils," her account of the looting of art by the Nazis from 1940 onward, it too is a profile but a profile of iniquity, minutely researched in often difficult circumstances. We can learn from all these pieces, but in doing so, we also have ourselves a very good time.

Richard Avedon

This is my introduction to the catalog for the Metropolitan Museum of Art's 1978 exhibition Avedon: Photographs, 1947–1977.

Fashion is theater. It has its authors and its directors, it has its actors and its actresses, and it has an audience that can be very large indeed. It is art, and it is also big business. It is trade, of a particularly complex and ramifying kind, and at its best it is poetry as well. It has successes that seem for a season or two to take the whole world and roll it flat, and it has its failures that are both gruesome and definitive.

It has variables—names that come and go—and it has constants. One of its constants over the last thirty years and more has been the activity of Richard Avedon. Avedon is self-evidently one of the best photographers of the day. But he is also a philosopher, a historian, a moralist, a poet, and a wit. He does not see fashion photography as a chore to be got through as quickly as possible. He gives it everything he has; and that "everything" includes those fantasies which take hold of us in childhood and never let go.

However implausibly, it was while serving in the Merchant Marine, during World War II, that he learned the techniques of photography that later served him so well in the world of high fashion.

He began his activity in that domain at a time right after the war, when nobody in this country knew anything about the state of high fashion in France, for the very good reason that there was nothing to work with and nothing to show. But the French fashion industry wasn't willing to lie down and die; and just to show that it was still alive, the French sent over to New York an exhibition of small and extremely lifelike dolls that were dressed just as real live full-sized people would be dressed when the couture houses could open again. The show was called *Le Théâtre de la Mode*, and among the people who came over with it was Christian Bérard, the most brilliant stage designer of his day.

It made a great stir, and when the French fashion houses began to open up again in 1946–47, American magazines thought it worthwhile to send people over to report on them. One of these people was Richard Avedon, who was seeing Paris for the first time. It was the decisive moment in his professional life. He knew nothing of Paris, beyond what he had picked up from the movies of the 1930s, and he was overwhelmed not only by the city itself but by the world of high fashion with its impassioned commitment to elegance and technical perfection.

He was in Paris when a soft-spoken, moonfaced man called Christian Dior showed his first collection. Such was the shortage of fabrics in France at the time that many women in the audience were still wearing skirts above their knees. His models came sailing through the crowded gray salons like sloops in a high wind. As they pirouetted this way and that, their long full skirts swooshed out around them, knocking ashtrays off the tables as they went. It was the New Look, the proof that Paris could still call a tune that the whole world would follow, and people wept to see it. It meant that miles of French cloth would be sold, and it meant years of work for the skilled French fingers that made braid, flowers, belts, buttons, and embroidery. The finely trained artisans of *la haute couture* were in business again.

Avedon the fashion photographer had his first great success in the atmosphere of high excitement and overflowing emotion that was the mark of Paris reborn. Those new fashions were a triumph for French intelligence, French wit, and French craftsmanship. For one or two men and women of genius and for a great many hardworking people of talent they foretold a lifetime of constructive activity; and for the pride and the dignity of a lately humbled France they were a tremendous tonic.

Coverage of the Paris collections was a serious matter in those days. Preparations were made long in advance. The girl who was to model the clothes was chosen way ahead in New York and worked over like a vestal virgin predestined for a magic ritual. Avedon went to Paris ahead of time to choose and rehearse his locations. The whole magazine team spent three weeks to record the showings. Nothing was left to chance. What looked like accident and spontaneity was nothing of the kind. There was not a breath of the reportage spirit. Every last effect was thought out in advance: the concierge in the doorway, the still-unchanged life of the street, the unexpected encounters, even the rising cloud of pigeons with their wings akimbo.

Avedon lived and worked in the closed world of couture and the clothes he was to photograph. He spent all day on location and all night in a small studio on the rue Jean Goujon. Paris for him was his little team: the model, his assistant, an electrician, the aged messenger who brought the big dressmaker's boxes round on his bicycle. He had no contact whatever with the glittering world that was conjured up in the photographs that would appear in *Harper's Bazaar* and later in *Vogue*.

Reclusive by choice as much as by necessity, Avedon at the age of twenty-four did not attempt to impress himself upon Paris. But when he shot in the Palais Royal, he knew that somewhere behind an upper window Colette was writing with her *fanal bleu* beside her. He also knew that at any moment Jean Cocteau, who also lived in the Palais Royal, might saunter down, with his carefully permed mane waving in the breeze, to have lunch at Véfour.

Paris after the liberation was full of bitterness and recrimination. Yet something was coming alive again, and behind that renewed vitality was the most imaginative of economic programs: the Marshall Plan.

Madeleine Renaud and Jean-Louis Barrault at their Théâtre Marigny under the bare chestnut trees delighted with their repertoire. A few years later the Barraults were to offer Pierre Boulez the hospitality of their small upstairs, where, on excruciatingly uncomfortable chairs, the Parisians heard Schoenberg, Berg, Webern, and Boulez's own music for the first time. Jean-Paul Sartre and Simone de Beauvoir were writing and holding court, first at the Café de Flore, then downstairs in the dark bar of the Pont Royal when too many gawkers invaded their Saint-Germain-des-Prés. Albert Camus came back from North Africa to run the most intelligent newspaper, *Combat*.

The austere and splendid Nadia Boulanger was still pouring out her enthusiasms, insights, and perceptions to a new generation of musicians in her freezing apartment on the rue Ballu (unchanged since Aaron Copland became her first composition pupil in 1921).

The tradition of intelligent popular entertainment continued. While over on the avenue George V Balenciaga showed superb black dresses as stiff with heavy embroidery as a jeweled icon, across the Seine on the Left Bank Juliette Gréco, in worn black slacks and sweater, sang *désabusé* songs written for her by Sartre and Raymond Queneau. And of course Piaf, diminutive sparrow of sorrow in a shapeless black shift, broke everybody's heart singing "La Vie en Rose."

These early photographs chart Avedon's evolution. From the start, he differed from the famous figures who preceded him: Baron de Meyer, Steichen, Man Ray, Hoyningen-Huene, Beaton, Horst. For one thing, he chose to observe, rather than to mingle with, the professionally elegant world. To that world he brought wit, vitality that never quite masked an underlying anxiety, and the ability to distill drama from frivolity. He did everything his own way. Not for him the backlighting that aureoled hair and profile, the ectoplasmic shimmer of a flattering background, the static pose by a Grecian column. Avedon's models are rarely still: they run, pivot, stride. (An early photograph of a girl gleefully speeding along on roller skates horrified officials of the Chambre Syndicale de la Couture, who thought it undignified.)

The clothes themselves take on a tautened nervous energy: panels fly, poufs billow, coats jut and twirl. Shoes become monuments. There is an acute sensitivity to texture: he is as alive to sunlit cigarette smoke against a cheek as he is to the mushroom bloom of a suede hat or the sheen of fur against the grain of wool.

These photographs reflect his romance with Paris: the loving side-look at uneven paving stones, the worn surface of a wall, the curve of a café chair, the watery lights on a bridge, the siphon of soda water on a bistro table, the old-fashioned lettering on a shop front, the Art Nouveau arabesques over a doorway.

An increasing interest in portraiture that was to blossom uncompromisingly in the 1960s creeps into the fashion photographs as the French fashion press crowd around girls in evening dress, members of the Dior *état-major* flank one of their creations. He knew just how to juxtapose everyday people with the improbable perfection of the professional beauty.

There are moments of cinematic quality—episodes from an unwritten story when the action is not yet defined. Something has happened, or is about to happen: we never know which. Tongue-in-cheek mini-dramas comment indirectly on the world they set before us. In one image a young woman sits in a French railway carriage (Avedon's Anna Karenina?). As she clasps her little dog, her frail face emerges, bathed in tears, from a sea of flowers. This photograph was refused by his magazine editor. "No one cries in a Dior hat" was the tart comment. Incidentally, while most of these photographs were done during assignments for *Harper's Bazaar* and *Vogue*, some favorites of his were never published.

Soon the romance is over. A new emphasis on humor, frenzy, and finally wry satire takes over. The gaiety is more frantic than exuberant, the openmouthed laughs look strident, everyone seems to be smoking nervously. Boredom creeps in as handsome bodies loll on beaches. There is a radical change in what is considered beautiful and acceptable. The first breasts are bared. The first black model appears. High fashion and the high stepper were one, at that moment in time. Avedon dealt with a world of performers. The anonymous models of the immediate postwar years were replaced by young women who became celebrities in their own right. At the same time, it turned out that the professional performers and the redoubtable heiresses to great fortunes asked nothing better than to put their persons in the public domain by modeling whatever was newest in high fashion. Beauty and notoriety and a certain stylish abandon were adroitly compounded by Avedon in images that quintessentialize one of the more curious moments in recent social history.

With the 1960s come the tough fashions, the clunks of jewelry, the face mask like Maori tattooing, the space-age glasses, the matted hair. The photographer-ringmaster urges his models to movement and yet more movement: they wheel, leap, cavort in midair.

These tough fashions corresponded to radical changes in a world that in the late 1960s and early 1970s was falling apart and did not know how to put itself together again. Fashion came out of the quilted silence of the couture houses and into the streets for its inspiration. Nothing could be too odd, nothing could be too extreme, nothing could contrast too abruptly with the fastidious perfection that had once been the aim of high fashion. It was a visual moment that got completely out of hand; and already after less than ten years the fashions in question look as remote from us as the costumes that went berserk under the Directoire. But Avedon was there; those frantic fashions were his material; and he went to work among them the way Claude Monet went to work among his water lilies.

The last room leaves the discotheque universe for the quiet privacy of Avedon's studio. It tells us as much about the man behind the camera and the journey he has undertaken as it does about the seven women who are enshrined there. Here is simplicity—of dress, of pose—with all artifice gone and nothing but the white studio wall behind the straightforward frontal pose. Alberto Giacometti used to say that what mattered to him in sculpture was to capture *le regard*—the gaze. The other features were only a framework for *le regard*. Once you had this, everything else fell into place. Richard Avedon has wrought this particular miracle, time and time again.

Irving Penn

My chapter in Irving Penn: A Career in Photography, *the catalog for a 1997–98 exhibition at the Art Institute of Chicago.*

At the end of World War II, *Vogue* magazine was a tumult of packaged high style. Superlatives swirled around like perfumed snowflakes in a heavy storm. The major players in the *Vogue* of those days had a distinctly cosmopolitan turn of mind. Iva Patcevitch, president of *Vogue*'s publishing house, Condé Nast, and Alexander Liberman, art director of *Vogue*, were recent arrivals from Paris, and both were of Russian origin; several of the magazine's photographers, such as Serge Balkin and Constantin Joffé, were also Russian.

Irving Penn was not like that at all. He was a plainspoken, plain-looking young American, recently back from the American Field Service. He wore sneakers, which at the time were anything but customary in the *Vogue* offices, and he rarely wore a tie. Quiet and reserved, he spoke little and he spoke softly. But there was no mistaking his steely—in fact, stubborn—resolve: he knew exactly what he wanted, and what he wanted had nothing to do with the accepted high gloss of the fashion photograph.

When I first met Penn in the New York office of *Vogue* in 1946, he showed me a photograph of a Venetian canal clogged with a lot of old rubbish. I said, almost to myself, that it looked like a painting by Paul Klee. His face lit up in surprise that a young editor should say such a thing. From that moment, there was a certain rapport between us.

From 1934 to 1938, Penn had attended the Pennsylvania Museum and School of Industrial Art, where he had hoped to become a painter, and during that time he spent two summers in the New York offices of *Harper's Bazaar* as the assistant and protégé of Alexey Brodovitch. While there, he glimpsed Salvador Dalí, Isamu Noguchi, and Richard Lindner on their way in or out, and he was present when new drawings by Jean Cocteau, Christian Bérard, and Jean Hugo arrived in the morning's mail.

But when the twenty-six-year-old Penn first came to work for Alexander Liberman at *Vogue* in 1943, he knew little of the multifarious and multinational avant-garde that he would be called upon to photograph. There was no reason to suppose that he would later excel as a portrait photographer, nor that between 1946 and 1950 Penn would shoot nearly three hundred portraits for *Vogue*, of which over one hundred would be published. His sitters were to include, among writers, T. S. Eliot, Edmund Wilson, W. H. Auden, Marianne Moore, Stephen Spender, Graham Greene, and Evelyn Waugh. There were masters of the keyboard, such as Wanda Landowska, Vladimir Horowitz, and Rudolf Serkin; filmmakers like Alfred Hitchcock and René Clair; among composers, Igor Stravinsky and Leonard Bernstein; jazz greats like Duke Ellington and Dizzy Gillespie; and a couturier, Christian Dior. There was also in 1947 a memorable group portrait that included, among other cartoonists, Charles Addams, Saul Steinberg, George Price, and William Steig.

In dealing with this formidable cast of characters, Penn turned out to be a gentle but implacable sorcerer—a sorcerer with an artist's eye. With a built-in divining rod he could pick up the inner vibration of his subjects, even if he had nothing to go on, except perhaps the notes written for him beforehand by a well-informed assistant. But when he peered through the lens, this reticent man showed no mercy as he ferreted out the secrets that the sitters might most have wished to hide. As early as 1942, during the year he spent trying to be a painter in Mexico, he shot a picture of chickens captured in a bottle. He has been doing something like it ever since.

For some of his portraits for *Vogue* in 1948, he built a set of two converging panels that forced his sitters into a constricted space. They were caught as surely as a specimen butterfly pinned to a panel.

Some of them took it (so to speak) in their stride. Marcel Duchamp stood in his corner, imperturbably puffing on his pipe. Spencer Tracy in the same year was as relaxed as if he were in his own living room.

Others were not so amenable. Georgia O'Keeffe so hated her portrait that she wrote to Penn in a very firm hand asking him to destroy it. O'Keeffe's reaction is not surprising. I saw the forbidden print, now part of the Penn Collection and Archives at the Art Institute of Chicago. Dressed all in black, she looks like a wizened waif, as much a captive as any of those Mexican chickens.

Penn's relentless perfectionism did not make him easy to work with. Even objects had to comply. Liberman once described a shoot involving the instant of a fall of a tray loaded with glasses. Penn insisted that only the finest Baccarat crystal would be right, so dozens and dozens of the most expensive glasses were used in recording the right moment of spill and break.

Insects, too, had to conform to Penn's wishes. He needed some flies to complete a color image, called *Summer Sleep*, of a dozing girl by a fan, shot through a screen. So dead flies were glued to the screen to keep them exactly in the spots where Penn felt they were needed.

A certain aloofness is often built into Penn's portraiture. One feels that he has deliberately set up a distance between himself and his subjects. He observes them but does not want to know them. He arranges their positions, their limbs, as meticulously but as impersonally as he organized the famous still lifes that were such a feature of his pages for *Vogue* (and one that was to be carried over in his commercial work).

The English actor Paul Scofield once noted that Penn liked to photograph strangers. But there were exceptions. Penn went to Barcelona in 1948 to try to recapture the atmosphere in which the young Picasso had matured in the late 1890s. Penn had introductions to Sebastià Junyer, Picasso's companion in those heady days and the friend who had accompanied him to Paris on that historic first trip in 1900. The Penn Archives have long, affectionate letters from Junyer, full of genuine delight in Penn's company. In Junyer, Penn made a friend for life.

Even in Paris, also in 1948, where he often started with only

minimal knowledge of his sitters, he got results that completely con-
tradicted expectation. Readers of *Vogue* who knew of Dora Maar as
Picasso's archetypal weeping woman were amazed to find her shown
by Penn as an immensely distinguished human being, no longer
quite young, who stared back at the camera as one photographer to
another.

Penn also captured something of the inner anxiety that underlay
Jean Cocteau's elegantly angular, show-off pose. The sideways glance,
the jacket worn off the shoulder, the contrasted patterns of tie and
waistcoat, and the famous hands ("like articulated jewels," Marcel
Proust had said)—all were trapped by Penn.

When faced with the quite young painter Balthus, who was then
known only to a small group of passionate admirers—Picasso among
them—Penn pounced on the reversed dandyism that Balthus af-
fected at the time: his torn and tattered old clothes, his painter's coat
belted with string, and the then-mandatory cigarette drooping from
his lips. Balthus adored being Balthus, and Penn's portrait captures
this to perfection.

One of the Parisian sitters, an expatriate American, was terribly
observant. Janet Flanner, who informed and delighted readers of
The New Yorker magazine for many years with her "Letter from
Paris," wrote with characteristic pungency and insight about her
portrait, "It is excellent of my face; that is exactly how worried I am
and look, especially when I fleetingly think of the universe today . . .
The only element which is not true is that I look tall; this comes
from your extraordinary and slightly falsified perspective, which is
your style signature and a highly interesting one, too. The top and
capital parts of the sitter go back, so that the head is idealizedly
small and the limbs come forward, giving, in my case, an impressive
but untrue height. You are very talented; your Hitchcock portrait in
Vogue this month is a fine piece of monstrosity, practically straight
Goya."

Not unexpectedly, Alfred Hitchcock himself had a different
opinion and telegraphed, "Have seen the picture taken by *Vogue*—
horrible! Please thank Mr. Penn with hope that it will be reshaped,
both in features and posture." It wasn't.

Penn was to photograph many figures from the world of dance, but the ecstatic arabesque was not his style: he brought a new poetry to immobility. For example, in 1948, after posing for her corner portrait, Martha Graham wrote how moved she was by Penn's "quietness and gentleness." The "inner stillness" of the confined space intrigued her, she said. In fact, while posing, she began to plan "a dramatic dance" drawn from the experience.

When Penn photographed him that same year, Merce Cunningham had just formed his endlessly innovative company. Not long before, in 1944, he had created the role of the preacher in Martha Graham's dance *Appalachian Spring*, with music by Aaron Copland. And then there is Jerome Robbins, barefoot, his slim black-clad body taking the measure of that corner and looking for once as defenseless as a puppet.

Acknowledgments

My first thanks go to my stepson, Olivier Bernier, for his steadfast encouragement and editorial acumen.

I will always be grateful to my stylish agent, Lynn Nesbit, for introducing my book and me to Jonathan Galassi. This led to the happiest of collaborations with Jonathan and his colleagues Jeff Seroy and Jesse Coleman, models all three of helpfulness and patience.

My longtime friend and now lawyer Virginia Rutledge has been, as always, a valued sounding board and counselor.

An *abrazo* to my nieces Natalia and Margarita Jimenez for keeping the Spanish accents going in the right direction.

My thanks to Elizabeth C. Baker, distinguished art editor, for taking a benign look at some of my text.

Another old friend, now the Rev. Susan J. Barnes, made helpful suggestions about a subject she knows intimately, the Menil family and collection.

Affectionate thanks to Michael Mahoney, who invented me as a lecturer and added a clarification to the Manet family text.

Thanks are due to Stephen Pascal, who delved into the *Condé Nast* archives for me.

More thanks go to Marcello Simonetti, who stepped in late with some helpful observations.

On the home front, I thank my assistant, Sue Spears, for plumbing the depths of the technological age for me.

And warm thanks to my housekeeper of thirty-five years, Lucy Montes, for her unselfish devotion.

A bouquet of thanks to the master florist Ronaldo Maia, for brightening my life with his uninterrupted, imaginative generosity.